Taking liberties

MANCHESTER
UNIVERSITY PRESS

Taking liberties

Problems of a new order from the French Revolution to Napoleon

edited by Howard G. Brown and Judith A. Miller

Manchester University Press
Manchester and New York

distributed exclusively in the USA by Palgrave

Published by Manchester University Press
Oxford Road, Manchester M13 9NR, UK
and Room 400, 175 Fifth Avenue, New York, NY 10010, USA
www.manchesteruniversitypress.co.uk

Distributed exclusively in the USA by
Palgrave, 175 Fifth Avenue, New York,
NY 10010, USA

Distributed exclusively in Canada by
UBC Press, University of British Columbia, 2029 West Mall,
Vancouver, BC, Canada V6T 1Z2

British Library Cataloguing-in-Publication Data
A catalogue record for this book is available from the British Library

Library of Congress Cataloging-in-Publication Data applied for

ISBN 0 7190 6430 9 *hardback*
      0 7190 6431 7 *paperback*

First published 2002

10 09 08 07 06 05 04 03 02   10 9 8 7 6 5 4 3 2 1

Typeset in Goudy Old Face
by Action Publishing Technology Ltd, Gloucester
Printed in Great Britain
by Biddles Ltd, Guildford and King's Lynn

Contents

Contributors

Rafe Blaufarb (Ph.D. University of Michigan): Assistant Professor, Auburn University, Alabama; author of *The French army 1750–1820* (Manchester University Press, 2002) and articles in the *Revue d'histoire moderne et contemporaine* (1996) and *French History* (2000).

Marie-Noëlle Bourguet (Doctorat Université Paris I – Sorbonne): Professeur d'histoire, Université Paris VII – Denis Diderot ; author of *Déchiffrer la France: la statistique départementale à l'époque napoléonienne* (Paris: Éditions des Archives Contemporaines, 1988) and co-editor of *L'invention scientifique de la Méditerranée. Égypte, Morée, Algérie* (Paris: EHESS, 1998).

Howard G. Brown (D.Phil. Oxford University): Associate Professor, State University of New York at Binghamton; author of *War, Revolution, and the Bureaucratic State* (Oxford: Clarendon Press, 1995) and articles in *French Historical Studies* (1995), *Journal of Modern History* (1997), *The Historical Journal* (1999) and *Historical Reflections* (2000). He is currently completing a book entitled 'Ending the French Revolution: Violence, Justice and Repression'.

Jennifer N. Heuer (Ph.D. University of Chicago): Assistant Professor, Middlebury College, Connecticut; author of articles in *French Politics, Society and Culture* (1999), *Radical History Review* (2000), *Clio: histoire femmes et sociétés* (2001) and *French History* (2002) and is currently preparing a book on women, families and citizenship in the years 1789–1830.

Annie Jourdan (Doctorat, University of Amsterdam; Habilitation, Université Paris I): Lecturer in European Studies, University of Amsterdam; author of *Les Monuments de la Révolution, 1770–1804: Une histoire de représentation* (Paris: Honoré Champion, 1997), *Napoléon: héros, imperator, mécène* (Paris: Aubier, 1998), and *L'empire de Napoléon* (Paris: Flammarion, 2000).

Judith A. Miller (Ph.D. Duke University): Associate Professor, Emory University, Atlanta, Georgia; author of *Mastering the Market: The State and the Grain Trade in Northern France, 1700–1860* (Cambridge University Press, 1999), a prize-winning article in *Journal of Modern History* (1992) and an article in *French Historical Studies* (2000). She is researching a book entitled 'Settling Accounts: Property, Law and Political Cultural in Post-Revolutionary France'.

Ronald B. Schechter (Ph.D. Harvard University): Assistant Professor, The College of William and Mary, Williamsburg, Virginia; editor of *The French Revolution: The Essential Readings* (Oxford: Blackwell Publishers, 2001) and author of *Obstinate Hebrews: Representations of Jews in France, 1715–1815* (forthcoming, University of California Press) as well as articles in *Past & Present* (1994), *Representations* (1998) and *Eighteenth-Century Studies* (1998).

CONTRIBUTORS

Michael D. Sibalis (Ph.D. Concordia University, Montreal): Associate Professor, Wilfred Laurier University, Ontario; author of articles in *French Historical Studies* (1987), *French History* (1989) and the *Annales de Bourgogne* (1992) as well as several book chapters on homosexuality in Paris.

Rebecca Spang (Ph.D. Cornell University): Lecturer, University College, London; author of the prize-winning book *The Invention of the Restaurant: Paris and Modern Gastronomic Culture* (Harvard University Press, 2000) and several book chapters on consumption during the French Revolution.

Acknowledgements

This volume arises from a two-day symposium first imagined a long time ago and finally held at Emory University on 12–13 November 1999 to coincide with the bicentennial anniversary of the coup d'état of 18 Brumaire VIII. The symposium, entitled 'The Impossible Settlement : Problems of a New Order in Post-Revolutionary France', brought together scholars from Australia, France, Canada, Great Britain, Ireland, the Netherlands, and the United States. All arrrangements for the symposium were made by Judith Miller with the able assistance of Rosalyn Page and Carol Cox.

The symposium combined papers from fourteen specialists in the field of Revolutionary and Napoleonic studies. Eight of those papers are included here. Other papers were prepared by Patrice Bret, Howard Brown, Suzanne Desan, James Livesey, Laura Mason, and Christine Peyrard. In addition, seven eminent historians of the period – Patrice Higonnet, Jean-Pierre Jessenne, Peter M. Jones, Martyn Lyons, Sarah Maza, D.M.G. Sutherland, and Isser Woloch – provided stimulating, even provocative commentaries. Discussion and debate were greatly enriched by the presence of numerous other specialists of the period, including Joshua Cole, Denise Davidson, John Dunne, Michael Kwass, and John Tone. We are grateful to all of them for their participation, and especially to Denise Davidson for filling a breach at the last minute.

The contributors have been most gracious in listening to editorial suggestions and undertaking revisions that were sometimes substantial. The chapter by Annie Jourdan was translated by Howard Brown. The chapter by Marie-Noëlle Bourguet was translated by the Center for Research in Translation at SUNY-Binghamton and revised by Judith Miller. Thanks are also due to Jennifer Pierce for her preparation of the final manuscript and index.

Above all we would like to thank those who generously provided funding for this entire enterprise: The Florence Gould Foundation, Emory University (especially the Institute of International and Comparative Studies and the Provost's Office), and the Dean's Office of Harpur College at the State University of New York at Binghamton.

New paths from the Terror to the Empire: an historiographical introduction

Howard G. Brown and Judith A. Miller

Historians have not ignored the years 1794 to 1804, but they have usually treated them as an addendum or a preface to more inspiring episodes in French history. Electoral coups, vigilante violence and the decadence of Parisian salons have generally had less appeal than the agonies of the *ancien régime*, the lofty ideals of 1789, the tragedy of the Terror, or the grandeur of Napoleon. Whereas historians have found ingenious ways to renew tired debates about the origins and course of the French Revolution, they have shown remarkably little interest in offering new conceptual approaches to the years beyond the Terror. An apparently insatiable public appetite for military history and Napoleonic biography have made it almost unnecessary, perhaps even inconvenient, to develop more sophisticated analyses of the drift to dictatorship. Thus, although not left entirely abandoned to some historical closet, scholarship on the Directory and Consulate is in great need of attention.

Yet, if the interval is worthy of sustained examination, much of the present scholarship derives from the debates and models created by work on the first years of the Revolution. Generally, the late Revolution continues to be considered by the standards set between 1789 and 1794, most often the extent to which the Thermidorian Convention, the Directory or the Consulate rejected the egalitarian and democratic ideals of year II. The character of the late republic has been largely fixed by several classic works and a few ageing syntheses aimed at a broader public.[1] The Marxist school was especially influential in generating the prevailing framework of a progressive revolution from 1789 to 1794, a conservative reaction from 1794 to 1804, and an ephemeral dictatorship from 1804 to 1814. Historians of this tradition contrasted the egalitarianism of year II with the various strategies developed

---

1   G. Lefebvre, *Les Thermidoriens* (Paris, 1937); and *Le Directoire* (Paris, 1946). Well-balanced overviews are D. Woronoff, *La République bourgeoise, 1794–1799* (Paris, 1972) and M. Lyons, *France under the Directory* (Cambridge, 1975).

1

to restrict power to the notables that followed.[2] Much of this literature emphasized that the coup d'état of 9 Thermidor II brought the bourgeoisie back to power.[3] Here, the concept of 'reaction' predominated, suggesting that the late republic must be understood primarily in terms of its repudiation of the program of year II, rather than as an interval in its own right. The regimes after Thermidor were defined primarily by what they were not: not popular, not egalitarian, not democratic. The essential development after Thermidor, therefore, was the steady affirmation of the social preponderance of the notables. Treated as a block, the years 1794 to 1804 were of interest primarily for having established the bourgeois republic and for having betrayed the Revolution's great promise.

Censure of the regimes after Thermidor did not wait for twentieth-century Marxists, however. Napoleon and his supporters first portrayed the Directory as four years of unending social and political chaos, of electoral coups and government corruption that only Bonaparte could surmount. This 'black legend' has been much elaborated since. Political narratives of the period are forced to follow the tragic demise of the republic one disappointing coup at a time.[4] Given the Directory's failure as a constitutional republic, the essence of much investigation has been to determine the relative blame to attach to constitutional impediments, inherited circumstances, political factionalism, and the inadequacies of political leaders in the Thermidorian and Directorial regimes. Did the separation of powers in the Constitution of Year III make the new republic unworkable? Had the revolutionary residue of foreign war, hyper-inflation and counter-revolution been simply overwhelming? How could the Directory, beleaguered as it was by political opponents on both extremes, have avoided invalidating elections and resorting to force? There is no doubt that its *politique de bascule* – tilting back and forth between subduing royalists and Jacobins – failed to generate a sizable constituency of moderate republicans, but could republican political culture have been altered enough to produce an alliance either with ardent democrats or constitutional monarchists?[5] Had the Thermidorian bourgeoisie adopted a liberal regime prematurely and thereby

2 G. Deville, *Thermidor et Directoire* (Paris, 1904), which appeared as vol. 5 of J. Jaurès, *Histoire socialiste de la France*; A. Mathiez, *Le Directoire jusqu'au 18 Fructidor* (Paris, 1934); G. Lefebvre, *Le Directoire* (Paris, 1946); A. Soboul, *La Première République: Le Directoire et le Consulat* (Paris, 1967).

3 For a discussion of this earlier literature, see F. Brunel, 'Sur l'historiographie de la réaction thermidorienne', *Annales historiques de la Révolution française* (hereafter *AHRF*) 337 (1979), pp. 453–74.

4 In descending order of censoriousness: L. Sciout, *Le Directoire*, 4 vols (Paris, 1885–87); A. Meynier, *Les coups d'état du Directoire*, 3 vols (Paris, 1938); M. J. Sydenham, *The First French Republic, 1792–1804* (Berkeley and Los Angeles, 1973).

5 L. Hunt, D. Lansky, P. Hanson, 'The Failure of the Liberal Republic in France, 1795–1799: The Road to Brumaire', *Journal of Modern History* 51 (December 1979), pp. 734–759; R. MacDougall, 'La consomption de la Première République et le coup d'état du 30 prairial (18 juin 1799)', *AHRF* (1989), pp. 52–74.

made a dictatorship inevitable?[6] And how should Napoleon's rule be understood? Was preserving liberty beyond his character? Was his image as the saviour of France only a myth? Had he rescued the nation or abandoned the goals of 1789? Did autocratic rule make him the last of the Enlightenment despots or is he better understood as the Louis XIV of the democratic state?[7] These questions have long dominated scholarship on the tumultuous years between two dictatorships.

Politics and political culture after Thermidor

More recently, the collapse of communism in Eastern Europe and the many transitions from dictatorship to democracy elsewhere have renewed interest in France's first effort to establish a liberal democratic republic. Suddenly the Thermidorian struggles over constitutionalism, the rule of law, and representative democracy have acquired contemporary relevance. The Constitution of Year III, for example, has been subjected to closer scrutiny than ever before. Scholars have discovered, almost to their surprise, how modern it sounds, how remarkably sensitive it was to issues of individual liberty, citizenship and separation of powers, all hitherto made impossible by the hold Rousseauian dogma had on the revolutionary imagination. This new work makes the constitutional project more than a matter of political reaction, and emphasizes its originality, modernity and sophisticated theoretical underpinnings.[8] However, this general admiration needs to be tempered by recognizing the Constitution's impractical aspects given the circumstances of 1795. The Thermidorians' attempt to end revolutionary politics through an inflexible constitutionalism led to overly mechanical means of ensuring the republic's durability. A rigid separation of powers, an inflexible bicameralism, and massive obstacles to amending the constitution stand out as especially egregious misjudgements. Yet even these mistakes are relative. The Constitution of Year III was not the Revolution's only failed attempt to create representative democracy. Marcel Gauchet takes an intellectual approach to this problem. He argues that the Thermidorians' failure was no different from that of their immediate predecessors and successors: the inability to conceive and

6   G. Lefebvre, *La France sous le Directoire* (Paris, 1944, nouvelle édition présentée par Jean-René Suratteau, 1984), pp. 727, 733.
7   A. Vandal, *L'Avènement de Bonaparte*, 2 vols (Paris, 1902–07); J. Tulard, *Napoleon or the Myth of the Saviour* (English ed., London, 1984); M. Lyons, *Napoleon Bonaparte and the Legacy of the French Revolution* (London, 1994); L. Bergeron, *France under Napoleon* (English ed., Princeton, 1981); F. Furet, 'Napoleon Bonaparte', in F. Furet and M. Ozouf, *Critical Dictionary of the French Revolution* (English ed., Cambridge, Mass., 1990), pp. 273–86.
8   R. Dupuy et M. Morabito (eds), *1795: Pour une République sans Révolution*, (Rennes, 1996); J. Bart, J.-J. Clère, C. Courvoisier and M. Verpeaux (eds), *La Constitution de l'an III ou l'ordre républicain* (Dijon, 1998); G. Conac and J.-P. Machelon (eds), *Boissy d'Anglas et la naissance du libéralisme constitutionnel* (Paris, 1999).

to constitute a 'third power' that would regulate the relationship between the legislative and executive organs, as well as the relationship between the sovereign people and its elected representatives. Only later did independent constitutional courts backed by the weight of public opinion provide this two-fold regulatory function.[9] Although strongly presentist and focused on ideas that were never implemented, Gauchet's approach has the merit of escaping the partisan mode of commemorative history so long associated with the French Revolution.

Recently the theoretical and practical problems faced by the First Republic have been explored by a spate of historians using a biographical approach. These biographies have gone a long way toward rescuing their subjects from older charges of cynicism and opportunism. Their goal has been to show that, in fact, a rational and even honourable, if occasionally naive, vision informed different leaders' political choices during extremely trying times. By following individual trajectories through this troubled period, these biographies help to reveal alternative outcomes and explain actual failures. Let us consider four examples, one representing each of four political traditions that struggled to determine the nature of the constitutional republic. Although unique in his stature as a political theorist, Sieyès represents the ambivalence of an erstwhile advocate of popular sovereignty disenchanted by its practical results. He was both a firm republican and a steadfast opponent of the Constitution of Year III. The constitutional ideas he presented in 1795 and 1799 have attracted much attention. Pasquale Pasquino highlights Sieyès' desire to found a workable form of constitutionalism based on a clear division of responsibilities and the creation of a *juré constitutionnel* to rule in cases of jurisdictional disputes. Thus, Pasquino argues that Sieyès had a very modern vision of the hierarchy of norms and of the super-legality of the constitution, an understanding not shared by his contemporaries, and one overlooked in previous scholarship.[10] In many ways, however, Sieyès' political engagement is more representative. A strong supporter of the Fructidor coup d'état of September 1797, as well as the subsequent crackdown on émigrés, priests, and nobles, he refused any cooperation with Jacobins. His intellectual egotism and endless conniving almost inadvertently made him the leading gravedigger of the democratic republic. Merlin de Douai, a fanatical defender of the Constitution of Year III, presents his biographer with exactly the opposite problem, for he was a man of little theory and disturbing pragmatism. Here was a renowned jurist during the *ancien régime* who became infamous for authoring the Law of Suspects in 1793 and notorious for his political intoler-

---

9 M. Gauchet, *La Révolution des pouvoirs: La souveraineté, le peuple et la représentation, 1789–1799* (Paris, 1995).

10 P. Pasquino, *Sieyes et l'invention de la constitution en France* (Paris, 1998). See also J.-D. Bredin, *Sieyès, la clé de la Révolution française* (Paris, 1988).

ance and casuistic legalisms as a minister in 1796–97 and a director in 1797–99. Hervé Leuwers' attempt to explain his choices risks appearing to sympathize with his political prejudices and undemocratic methods.[11] However, Merlin is precisely the sort of complicated figure who needs thorough probing. He embodied the regime's essential tension between using the law to trammel local officials and resorting to extra-legal measures to save the republic. His actual choices played a key role in shaping the ideology of order that later underpinned the Consulate and Empire.

Other biographies follow oppositional figures within the republican camp. On the republican right, Christine Le Bozec's Marxist analysis explores Boissy d'Anglas' status as a bourgeois liberal whose prosperity committed him to property and legality, and whose experience of Parisian *journées* left him utterly unsympathetic to the 'mob'.[12] Proscription on trumped-up charges of royalism in 1797 gave way to a highly successful career in government after 1800. Had the Directory found ways to accommodate such men, it might have survived. On the republican left, Antonelle, an eccentric nobleman and Jacobin mayor of Arles, became a radical journalist and co-conspirator with Babeuf. Pierre Serna has made the most of Antonelle's scribblings, but succumbs to the biographer's temptation to exaggerate their significance.[13] According to Serna, the autumn of year IV held the potential for genuine republican renewal – one capable of weathering the challenges of counter-revolution and reaction. He insists that the Directory was responsible for pushing the democratic opposition into illegality, a strong claim considering Jacobins' behaviour in the Revolution to date. Nonetheless, whatever their individual strengths or weaknesses, read collectively, these political biographies enable us to see the diversity within republicanism and how difficult it was to build consensus for the new regime.[14]

Approaching the period through biography helps to raise awareness of the difficulties facing the republic after six years of unprecedented upheaval. However, appreciating the extent of Thermidorian and Directorial achievements requires a greater breadth of vision. For whatever reason, English historians alone have undertaken periodic general reassessments that shed a more positive light on the period. These authors stress that the Directory inherited an immeasurably greater burden of social, economic, financial and political

---

11 H. Leuwers, *Un juriste en politique, Merlin de Douai (1754–1838)* (Arras, 1996).
12 C. Le Bozec, *Boissy d'Anglas, un grand notable libéral* (Privas, 1995).
13 P. Serna, *Antonelle: Aristocrate révolutionnaire, 1747–1817* (Paris, 1997). See also his 'Comment être démocrate et constitutionnel en 1797', *AHRF* 308 (1997), pp. 199–219.
14 Other recent biographies on republican figures of influence during the Directory include: B. Fontana, *Benjamin Constant and the Post-Revolutionary Mind* (New Haven and London, 1991); J.-R. Suratteau and A. Bischoff, *Jean-François Reubel: L'Alsacien de la Révolution française* (Steinbrunn-le-Haut, 1995); M. Sydenham, *Léonard Bourdon* (Toronto, 2000); R. Hermon-Belot, *L'Abbé Grégoire, la politique et la vérité* (Paris, 2000).

dislocation than it bequeathed to the Consulate.[15] On a far more ambitious scale, Isser Woloch has provided a monumental synthesis of the changes wrought in France's 'civic order'.[16] He uses this phrase to encompass the values, policies, and institutions that formed the basis for French public life from the Revolution to the Restoration. Although he regrettably omits any discussion of religion or gender,[17] especially thorny problems during the years 1795 to 1801, this period emerges from his study as one of much innovation and consolidation. It is true that the Directory oversaw retrenchment on revolutionary ideals in such areas as electoral participation, public assistance, and primary education. But he is careful to take a broader perspective, noting the impressive scope of change since the pre-Revolution. His yardstick is his own vision of progress, not the visionary ideals of year II. Subsequent research on republican government also describes major strides toward modern bureaucratic structures. New methods of organizing and controlling administrative expertise created a more powerful state capable of defending the young republic abroad and penetrating the village at home. These methods helped to make the bureaucracy more responsive to a democratic state elite, but even after democracy disappeared, the restored ministries of the Directory became lasting monuments to the period.[18] Finally, those overly focused on the sordid nature of politics at this time need to be reminded that these years gave birth to lasting scientific and educational institutions such as the *École polytechnique*, the *École normale supérieure*, the *École des langues orientales*, the *Conservatoire des arts et métiers*, the *Musée des monuments*, the *Institut de France*, and not least, the metric system. Furthermore, the formation of *écoles centrales* in 1795 provided a major step toward the *lycées* of 1802.[19] Such evidence makes it difficult to dismiss these years as a dark age during which succeeding regimes merely eroded representative government and finally placed a broken republic at the mercy of a personal dictatorship.

15   For useful historiographic introductions which moderate the 'black legend', see A. Goodwin, 'The French Executive Directory: A Re-evaluation', *History* 22 (1937), 210–18; C. H. Church, 'In Search of the Directory', in J. Bosher (ed.), *French Government and Society, 1500–1850, Essays in Memory of Alfred Cobban* (London, 1973), pp. 261–94; and M. Crook, *Napoleon Comes to Power: Democracy and Dictatorship in Revolutionary France, 1795–1804* (Cardiff, 1998).

16   I. Woloch, *The New Regime: Transformations of the French Civic Order, 1789–1820s* (New York, 1994).

17   Some aspects of gender and the polity have been treated since Woloch's book appeared. See X. Martin, 'Fonction paternelle et Code Napoléon', AHRF 305 (1996), pp. 465–75; S. Desan, 'The War between Brothers and Sisters: Inheritance Law and Gender Politics in Revolutionary France', *French Historical Studies* 20 (1997), pp. 597–634 and 'Reconstituting the Social after the Terror', *Past and Present* 164 (1999), pp. 81–121.

18   C. H. Church, *The Revolution and Red Tape: French Ministerial Bureaucracy, 1770–1850* (Oxford, 1981); H. G. Brown, *War, Revolution, and the Bureaucratic State* (Oxford, 1995); C. Kawa, *Les ronds-de-cuir en Révolution* (Paris, 1997); and K. Alder, *Engineering the Revolution: Arms and Enlightenment in France, 1763–1815* (Princeton, 1997).

19   D. Julia, *Les trois couleurs du tableau noir: La Révolution* (Paris, 1981); R. R. Palmer, *The Improvement of Humanity: Education and the French Revolution* (Princeton, 1985); J. Godechot, *Les Institutions de la France sous la Révolution et l'Empire* (Paris, 1968).

Fifteen years ago, scholarship on the French Revolution made a massive return to issues of political history, drawing on a range of linguistic, anthropological, gender and cultural models to reveal new forces at work in late eighteenth-century French society.[20] At the heart of 'political culture,' however, has been the study of revolutionary discourses crafted by politicians and journalists. This research sought to recover the discursive and imaginative dynamics that moved the Revolution toward the Terror. In this body of work, the end of the discourse of the general will and popular sovereignty on 9 Thermidor – rather than the defeat of any social movement – signalled the Revolution's collapse. Such an approach ignores many post-Thermidorian perspectives. However, making the period beyond Thermidor a subject in its own right generates considerable insight. For example, Bronislaw Baczko, while ignoring any influence social struggles, military victories, or religious resurgence might have had after the overthrow of Robespierre, explores the prolonged political ambiguities of Thermidor.[21] The Convention's contorted efforts to disavow the Terror and yet preserve the continuity of revolutionary government belie previous claims that this was a period of political reaction, at least until well after the coup. Only then did it become impossible to resist demands for revenge. Being deeply implicated in the Terror, the Thermidorians initially tried to avoid organizing retributive justice. The double game of proclaiming rupture and asserting continuity, all while resisting calls for vengeance, perpetuated many of the political practices of the Terror: calumny, denunciations, exclusions and executions. The essential change, therefore, took place in the rhetoric of revolutionary legitimacy accompanying these practices. However, once show trials exposed the intimate horrors of the Vendée and the arbitrariness of revolutionary justice, victims of the Terror throughout the country came to see their own suffering as part of a great national tragedy and thereby justified their desire for vengeance. Thus, the twin discourses of justice and vandalism generated by exiting the Terror soon turned revenge into a full-scale political reaction that threatened the Republic's survival. In this way, dismantling the Terror led inexorably to searching for ways to end the Revolution itself.[22]

The recent focus on the rhetoric of revolution might not always provide satisfactory causal explanations, but it has certainly detected unexpected forces at work in otherwise conventional subjects. Perhaps the best example

20 For the range of possibilities 'political culture' entailed, see the following seminal works: L. Hunt, *Politics, Culture and Class in the French Revolution* (Berkeley, 1984); K. Baker, C. Lucas and F. Furet (eds), *The French Revolution and the Creation of Modern Political Culture*, 4 vols (Oxford, 1987–94); and F. Furet and M. Ozouf, *The Critical Dictionary of the French Revolution* (English ed., New York, 1990).

21 B. Baczko, *Ending the Terror: The French Revolution after Robespierre* (English ed., Cambridge, 1994).

22 For some sharp criticism of this discursive approach to the Thermidorian Convention, see F. Brunel and S. Goujon, *Les martyrs de prairial: textes et documents inédits* (Geneva, 1992).

of this for the late 1790s is Eric Walter's study of Gracchus Babeuf. Walter moves beyond the question of Babeuf's over-studied role as ideological precursor of nineteenth-century Communism and instead uses a literary analysis to reveal prophetic strains in Babeuf's writings. Babeuf drew on the egalitarian millenarianism of his time, a discourse that Jean-Paul Marat, Jacques Roux and other revolutionary radicals had secularized. While in prison from February to October 1795, Babeuf apparently began going into trances and using feverish language. By the time the 'conspiracy of equals' took shape, he had polished his style. At times, his writings burst into a fiery prophetic voice, linking transformative violence to his vision of the future. Walter interprets these not as statements of doctrine, but as messianic epiphanies most fully realized in his great show trial. This innovative treatment of a revolutionary icon invites others to explore the legacy of Christian metaphors and tropes in political rhetoric under the secular republic.[23]

Other historians who examine political culture after Thermidor pay more attention to grass-roots political practices and the impact of the Convention's policies on the most vulnerable. For Florence Gauthier, one of the most disturbing elements of the Thermidorian vision was its impact on colonial issues. By attaching citizenship to property, and not to the individual, the Thermidorians turned their backs on the Revolution's earlier vision of colonial emancipation. The true parliamentary coup, according to Gauthier, came when the Convention suppressed the Constitution of 1793, disenfranchising not only the poor, but also people of colour. This led to a twofold politics aimed at military hegemony on the continent and the colonial empire abroad.[24] At the heart of this empire, that is, in Paris itself, Raymonde Monnier argues that the key to the 'Thermidorian transition' was the systematic contraction of a Habermasian 'public space' in the capital. By this she means the dissolution of popular societies, then the closure of section meetings, and finally the limiting of political activity to electoral assemblies based on censitary voting.[25]

Long before notions of 'the bourgeois public sphere' had an impact on revolutionary studies, Isser Woloch wrote a pioneering social and political history of the democratic movement in the years 1795–1800.[26] Historians sympathetic to Jacobinism continue to gather evidence for his argument that the Directory failed because it refused to accept the Jacobins as partners in

23 See the pieces by E. Walter in A. Maillard, C. Mazauric, and E. Walter (eds), *Présence de Babeuf: Lumières, révolution, communisme* (Paris, 1994). Two other pieces notable for their original perspectives on the revolutionary imagination are: D. Margairaz, 'François de Neufchâteau en Révolution ou les figures de la ville', in B. Benoit (ed.), *Ville et Révolution française* (Lyon, 1994), pp. 256–72; and B. Gainot, 'Enquête sur le « suicide » de Victor Bach', *AHRF* (1999), pp. 615–27.

24 F. Gauthier, *Triomphe et mort du droit naturel en Révolution 1789–1795–1802* (Paris, 1992).

25 R. Monnier, *L'espace démocratique: Essai sur l'opinion à Paris de la Révolution au Directoire* (Paris, 1994).

26 I. Woloch, *Jacobin Legacy: The Democratic Movement under the Directory* (Princeton, 1970).

defending the Republic. Careful regional work of this nature has also begun to shed light on patterns of democratic participation. The study of electoral politics is moving beyond the obvious analysis of plotting results on a political spectrum running from royalist to radical democrat.[27] The meaning of low voter turnout during the Directory is now contested. In fact, the whole context of electoral participation, ranging from secret societies to public processions, from voter registration to physical intimidation, is being investigated for signs of democratic vitality right down to 1799.[28] Bernard Gainot in particular has conducted extensive research into the provincial networks of the so-called 'neo-Jacobins' of the late Directory. He finds them surprisingly vigorous and argues that they were united by a set of democratic principles: freedom of the press, right of political association, right of peoples to self-determination, and republican assimilation of the colonies.[29] Despite these admirable efforts to reanimate the study of republican politics, it is clear that more attention needs to be paid to the undemocratic ways in which local elites operated to gain or retain power. After all, it was a 'political culture' which mixed lofty principles and base practices that gave the new regime its true definition at the local level.[30]

Regional dimensions, 1794–1804

Resistance to the Revolution constitutes another crucial arena of politics. However, here the linguistic analysis deployed in studying 'political culture' has had less influence. Instead the disciplines of sociology and anthropology have been used to expand the tool kit of historians, enabling them to improve upon the crude labels of royalism or counter-revolution. The phenomena of civil war and guerrilla resistance in western France, for example, have acquired added layers of complexity. Older explanations of resistance based

27   J.-R. Suratteau, Les élections de l'an VI et le coup d'Etat du 22 floréal (Dijon, 1971); 'Les élections de l'an IV', AHRF 123 (1951) pp. 374–93 124 (1951) pp. 32–62; 'Les élections de l'an V', AHRF 154 (1958) pp. 20–63.

28   See M. Crook, Elections and the French Revolution: An Apprenticeship in Democracy, 1789–1799 (Cambridge, 1996) and P. Gueniffey, Le nombre et la raison: La Révolution française et les élections (Paris, 1993). Among the many local studies are: C. Peyrard, Les Jacobins de l'Ouest: Sociabilité révolutionnaire et formes de politisation dans le Maine et la Basse-Normandie (1789–1799) (Paris, 1996); M. Gentry, 'Les élections municipales à Paris sous le Directoire', AHRF 319 (2000), pp. 47–70; S. Bianchi, 'Vie, pratiques et sociabilité politiques en milieu rural dans le sud de l'Ile-de-France (1787–1800)', Université de Paris-I (1996).

29   B. Gainot, 1799, un nouveau Jacobinisme? (Paris, 2001).

30   On the stratagems used in exercising power at the local level, see C. Lucas, 'The First Directory and the Rule of Law', French Historical Studies 10 (1977), pp. 231–60 and 'The Rules of the Game in Local Politics under the Directory', French Historical Studies 16 (1989), pp. 345–71; and P. Jones, 'La République au Village in the Southern Massif Central', The Historical Journal 23 (1980), pp. 793–812; and the papers published in Du Directoire au Consulat, vol. 1: J. Bernet, J.-P. Jessenne, and H. Leuwers (eds), Le lien politique local dans la Grande Nation (Lille, 1999).

mainly on the leadership of nobles and priests have long given way to arguments based on changing economic structures and the peculiar nature of tenant farming in the region.[31] More recently, historians have tried to take stock of the awful carnage wrought by the civil war from 1793 to 1796 and then blamed it all on the murderous ideological zeal of the revolutionary government.[32] Unfortunately, the polemical thrust of this work rules out any investigation of efforts at reconciliation following the military pacification. Certainly *chouannerie* persisted down to Napoleon. Though not uniform across time and place, it has yet to receive the sort of subtle analysis done of the reactionary violence of the Midi.[33]

A generation ago, Richard Cobb, eschewing all social science methods, published two remarkably evocative and astute passages on the White Terror of 1795–97 in the Rhône Valley and Mediterranean basin. He preferred the terms anti-revolutionary or counter-terrorist violence to distinguish the prison massacres and vendetta killings from other forms of so-called counter-revolution. Whereas Cobb remained resolutely impressionistic, Colin Lucas and Gwynne Lewis have sought to be more precise in explaining causes. Taking a more anthropological approach, Lucas argued that most of the grizzly anti-republican violence that occurred in lowland areas of the Midi derived from a defence of the local community and was expressed as retribution for violating its traditional mores. Lewis, on the other hand, stressed the role of long-standing religious animosities, property disputes, and widespread counter-revolutionary conspiracy.[34] Together these studies demonstrate the importance of assessing local patterns of resistance for understanding the ultimate failure of the constitutional republic.

Even in areas where violence was less common and not so dramatic, resistance was often pervasive. D. M. G. Sutherland has convincingly argued that the entire history of the 1790s is best understood as a struggle against a

31 P. Bois, *Paysans de l'Ouest* (Paris, 1960); C. Tilly, *The Vendée: A sociological analysis of the counterrevolution of 1793* (Cambridge, MA, 1964); D. M. G. Sutherland, *Chouans: The Social Origins of Popular Counter-Revolution in Upper Brittany, 1770–1796* (Oxford, 1982).

32 R. Secher, *Le génocide franco-français: La Vendée-Vengé* (Paris, 1986); J. Hussenet, 'La guerre de Vendée: Combien de morts?' *Recherches vendéennes* (1994), pp. 39–89; (1995), pp. 31–95; (1996), pp. 301–66 ; (1997), pp. 97–218; A. Gérard, '*Par principe d'humanité* . . .' *La Terreur et la Vendée* (Paris, 1999). For a more balanced assessment, see J.-C. Martin, *La Vendée et la France* (Paris, 1987). On certain aspects of recovery, see the collection of papers in *La Vendée: Après la Terreur, la reconstruction* (Paris, 1997).

33 Two recent works are helpful, but limited in ambition: R. Dupuy, *Les Chouans* (Paris, 1997) in the Hachette series 'La vie quotidienne' and E.-M. Guyot, *Vendéens et chouans contre Bonaparte (1799–1814)* (Toulon, 1990).

34 R. Cobb, *The Police and the People: French Popular Protest, 1789–1820* (Oxford, 1970), pp. 131–67; R. Cobb, *Reactions to the French Revolution* (Oxford, 1974), pp. 19–62. See their separate contributions to C. Lucas and G. Lewis (eds), *Beyond the Terror: Essays in French Regional and Social History, 1794–1815* (Cambridge, 1983) as well as C. Lucas, 'The Problem of the Midi in the French Revolution' *Transactions of the Royal Historical Society*, 5th series, 28 (1978), pp. 1–25 and G. Lewis, *The Second Vendée* (Oxford, 1978).

counter-revolution (broadly defined) that was 'massive, extensive, durable, and popular'.[35] As his book makes clear, this resistance was more often than not provoked simply by trying to impose a modern, secular state on a predominantly agrarian and still profoundly religious populace. Such conclusions are given ample support by subsequent specialized studies of religious rioting under the Directory, draft-dodging during the Revolution and Napoleonic period, and town administration across half a century.[36] The more this explanation expands, however, the more it begs the question. State-formation and resistance to it have always had a symbiotic relationship. However, apart from the Terror, repression during the period has received little attention. Historians have tended to lose interest in resistance when it deteriorated into widespread banditry and have totally ignored responses to it. Nonetheless, studying the relationship between resistance and repression in the late Revolution leads to a new periodization. Although less spectacular, the violence of 1797–1802, both state and non-state, did more to change the state's role in society than did the violence of 1793–94. By 1802, France had become a security state based on 'liberal authoritarianism'. This was as enduring a feature of the nineteenth century as any other product of the Revolution.[37]

As must be abundantly clear by now, understanding the turmoil of the Directory requires a form of political history that gets out of Paris. Some of the basic features of politics in the period – the persistence of counter-revolution and the resilience of Jacobinism, for instance – cannot be grasped without detailed local studies. The violence of the period is especially susceptible to interdisciplinary methods. Anthropological, discursive and literary approaches have helped to uncover the workings of brutality in other periods and may well illuminate the forces at work in the Directory.[38] Moreover, regional examples are still needed in order to explain how the Consulate was received in different parts of the country. Equally, it is in provincial towns and

35 D. M. G. Sutherland, *France 1789–1815: Revolution and Counterrevolution* (London, 1985), p. 14. Cf. J.-C. Martin, *Contre-révolution, révolution, et nation en France, 1789–1799* (Paris, 1998), where 'the Counter-Revolution' is defined as a concept which embraced all the failed opponents (including Feuillants, Girondins, Dantonistes, Hébertistes and Robespierristes) of successive revolutionary regimes whose legitimacy derived from creating national unity.

36 S. Desan, *Reclaiming the Sacred: Lay Religion and Popular Politics in Revolutionary France* (Ithaca, 1990); A. Forrest, *Conscripts and Deserters: The Army and French Society during the Revolution and Empire* (New York, 1989); G. Fournier, *Démocratie et vie municipale en Languedoc du milieu du XVIIIe au début du XIXe siècle*, 2 vols (Toulouse, 1994). See also F. Lebrun and R. Dupuy (eds), *Les résistances à la Révolution* (Paris, 1987).

37 H. G. Brown, 'From Organic Society to Security State: The War on Brigandage in France, 1797–1802', *Journal of Modern History* 69 (1997), pp. 661–95 and 'Domestic State Violence: Repression from the Croquants to the Commune', *The Historical Journal* 42 (1999), pp. 597–622.

38 See the remarks on this point in J.-C. Martin, 'Un bicentenaire en cache un autre: repenser la Terreur?' *AHRF* 297 (1994), pp. 517–26.

villages that historians must search for the full implication of gendered resistance based on the defence of Catholicism. Was it really a determined boycott
by women that led to the ultimate demise of the constitutional church,
effectively forcing Bonaparte into the Concordat for the sake of domestic
tranquillity?[39] More than at any other time in the decades before or after,
provincial politics during the years 1795 to 1801 decided the fate of the
regime in power. Whether it is through a study of 'political culture', anti-
republican resistance, or state repression, the transition from democracy to
dictatorship requires many local studies.

The impending dictatorship

If the workings of local politics during the late Directory are still open to
question, the ways in which the Consulate de-politicized a society torn by
ideologies and factions remains even more obscure. The process by which
the Consulate put forth a programme and the broader responses of French
society to the end of the Republic have generated little monographic
research. Nonetheless, the subject is at last getting attention. An abundance
of research at the local level has been undertaken recently, some of it breaking through to re-conceptualize problems of social order and state consolidation.[40] Even at the level of high politics historians are beginning to
recognize the genuine republicanism of the early Consulate, the continued
importance of political debate in these years, and, perhaps above all, the
significance of the men who then assisted in constructing the Empire. Why
did so many republicans and constitutional monarchists willingly collabo-
rate with Napoleon Bonaparte even as he betrayed their most cherished
ideals? Isser Woloch is inclined to temper charges of cynicism with understanding explanations, accepting the idea that at least they would be at
hand to preserve some semblance of liberal principles. Furthermore, it was
not easy to decide when a timely resignation done with *éclat* might have
had a serious impact; after all, these Brumairians were dealing with 'the
gradually unfolding, gilded authoritarianism of Napoleon Bonaparte, the

---

39 O. Hufton, 'The Reconstruction of a Church, 1796–1801', in Lucas and Lewis, *Beyond the
    Terror*, pp. 21–52.
40 A series of French conferences have commemorated various bicentennial moments of the late
    Revolution. These generally contain short papers of variable quality; furthermore, some of the
    collections are not widely available. M. Vovelle and R. Monnier (eds), *Révolution et République:
    L'exception française* (Paris, 1994); R. Dupuy (ed.), *Pouvoir locale et Révolution: La frontière intérieure*
    (Rennes, 1995); R. Dupuy and M. Morabito (eds), *1795, Pour une République sans Révolution*
    (Rennes, 1996); B. Gainot and P. Bourdin (eds), *La République directoriale*, 2 vols (Clermont-
    Ferrand, 1998); J.-P. Jessenne, J.-P. Hirsch, and H. Leuwers (eds), *La Grande Nation* (Lille, 2000);
    and M. Arrous, *Napoléon: de l'histoire à la légende* (Paris, 2000); J.-P. Jessenne (ed.), *Du Directoire au
    Consulat*, vol. 3: *Brumaire dans l'histoire du lien politique et de l'État-nation* (Rouen, 2000). Finally, the
    first local history of the Napoleonic period in English has just appeared: G. Daly, *Inside Napoleonic
    France: State and Society in Rouen, 1800–1815* (Aldershot, 2001).

dictatorship that 'dared not speak its name'.[41]

Other broader studies have also examined the new elites, assessing their origins and whether a distinctly different group of notables had emerged. The financially powerful have been the subject of detailed prosopographical analysis by Louis Bergeron, Guy Chaussinand-Nogaret and Michel Bruguière.[42] On the local level, long-term studies by Jean-Pierre Jessenne and Peter M. Jones have assessed the extent to which notables were able to redefine and consolidate their strength across the Revolution.[43] Other important work has examined military desertion, an important feature of resistance to these regimes.[44] Nonetheless, our overall knowledge of the activities and adherences of those living under the Napoleonic state, in particular, remains rather fragmentary. Napoleon and his servitors – and not French society – continued to be the focus of most work on the years 1799–1815.

Yet, while there is much to be done on many aspects of Napoleonic France, recent scholarship on the economy at least suggests sources of stability by the early nineteenth century. Unlike other areas of work on the Revolution, that of the economy has broken free of the traditional focus on the radical or conservative nature of the era's ideologies. This trend might seem surprising given the significance of economic matters for several generations of Marxists and revisionists alike. Nonetheless, several areas of new research have opened, although, in some cases, they depend to a large extent on somewhat older scholarship. The first looks at the impact of the Revolution on the country's long-term economic rhythms. The second examines the potential for theoretical innovation in the economic ideologies of the late Revolution. The third assesses the new structures put in place after the abolition of the Maximum in late 1794 and the responses they elicited at both the national and local levels. Together, these three strands of scholarship reveal convincingly the presence of new behaviours, economic structures and fresh debate about how to activate the economy.

Scholars looking at the economy's long-range movements now try to avoid the politicization that has stimulated much work on the Revolution. Rather than blaming the Revolution for economic upheaval, scholars are assessing its long-term consequences and placing these in an international

---

41 T. Lentz, Le Grand Consulat, 1799–1804 (Paris, 1999); J.-O. Boudon, Histoire du Consulat et de l'Empire (Paris, 2000); I. Woloch, Napoleon and His Collaborators: The Making of a Dictatorship (New York, 2001), quotation from p. 239.

42 L. Bergeron and G. Chaussinand-Nogaret, 'Les Masses de granit:' Cent mille notables du 1er Empire (Paris, 1979); M. Bruguière, Gestionnaires et profiteurs de la Révolution: L'administration des finances françaises de Louis XVI à Bonaparte (Paris, 1986). See also J. Tulard, 'Les composants d'une fortune: le cas de la noblesse d'Empire', Revue historique 513 (1975), pp. 119–38.

43 J.-P. Jessenne, Pouvoir au village et révolution: Artois, 1760–1848 (Lille, 1987); P. M. Jones, Politics and Rural Society: The Southern Massif Central, c. 1750–1880 (Cambridge, 1985).

44 A. Forrest, Conscripts and Deserters: The Army and French Society during the Revolution and Empire (New York, 1989).

context. Thus, these studies set out to establish trustworthy data series and to determine the new departures that the Revolution offered the economy. This work highlights the move inland of the French economy during the Revolution, away from ports and toward Paris. That tendency increased the power of Parisian banking over the provinces. In agriculture, this work suggests that the Revolution's greatest impact lay not in its abolition of feudal dues or even the sale of *biens nationaux*, the focus of traditional explanations.[45] Instead, other forms of economic transfer, such as debt repayment after hyper-inflation and the rise of wages for farm labour, seem to have had a greater impact. Moreover, de-urbanization and the disruption of commercial networks turned the rural world in on itself. Overall this work finds that the Revolution consolidated many of the agrarian structures of eighteenth-century France and prolonged the weight of rural France far into the nineteenth century.[46]

Moving from hard economic realities to theoretical debates, one finds sophisticated new work on contemporary discussions of political economy. Notions of how to regenerate the economy and re-establish social harmony were constantly being presented and debated in the pages of the *Décade philosophique* and at the National Institute's Class of Moral and Political Sciences. *Idéologues* such as Destutt de Tracy, Cabanis, and Garat might have won the battle of posterity. All the same, recent research has shown that at the time their ideas did not overwhelm alternative viewpoints presented by men like the writer Louis-Sébastien Mercier, the deputy Antoine-François Delpierre, and the minister François de Neufchâteau, advocates of what James Livesey has called 'commercial republicanism'.[47] Taking a longer view, and examining the intersection of practices and ideas, other work has tried to assess the influence of liberal ideologies on the commercial world itself. These studies stretch into the nineteenth century,

45 For almost definitive studies of these issues from a non-economic perspective, see J. Markoff, *The Abolition of Feudalism: Peasants, Lords and Legislators in the French Revolution* (University Park, PA, 1996), who stresses the unique and precocious nature of peasant emancipation in France, and B. Bodinier and É. Teyssier, *L'Évènement le plus important de la Révolution: La vente des biens nationaux* (Paris, 2000), who conclude that the total *biens nationaux* sold in the first decade was about ten per cent of French territory, two-thirds of which came from the Church, and that the number of purchasers amounted to one in ten French households, both smaller figures than previously assumed.

46 Compare the more conventional perspectives in G. Koubi (ed.), *Propriété et Révolution* (Toulouse and Paris, 1990) with other recent literature, such as F. Hincker, *La Révolution française et l'économie: Décollage ou catastrophe?* (Paris, 1989), T. J. A. Le Goff and D. M. G. Sutherland, 'The Revolution and the Rural Economy', in A. Forrest and P. M. Jones (eds), *Reshaping France: Town, Country and Region during the French Revolution* (Manchester, 1991), and the dozen articles in *Révolution de 1789: Guerres et croissance économique*, Revue économique 40 (1989), many of which go well beyond 1794.

47 G. Faccarello and Ph. Steiner (eds), *La pensée économique pendant la Révolution française* (Grenoble, 1990); M. S. Staum, *Minerva's Message: Stabilizing the Revolution* (Toronto, 1996); J. Livesey, *Making Democracy in the French Revolution* (Cambridge, Mass., 2001).

following the activities of authorities and businessmen as they negotiated the state's commitment to freer trade and new juridical structures. Jean-Pierre Hirsch's exceptionally rich study of Lille provides evidence of a dualist vision combining a desire for protectionism and effective institutions with elements of economic liberalism.[48] A study of the grain trade, a topic central to understanding food riots and popular radicalism, also reveals the complex relationship between free-market ideals and continued state intervention. Repeated crises in production and distribution inspired several efforts to restructure the supply system, affecting everyone from small-town bakers to huge import conglomerates. The many early nineteenth-century central and regional authorities did not see their massive efforts as antithetical to free trade, but rather as necessary complements to liberal reforms.[49] Such work suggests that this period was one of profound debate about the new norms of the economy, debates that defy earlier dismissals of the late Revolution as merely installing elements basic to the cold capitalism of the nineteenth century.

Beyond the social, political and economic investigation of recent years lies a vast field of cultural approaches that could be used to uncover aspects of negotiation, contestation or resignation encountered along the various paths leading from the Terror to the Empire. Overall, the interdisciplinary approaches that have enlivened the study of other periods have yet to make an equal impact on the period after Thermidor. While legal historians have organized conferences on the creation of revolutionary law and the making of the Civil Code, little of that work crosses over into the more orthodox periodical or monographic publications on the Revolution.[50] Literary criticism and art history are only beginning to enter mainstream work on the era, although they could point the way toward new conceptualizations of the individual and the impact of images.[51] Annie Jourdan has reminded historians of the power of artistic and architectural achievements in providing cultural propaganda for revolutionary and Napoleonic regimes desperate to establish

48   J.-P. Hirsch, Les deux rêves du Commerce: Entreprise et institution dans la région lilloise (1780–1860) (Paris, 1991) and 'The French Revolution, Cradle of Free Enterprise', American Historical Review (1989). See also S. Chassagne, Le coton et ses patrons, France, 1760–1840 (Paris, 1991); and D. Woronoff, L'industrie sidéurgique en France pendant la Révolution et l'Empire (Paris, 1984).

49   J. A. Miller, Mastering the Market: The State and the Grain Trade in Northern France, 1700–1860 (Cambridge and New York, 1999).

50   La Famille, la Loi, l'Etat: de la Révolution au Code civil (Paris, 1989); X. Martin (ed.), Nature humaine et Révolution française: du siècle des Lumières au Code Napoléon (Paris, 1994); J.-L. Halperin, L'Impossible Code civil (Paris, 1992).

51   A variety of works provides suggestive alternatives for exploring the late Revolution, especially its imaginative dimensions: D. Denby, Sentimental Narrative and the Social Order in France (Cambridge, 1994); T. M. Kavanagh, Enlightenment and the Shadows of Chance: The Novel and the Culture of Gambling in Eighteenth-Century France (Baltimore, 1993); T. Crow, Emulation: Making Artists for Revolutionary France (New Haven, 1995); L. Nochlin, The Body in Pieces: The Fragment as a Metaphor of Modernity (London, 1994).

their legitimacy.[52] Economic work rarely appears in conference programs and publication series, whereas it would certainly help to explain the debates and strains of the era. Moreover, few scholars have asked about women – whether in the crowd or the salon. Widespread scholarly interest in European colonial expansion, together with a timely bicentennial, has led to a spate of work on the broader implications of the French expedition to Egypt in 1798.[53] There has also been a flurry of work on slave emancipation, although the focus remains largely on legislative debates and pamphlet wars, rather than exploring the experiences of people of colour, especially those who lived in France.[54] In other words, some of the sources and inquiries that could revolutionize the history of the years after Thermidor are still struggling to gain the *droit de cité*.

Recovering the contingent

The articles in this volume offer an original perspective on the post-revolutionary order. Most important, these authors escape the hegemonic influence that the categories of year II have exercised over the field. Instead, they seek to recover the ambiguities of the period and to explore diverse issues not confronted earlier in the Revolution. The point of entry for this fresh discussion of the late Revolution is Howard G. Brown's interpretive overview of the transition from Thermidor to the Empire. He replaces the common notion of a revolutionary decade (1789–99) with an alternative decade dominated by prolonged efforts to end the Revolution (1794–1804). This challenges widespread assumptions that the coup d'état of 18 Brumaire VIII constituted a major rupture in French history. Furthermore, he argues for a strange unity in this fractured decade and highlights the continuity of contingency in the search for stability. Tracing the progressive resolution of basic issues facing France in 1794 without assuming the outcome of 1804 allows him to provide a stimulating introduction to traditional issues of domestic politics, foreign affairs, economics, religion and

---

52 *Les Monuments de la Révolution, 1770–1804: Une histoire de représentation* (Paris, 1997) and *Napoléon: Héros, imperator, mécène* (Paris, 1998).

53 See M.-N. Bourguet, B. Lepetit, D. Nordman, and M. Sinarellis (eds), *L'invention scientifique de la Méditerranée. Égypte, Morée, Algérie* (Paris, 1998); H. Laurens, *Les origines intellectuelles de l'expédition d'Égypte* (Istanbul and Paris, 1987); P. Bret, *L'Égypte au temps de l'expédition de Bonaparte (1798–1801)* (Paris, 1998); P. Bret (ed.), *L'expédition d'Égypte, une entreprise des Lumières* (Paris, 1999).

54 See for instance M. Dorigny and B. Gainot, *La Société des Amis des Noirs, 1789–1799. Contribution à l'histoire de l'abolition de l'esclavage* (Paris, 1998); Y. Bénot, *La démence coloniale sous Napoléon* (Paris, 1992); F. Gauthier, *Triomphe et mort du droit naturel en Révolution, 1789–1795–1802* (Paris, 1992). The Atlantic World, a formulation more common in North American scholarship, places such questions in an international context. See D. Geggus, 'Esclaves et gens de couleur libres de Martinique pendant l'époque révolutionnaire et napoleonienne: trois instants de resistance', *Revue historique* 597 (1996), pp. 105–32; R. D. Meadows, 'Engineering Exile: Social Networks and the French Atlantic Community, 1789–1799', *French Historical Studies* 23 (2000), pp. 67–102.

the social order. His contribution is valuable both for provoking debate and providing a context for the chapters that follow.

One of the central issues in this collection is the multivalent role played by the law in shaping revolutionary outcomes. The torrent of laws unleashed by one revolutionary government after another did not make everyone legalistic, but it certainly altered the nature of legitimate authority and therefore also changed how it was contested. Furthermore, the arbitrariness associated with the *ancien régime* and the Terror propelled republican leaders into a veritable cult of the law. Recent cultural methodologies based on literary, rhetorical and theatrical concerns enrich several of the contributors' approaches to the law.

The centrality of the law in reorganizing French society comes through in two papers on civil litigation, a topic that has received scant coverage elsewhere. Introducing the question of the construction of women's rights under the Directory, Jennifer Heuer reveals the tensions between sex and citizenship and seeks to identify the gendered structures that emerged. Moving beyond the focus of recent scholarship on women's formal exclusion from politics, Heuer examines the laws regarding their claim to French citizenship as individuals apart from their status as wives or daughters. She treats the Directory's laws on émigrés as another arena in which the revolutionaries struggled to sort out the gendered implications of their reordering of the state around the household. Judith A. Miller's contribution explores the legislative remedies to the hyper-inflation of 1795–97. The Councils issued numerous decrees allowing parties to rewrite contracts and recalculate debts – even permitting former landowners to sue for damages or to evict those who had purchased their homes and farms. These lawsuits proved no mere Directorial aberration, however; the Civil Code retained them. Taking up the debates of the Code on such suits, her article reveals the surprising ways in which the Code's authors used sentimental literary narratives rather than legal arguments to justify preserving highly problematic laws. Ultimately, such discourses enabled the Code's authors to present Napoleonic law as both apolitical and universal, utterly severed from the world of its making.

The law remained a language of negotiation well into Napoleon's reign. Ronald S. Schechter's study of the 'Festival of the Law' that accompanied Napoleon's establishment of the Sanhedrin, the council created to advise him on Jewish life in France, shows great sensitivity to divergent representations of a familiar event. Inverting the image of Napoleon as the supreme lawgiver, the Sanhedrin presented themselves as the guardians of the law and God as the ruler over the Emperor. Thus, Schechter boldly argues, they ultimately subverted Napoleon's attempt to use this assembly as a means of reinforcing his own authority. Michael Sibalis moves from the discursive and representational to the all-too-real physical experiences generated by post-revolutionary law. He explores the interaction between the Napoleonic Senate's Commission on Human Rights and the actual workings of the Napoleonic police. Having painstakingly followed up hundreds of petitions that came before the Commission, he persuasively argues that when it came to protecting French citizens from arbitrary police power, the Commission provided little more than window dressing for liberal principles. Furthermore, Sibalis's wealth of evidence creates a vivid picture of arbitrary police power under Napoleon.

It is often said that by abolishing the nobility and all its privileges, the French Revolution opened careers to talent. But were the changes really so profound? Had the *ancien régime* not already found ways to accommodate the need for talent by enshrouding it in the discourse of merit? Rafe Blaufarb further undermines the textbook cliché by reversing the analytical perspective and demonstrating that Napoleon turned the *ancien régime*'s discourse on merit into a guise covering privileged access to military careers for the wealthy and well-connected. Blaufarb's extensive prosopographical work on officers shows how the army's recruitment strategies shifted away from revolutionary ideals toward drawing men from the social elite. This unexpected change in policy met not only the military need for an educated, orderly officer corps, but also satisfied the Emperor's desire to weld the notables to his regime. Ironically, despite the overwhelming role of military success in Napoleon's rise to greatness, his dependence on sheer talent might have been greater in the arts than the army. Annie Jourdan's look at Napoleon and his artists, David in particular, emphasizes that when it came to creating his image as a modern hero, Napoleon knew what he wanted and artists quickly learned how much he was willing to pay to get it. Incessant war and the Emperor's conceit caused artists' political enthusiasm to decline at the same time as their fees rose. Jourdan sees this not as cynical venality. Instead, the artists revealed not only a growing belief that their talent constituted a rare form of genius fully deserving the ample rewards and honours bestowed upon them, but great skill at negotiating the cultural demands of the Napoleonic state.

The politics of culture have never been confined to artists alone. Areas as diverse as colonial contact and the political economy of personal pleasure allow two other contributors to explore the meaning of cultural modernity in the aftermath of revolution. Their essays show further unanticipated forces and consequences at work. Marie-Noëlle Bourguet's imaginative study of Bonaparte's expedition to Egypt moves deftly from the practical aspects of exploration and discovery to the cultural legacy they generated. The military defeat and Napoleon's demand that the scientists remove any topographical elements from their publications forced them to reorient their volumes to emphasize Egypt's antiquity rather than its geography. Its monuments overshadowed its people and its cities; in short, its ancient past triumphed over its present. This orientation bore unanticipated results, however, causing Egyptians to find in their ancient heritage novel opportunities for constructing a national identity in a colonial age. Rebecca Spang rejects the notion of 'a return of the repressed' advanced by previous historians to explain the image of the post-Thermidorian years as an age of frivolity and decadence. By looking through the diaphanous dresses and beyond the conspicuous consumption of the period, she sees a previously unrecognized conceptual shift from luxury to pleasure. The eighteenth century and the Revolution gave luxury a negative connotation. Therefore, as a category of legal and economic analysis, it gradually gave way to the individualized category of pleasure. On such a construct rested both modern capitalism and the consumer's realization of individual liberty. Thus, Spang explores a cultural turn that has been missed in the mass of criticism levelled at the regime's *nouveaux riches* and yet one which has broad social and economic significance.

These contributions highlight the contingent aspects of bringing the French Revolution to a close. Taken together, the articles suggest the uncertain, rather than over-determined, nature of the outcomes in the period after Thermidor. Moreover, they reach beyond the questions presently defining the field to introduce new perspectives – legal, gendered and cultural, for instance. As these articles reveal, the dynamics of the period extend well beyond the simple recapitulation of the programmes of the early Revolution. The aftermath of the French Revolution presented its own problems and produced original responses. One cannot understand the birth of modern France without paying close attention to these years.

1

The search for stability

Howard G. Brown

Historians tend not to dwell on the years between Robespierre and Napoleon, often dismissing them as confused, vapid and uncertain. The papers in this volume cover a wide range of topics and assume different levels of familiarity with the period. Therefore, the following survey has been written to complement these other contributions, filling in their context without treading on their terrain. But this is an interpretive overview, a survey with an argument. It makes the case for treating the years 1794 to 1804 as an era in its own right. Taking this approach brings a fresh perspective to developments in politics, social structure, the economy, warfare, foreign affairs, colonial policy, the status of religion and the nature of civil society. This unorthodox periodization highlights the continuity of contingency; that is, it traces the progressive resolution of some basic issues facing France in 1794 without assuming the outcome of 1804.

Moments of rupture

The coup d'état of 18 Brumaire VIII (9 November 1799) has long been treated as a momentous rupture in French history. This essay questions such an assumption. However, its purpose is not to determine whether the coup was the political assassination of a thriving democracy or an act of euthanasia that spared the polity further suffering. Rather, it seeks to reintegrate this single event into the fluid political, social, and cultural climate of that era. To do this, the notion of a revolutionary decade (1789–99) has been abandoned in favour of a decade in which France struggled to move beyond the Revolution (1794–1804). This is unusual. For the past three decades, the study of the French Revolution has been dominated by two concerns: understanding its origins and explaining the Terror. Therefore, many recent histories of the Revolution conclude with 9 Thermidor II (27 July 1794) and its immediate aftermath, when Jacobins were ousted from power and the Terror ended.[1] This was not, however, the end of the French Revolution, it was only the beginning of imagining its end.

The years 1789–94 witnessed the sudden emergence of a revolutionary imaginary.[2] The absolutist monarchy had tried for decades to reform the polity, but in one way or another botched every effort. These failures weakened the existing structure and alienated an emerging public opinion. Therefore, finding solutions to the combined economic and political crises of 1787–88 required imagining profound changes in the polity, ones that would redefine the very essence of society and politics. Thus, the death throes of French absolutism generated a political sphere common to society rather than derived from monarchy, that is, an arena of politics in the modern sense, a heady, self-conscious expression of collective possibilities. When this revolutionary imaginary erupted in 1789, an awesome combination of destructive power and creative energy ripped France from its moorings and launched it on a stormy sea. Not until 1794 did the men whose imaginations had taken the ship furthest from shore begin to search for land again. Overthrowing Robespierre, closing the Paris Jacobin Club, and putting the terrorist Carrier on trial broke the grip of the revolutionary imaginary. By the end of 1794, France was charting a new course based on revolutionary realism. This was still revolutionary, and therefore contained both the destructive and creative elements of the previous half-decade, only henceforth they were increasingly restrained by the power of pragmatism. Now finding solutions required imagining an end to revolution. This would involve setting limits on politics and validating the interests of civil society. However, the troubled legacy of the French Revolution's early years weighed heavily on succeeding regimes: the Thermidorian Convention (1794–95), the Directory (1795–99), the Consulate (1799–1804) and even the Empire (1804–14).

In 1789, the Revolution had promised individual liberties, representative government, prosperity and the rule of law. By 1794, however, it had brought war, famine and violent conflict over the nature of the body politic. The republic that emerged from the Jacobin Terror faced the task of generating political and social stability while its core concepts – individual rights, religious tolerance, representative government, economic freedom, and civil equality – had been rejected or vitiated by one or all of the regimes since 1789. Thus, as Benjamin Constant and Germaine de Staël understood so well, consolidating the revolutionary settlement through a constitutional republic required a remarkably dexterous handling of the recent past. The idea of

---

1   Most of the specialized scholarship on the years after the Terror has been incorporated into more substantial surveys of the period noted in the introduction and will not be cited here. Where citations follow they are to works whose findings have yet to be absorbed into survey histories.

2   This concept is adapted from B. C. J. Singer, *Society, Theory and the French Revolution: Studies in the Revolutionary Imaginary* (London, 1986).

republicanism would have to be separated from France's experience of the republic in 1792–94 and instead be anchored in the principles of 1789–91. This proved impossible.

By the autumn of 1795, the republic had erected a constitutional fence between political power and individual freedom, and asserted an even-handed application of the laws as the key to personal security. At the same time, republicans sought to become more respectable by repudiating the demagoguery of populist democracy and restricting power to the hands of property owners. However, even this moderate, constitutional republic had harsh qualities. It excluded refractory priests, émigrés, and the relatives of émigrés from the body politic; it accepted military expansion as an essential source of legitimacy; and it resorted to coercive state power to transform social mores. This aggressive republicanism did not go unchallenged. Political debate during the years 1794–1804 often brought out strains of democratic liberalism. However, arguments in favor of strict constitutionalism, freedom of the press, citizenship, and voting rights were motivated as much by factional advantage as political principles. Furthermore, most republicans were too conditioned by their revolutionary past to renounce authoritarian responses to real or perceived threats to the nascent regime. Thus, like so many fledgling democracies over the past two centuries, the French First Republic found itself torn between adhering to high-minded principles and resorting to dubious expedients. The ultimate expedient was the coup d'état, repeated four times in two years, twice by the government and twice against it. A few weeks after the final coup, the Consulate made a famous proclamation, 'The Revolution is established upon the principles with which it began: it is over.' This contained two lies: the Consular regime was not based on the principles of 1789 and only further movement away from many of them finally brought the Revolution to a close.

Seeking political stability

France's tortuous journey from a bloody reign of virtue to an even bloodier reign of military prowess had a unity of character – the search for stability. However, France did not take a straight and narrow path to authoritarianism. Rather, it lurched from right to left, sometimes doubling back, but more often stumbling forward. This erratic movement was most pronounced in the arena of domestic politics. Constitutional changes gave the Directory and Consulate their names, but two broader political themes divided the period into distinct phases.

The first phase should be called the Thermidorian republic. This period ran roughly from the dismantling of the Jacobin dictatorship in the autumn of 1794 to the defeat of domestic royalism in the autumn of 1797. These years were dominated by economic chaos, continuous warfare, and vigilante violence. They were also characterized by a desperate struggle to define the nature of republican democracy and the type of political elite it would generate. Above all, this period was shaped by the Thermidorians' belief in the power of constitutionalism. Despite a great diversity of opinion on ideological and practical matters, Thermidorians shared the common assumption that by designing, implementing and defending a republican constitution based on the principles of 1789–91 they would be able to resolve the greatest challenges facing the country. This belief stood unshaken until 1797. In the meantime, the range of democratic possibilities narrowed considerably.

Populist democracy was one of the great forces propelling the Revolution from 1789 to 1794, but it disappeared quickly thereafter. The *sans-culottes* movement began its decline under the Revolutionary Government. This facilitated the overthrow of Robespierre and made it easier for the Thermidorians to chart a more conservative course. The massive hunger riots of Germinal and Prairial III (spring 1795) became the paroxysm of *sans-culottisme*. For the first time, revolutionary leaders used the army to repress the urban populace. The subsequent disarmament and arrest of over a thousand militants emasculated Parisian radicalism. Thereafter, the rapid disappearance of the *sans-culottes* movement made it appear a political freak of nature in the first place. Although Babeuf's 'conspiracy of equals' unearthed in 1796 supported the ideals of direct democracy, it contained only a modest number of former *sectionnaires*. It relied instead on provincial militants eager to use coercive force to build a new social and economic order. The show trial of Babeuf and a few co-conspirators publicized the Directory's hostility to radical democrats. This was a popular response to the 'anarchists' who had benefited from the amnesty of October 1795. All the same, the Directory bungled the long trial and alienated many staunch republicans in the process.

Thermidorian politicians found it easier to exorcize the demons of radical democracy than to convert the rural masses to republicanism. Only a good many royalist blunders and some timely interventions by the army prevented a groundswell of anti-Jacobin reaction from bringing down the fledgling republic. The alliance between French émigrés and foreign powers was never the greatest threat to the republic. When the British sponsored an ill-conceived invasion of Brittany at Quiberon Bay in June–July 1795, General Hoche quickly bottled up the émigré army and their *chouan* allies. Almost eight hundred prisoners of war were tried and shot using a revolutionary definition of treason. Meanwhile, after the dauphin died in a Paris prison, his uncle proclaimed himself Louis XVIII and issued the hard-line Declaration of Verona in which he promised a full return to the *ancien régime*. This permanently crippled the royalist cause by alienating constitutional monarchists. His timing could not have been worse.

23

The insult of Verona added to the injury of Quiberon just when a right-wing reaction was sweeping the country. The surge of vigilante violence in the summer of 1795 was directed against the ideologues and opportunists of the Terror. Although motivated more by revenge than royalism, the prison massacres and rural ambushes that took place throughout southern France could easily have destroyed the base of republicanism in the region. In Paris, the politics of revenge triumphed so thoroughly that a royalist rebellion against the Convention erupted in early October. The insurrection of 13 Vendémiaire IV (5 October 1795) almost aborted the new republican constitution. Bonaparte's ruthless 'whiff of grapeshot' preserved the Thermidorians in power and ironically made him midwife to the Directorial regime.

The elections held to implement the Constitution of 1795 did not bode well for the new regime. With a few regional exceptions, the mass of administrative and judicial officials were moderates or conservatives. Only a law requiring two thirds of deputies to be chosen from the Convention prevented monarchists from winning a majority of seats and hijacking the republic. The social and economic chaos left after three years of republicanism enabled royalists of all stripes to regain influence. The civil war zone of western France would have gone completely royalist had it not been for a massive military occupation. In fact, the constitution could not be implemented in western departments until six months after the Directory took office. Not surprisingly, the elections of spring 1797 produced a right-wing majority in the bi-cameral legislature. Hostility to the republic mounted on a tide of returning émigrés, emboldened refractory priests, and unsparing criticism from the right-wing press. Anti-republican riots broke out around the country. In Paris, the new legislative majority sought to hamstring the Directory and roll back its exclusionary policies. For weeks, people waited anxiously for one side or the other to strike.

Once again, the army saved the republic, but badly damaged Thermidorian constitutionalism in the process. On 18 Fructidor V (4 September 1797), three members of the Directory launched a coup d'état against the right wing. The purge included two Directors and 177 deputies. The election results in over half the departments were also annulled. The hundreds of resulting vacancies were filled by co-option, or in the case of the judiciary, by outright appointment. The purge was more systematic than during the Terror, extending down to thousands of cantonal administrators across the country. This destroyed all chance of restoring a monarchy. Thus, the royalists' efforts to overthrow the republic by armed force failed in 1795, and their efforts to overthrow it by democratic means failed in 1797. In the process, the Thermidorians learned how ineffective a mere constitution was in restoring stability and how essential the army had become to the republic's survival. The depth of popular disaffection in the country also forced the regime to lean on the anathematized left for support. As a result, many former Jacobins regained positions of power. However, after the Fructidor coup, the greatest domestic obstacle to stabilizing the republic no longer came from royalists, but from ardent republicans.

Whereas the years from 9 Thermidor II to 18 Fructidor V constituted the Thermidorian republic, the subsequent phase from the Fructidor coup to the Life Consulate should be called the authoritarian republic. This period was characterized by constitutional violations and revisions, renewed warfare, a continual erosion of democracy, the elimination of Jacobinism, and a steady increase in centralized state power. Readers will quickly note that this is an unorthodox periodization and that the authoritarian republic straddled the coup d'état of 18 Brumaire VIII.

The Fructidor coup greatly expanded the Directory's arbitrary powers. The government revived the persecution of émigrés and priests, and once again tried to impose cultural conformity. This so-called 'Fructidorian Terror' included forming ad hoc military commissions to execute émigrés caught back in France, selectively deporting 1,400 priests on the grounds of 'agitation,' closing dozens of opposition newspapers, and excluding former nobles from political office. The Second Directory's republican *Kulturkampf* extended to an elaborate panoply of festivals and a serious attempt to enforce the ten-day week of the republican calendar. This became a protracted struggle to close local markets on the *décadi* and churches on Sundays. Public manifestations of Catholicism ranging from confraternity processions to the ringing of church bells were all banned. Naturally, villagers responded with greater hostility than ever before. However, such policies gave great power to local republicans willing to coerce their fellow citizens. These ardent republicans took advantage of their sudden return to power and staged a major comeback in the elections six months later. The more moderate politicians in Paris soon panicked.

The government quickly confiscated the elections of 1798. The legislative coup of 22 Floréal VI (11 May 1798) totally annulled the elections in eight departments, validated the choices of nineteen 'schismatic' assemblies organized by government supporters, and sanctioned the election of only preferred candidates in a dozen other departmental contests. This crass manipulation excluded a quarter of the would-be deputies and a third of the elected judicial and departmental officials. The bulk of those denied office were Jacobins. Unlike the two-thirds law of 1795 and the annulling of election results in 1797 and 1798, the elections of 1799 took place largely as intended. By this time, however, previous election fraud had created widespread cynicism and only about 11 per cent of the electorate bothered to vote.[3] This yielded a mix of political novices and 'Floréalized' Jacobins bent

3   M. Crook, *Elections in the French Revolution* (Cambridge, 1996), p. 155.

on avenging their exclusion the year before. A virulent propaganda campaign against the Directory's handling of the war effort fuelled the coup of 30 Prairial VII (18 June 1799). This legislative assault on the executive drove three Directors and three ministers from office. The coup was quickly followed by a spate of emergency measures reminiscent of 1793 – massive conscription, a forced loan on the rich, and a law of hostages. The new government then conducted another extensive purge of local administrations, this time without even a pretext of electoral irregularities. While Jacobin legislators tried to wreak revenge on the ousted members of the government, moderate republicans plotted a coup to revise the constitution along authoritarian lines. When Bonaparte abandoned his army in Egypt, Sieyès, recently elected to the Directory, accepted him as the necessary sword for a coup against the regime. Orchestrated rumours of a Jacobin plot created a plausible excuse to intervene. However, the planned parliamentary manoeuvre went famously awry. The need to use bayonets to drive out legislators gave Bonaparte the biggest break of his life. Plenty of legal window dressing accompanied the transition from Directory to Consulate, but nothing hid Bonaparte's central place in the new regime. The Constitution of Year VIII was adopted within six weeks and the entire administrative and judicial hierarchy reorganized in a more authoritarian manner. Elected offices at the departmental and municipal levels were abolished and replaced by appointed officials. This included judges and public prosecutors. Juries remained in place, but soon they were hearing cases prepared by special security magistrates who took over the investigative functions of justices of the peace, deemed compromised by their localism.

The Brumaire coup was not planned as a personal seizure of power; rather it was the overthrow of a discredited government by a coalition of constitutional revisionists – the Brumairians. The new system was the product of a broad consensus within the political elite. The Fructidor coup had almost led to a formal revision of the constitution to strengthen the executive so this was hardly a surprising development after Brumaire. But this was not Bonaparte's achievement. Nor was it as radical a rupture with the recent past as has often been claimed. The Directory had selectively nullified elections, disfranchised former nobles, and regularly appointed officials to elective offices. This pattern characterized the Second Directory and belied the regime's democratic claims. After the constitutional rupture of Fructidor, the Directory sacked and replaced so many elected officials, and did it so frequently, that the Consulate's transition to appointed prefects, judges and mayors appeared to be little more than streamlining an already undemocratic system of local administration. How much did it matter when the rigged plebiscite of 1800 replaced the election tampering of the late 1790s? How many Frenchmen saw more democracy in the Directory's discriminatory exclusion laws than in the

Consulate's electoral lists? The Directory had banned forty-two newspapers in the wake of Fructidor, closed down at least twenty more over the next two years, co-opted some of the most important remaining papers, and systematically created obstacles to the circulation of others.[4] How much freedom of the press was really left when the Consulate stifled it in 1800?

To be fair, the Directory did constitute an opportunity for an apprenticeship in democratic practices. Even if elections were often the source of violence or simply prompted general apathy, they sometimes generated real democratic outcomes – usually to the regime's embarrassment. The formation of 'constitutional circles' appeared to be promising forms of political engagement, although many contemporaries feared them as new Jacobin clubs and the government twice ordered them all closed. There was also a vibrant left-wing press. These papers relentlessly attacked their political rivals and anyone in the government unwilling to heed their *cris d'alarme* about the mounting threat of royalism. Those scholars who put these democratic practices in their most favourable light refer to men on the radical left as neo-Jacobins or democratic republicans. These terms serve to distinguish them from the Jacobins of the Terror and to denigrate directorial republicans as undemocratic. These are somewhat false distinctions. Little was new about the neo-Jacobins – they were the men of 1793–94 minus their national leaders. Although they stubbornly resisted the regime's social conservatism and hoped to base their own political power on grass-roots support, whenever they acquired local office or legislative influence they once again resorted to undemocratic tactics of coercion and exclusion. This was made perfectly clear by the measures adopted in the summer of 1799. The ease with which the Consulate overcame any opposition from 'democratic republicans' shows how little support they had among the mass of Frenchmen by the end of the revolutionary decade. A genuinely loyal democratic opposition would not have found itself so totally isolated. In sum, theories of democratic practice generated in these years resonate well in the late twentieth century, but an examination of local political practices at the time makes 'neo-Jacobins' much less original or appealing.

Achieving a truly democratic republic would have been an exceptional outcome. Most analyses have had a basically ahistorical framework, assuming that France was ready for democracy. Any analysis of the Directory must not forget how radical the revolutionaries' goals had been. Making all offices of local administration, including judges and justices of the peace, into elected positions gave the national executive very little power to control the apparatus of local administration. Even under the somewhat regressive terms of the Constitution of 1795, three-quarters of adult men could vote and over a million of these (or about ten per cent of the adult male population) met the

4   H. Gough, *The Newspaper Press in the French Revolution* (Chicago, 1988), pp. 141–59.

criteria necessary to hold political office. The annual elections built into the Constitution of 1795 put the country in a state of almost continuous political turmoil. In order to prevent this from generating a separate class of political activists, however, the Constitution prohibited citizens from being chosen as electors two years in a row. Together these procedures resulted in a distressing level of agitation as well as incoherence in local and national politics. The prevailing status hierarchies, economic dependencies and patterns of deference in eighteenth-century France made this an excess of democracy. It would have been extraordinary for fully democratic practices to have determined the exercise of political power.

The coup d'état of 18 Brumaire has become synonymous with an authoritarian reaction against republican democracy. This is due in large part to later struggles over republicanism in France, especially Napoleon III's massive repression of 1851 and Marx's analysis of it. Judging the necessity, inevitability or criminality of the Brumaire coup is no longer so compelling. Once divested of its significance for later political struggles, the coup can be returned to its proper context – the period of contingency necessary to create a post-revolutionary order. True, the sordid events of 18–19 Brumaire VIII brought a general to power and, true, Bonaparte soon became Napoleon, a thoroughly Machiavellian prince running a new model empire. But Brumaire should not be used as historical shorthand for the transition from democracy to dictatorship. Both the demise of democracy and Bonaparte's role in it cannot be confined to the coup and the Consulate.

Just as republican historians have failed to describe the comatose state of democracy before the Consulate nailed the coffin shut, Bonapartist historians have emphasized the Consulate's return to law and order without acknowledging the Directory's preparatory work. The endemic lawlessness of rural France was not ended by the Consulate's ecumenical choice of officials or its reopening of churches alone; it also took ruthless repression. The Fructidor coup began this process. Military commissions tried at least a thousand people as émigrés and summarily executed 275 of them. By the Brumaire coup over 200 cities, towns and villages had been put under a form of martial law known as a 'state of siege'. Starting in January 1798, military courts tried hundreds of civilians accused of highway robbery or housebreaking. Mobile military commissions attached to flying columns followed in early 1801 in order to break the back of brigandage in the west and south. Once the balance of fear had tipped in the state's favour, Special Tribunals were created to ensure that the regular criminal courts would not be corrupted by sympathy or intimidation. Between 1797 and 1802 the gendarmerie doubled in size and public prosecutors gained considerable investigative powers. In the process, France became a security state. Eliminating representative democracy and fortifying criminal justice went hand in hand with a vast administrative analysis of society that gave the state an unprecedented ability to chart social change, and thereby respond more effectively to it. Thus, local communities became enmeshed in the security state, at first through repression and then through supervision.[5] The Revolution turned subjects into citizens; the security state turned citizens into *administrés*.

The formation of an authoritarian republic went hand in hand with the emergence of a state-defined political notability. This was the authoritarian conclusion drawn from the idea of citizenship developed in 1795.[6] The Constitution of 1799 created a complex procedure combining popular election and government selection, but suspended its application till 1801. The lists of communal, departmental, and national notables generated that year contained a heavy dose of officials but few former nobles and virtually no returned émigrés. If the regime were really to take root, however, these last groups needed to be better represented. In a clear break with republican thinking, Bonaparte granted an amnesty to émigrés who had not fought against the republic. He extended this in April 1802 to include all but the most notorious opponents of the regime. Therefore, when the Constitution of 1802 made Bonaparte First Consul for Life, it also created new criteria for official departmental and national notables. Henceforth, electoral colleges would be composed of men elected from the six hundred biggest taxpayers in a department plus a few government appointees. Members of the new electoral colleges served for life. Thus, after 1803 France had an official socio-political elite based on the most consistently taxed asset: landed property. This elite blended former nobles and returned émigrés into the larger mass of prosperous landowners, local officials, and educated professionals, most of whom had enhanced their economic standing through the purchase of 'national property'. This ability to combine revolutionary winners and losers in a semi-permanent political elite provided one of the key conditions of stability under Napoleon.

Just as the nature of the socio-political elite remained contingent until late in the Consulate, so did the role of the tri-cameral legislature. The continuity of legislative personnel from the Directory was remarkable, belying claims that the coup constituted a profound rupture. Fully ninety per cent of the Legislative Body and seventy per cent of the Tribunate had held seats in the Councils of the Directory.[7] Although this did not include radical democ-

---

5   H. G. Brown, 'From Organic Society to Security State: The War on Brigandage in France, 1797–1802', *Journal of Modern History* 69 (1997), pp. 661–95.

6   The Constitution of Year III granted civil rights to those who met the conditions of French national identity, but granted political rights only to 'citizens', i.e. French adult male taxpayers. M. Troper, 'La mutation du concept de citoyen en l'an III' in J. Bart, J.-J. Clère, C. Courvoisier, and M. Verpeaux (eds), *La Constitution de l'an III ou l'ordre républicain* (Dijon, 1998), pp. 85–97.

7   Calculations based on I. Collins, *Napoleon and his Parliaments, 1800–1815* (New York, 1979), pp. 19–20.

rats, there were plenty of constitutional liberals. Naturally, some of them tried to check the new government's arbitrary tendencies. But opposition from these 'metaphysicians' infuriated Bonaparte. Purging them in the spring of 1802 marked the limits of an authoritarian republic and started the descent into dictatorship. The legislative purge proved essential to passing both the Concordat and the Legion of Honor, landmarks in the post-revolutionary settlement. The now supine legislature also agreed to a national plebiscite on making Bonaparte First Consul for life. It would have been astonishing if the plebiscite of 1802 had not been an overwhelming endorsement of Bonaparte's rule. After all, he personally deserved most of the credit for both the Peace of Amiens and the Concordat. The Life Consulate was embodied in the Constitution of Year X, promulgated on 3 August 1802. This gave the First Consul dictatorial powers. He could now negotiate treaties on his own, convoke the various legislative bodies when he wanted, and appoint the presidents of all electoral colleges. The newly formed *Conseil Privé* enabled him to control changes in the constitution or suspend it in select departments, to annul criminal court judgments, to extend the powers of arrest, and to suspend juries, as well as to grant pardons and dissolve the Tribunate and Legislative Body. Thus, the Life Consulate eliminated all institutional bases for seriously contesting Bonaparte's rule. Putting such sweeping powers in the hands of one man ended the republic in all but name.

It was Fructidor, and not Brumaire, which turned the page on representative democracy and the rule of law, and it was the Consulate for Life, not the Imperial coronation, which closed the book. The Thermidorian years convinced the republican elite that genuine democracy was not yet viable in France. The turn to liberal authoritarianism occurred in 1797 and by 1802 the security state was in place. Only after the power of the post-revolutionary notability had been solidified was the Revolution truly over. The Constitution of Year X completed this process by restricting political participation to the biggest taxpayers. The state's basis of legitimacy had shifted from providing the people with access to politics to providing personal security and social stability.

This does not mean that the Revolution had inevitably to end in dictatorship. Nonetheless, authoritarian rule was probably unavoidable. The people were culturally prepared for it by the *ancien régime*; they were further persuaded of its benefits by widespread violence, arbitrary abuse of authority by rival factions, and the turmoil of republican elections. Frenchmen favoured a personalized form of political leadership – after all, look what collective government had produced – and the propertied classes wanted to escape egalitarian impulses and the uncertainty surrounding *biens nationaux*. The Brumaire coup accelerated the trend toward authoritarian rule. All the same, it took Bonaparte several years to turn these basic instincts into a personal dictatorship. Despite his proclamation, the Revolution was not over in 1799; however, it certainly was in 1802, but not based on the principles with which it began.

Between 1802 and 1804, Bonaparte put the finishing touches on his personal dictatorship. For once, rhetoric lagged behind reality and France remained officially a republic till 1804. War with England was renewed in 1803, making Bonaparte's continued leadership all the more important. Serious opposition merely furnished opportunities to tighten his grip. In desperation, Georges Cadoudal, the last great *chouan* supported by the British government and the Bourbon pretender, again plotted an assassination. He used General Pichegru, a royalist deputy exiled at Fructidor, to solicit the support of General Moreau, the victor of Hohenlinden and Bonaparte's greatest republican rival in the army. When Bonaparte learned about this parody of revolutionary conspiracy theories, he closed the gates of Paris and rounded up all the principal players. He also had the one Bourbon he could lay his hands on, the Duke of Enghien, kidnapped in Baden and summarily executed outside Paris. This famous crime made Bonaparte a regicide and erased any hope that he might restore the monarchy. The conspiracy alarmed politicians and citizens alike, prompting them to complete his dictatorship. Even before the conspirators were put on trial, the Senate transformed France into an Empire and named Bonaparte its Emperor. A national plebiscite then confirmed this position as hereditary. The Imperial *sacre* at Notre Dame with the Pope and the entire Bonaparte clan in attendance illustrates how quickly the personal dictatorship would become an imperial dynasty.

Continental war and colonial power

At the height of the Terror, France had fourteen armies fighting on every front, including a civil war in the west. Although Austria and Prussia were distracted by the scramble for Poland, France's unprecedented mobilization stunned the coalition arrayed against her. The French victory at Fleurus (June 1794) made it possible to overthrow Robespierre and end the Terror. Thereafter, revolutionary armies no longer fought to defend an endangered fatherland, but to defeat the republic's enemies abroad. Achieving peace through victory quickly became an essential goal of French republicanism. Anything less risked sapping the republic's credibility and depriving it of a plausible excuse for using coercion to maintain itself at home. The formula of peace through victory became a leitmotif of the Thermidorian Convention, Directory, and early Consulate. The vagaries of military campaigning did not change this goal until it was finally realized in 1802. This constant pursuit of peace through victory had three important consequences for the outcome of the French Revolution: it militarized the polity, expanded France, and consolidated Bonaparte's power. Each of these can be explored separately.

By the time Bonaparte seized power, most Frenchmen experienced the republic as a polity that privileged war over democracy. Coercive mobilization and the glorification of arms had a greater impact on village life than holding elections or living under a so-called rule of law. In this respect, Brumaire made little difference. The republic was founded on a war emergency and only military expansion enabled it to survive as long as it did. Bonaparte acknowledged this fact in exile on St. Helena, stating that 'the Directory was overpowered by its own weakness; to exist it needed a state of war as other governments need a state of peace'.[8] He knew what he was talking about because his regime lived by the same rules. Even when the Empire was at its zenith he remarked, 'My power is dependent on my glory, and my glory on my victories. My power would fall if I did not base it on still more glory and still more victories.'[9] Treating the revolutionary and Napoleonic periods separately, as is usually the case, has obscured the importance of continuous warfare in determining the shape of the post-revolutionary settlement.

The 'municipal revolution' of 1789 created bourgeois militias across the country. Although they soon became units of the National Guard, they were really expressions of the new power structure at the communal level. The revolutionaries' rupture with the church displaced Sunday mass and religious processions as the traditional expressions of communal solidarity. This made service in the National Guard one of the few approved ways to embody the local community. Fear of war made the National Guard into a critical nexus between hundreds of urban communities and the revolutionary state. The two hundred thousand volunteers drawn from the National Guard in 1791 and 1792 were recruited, organized and equipped by local authorities. Much vaunted as citizen-soldiers, these volunteers nonetheless remained tangible expressions of localism. Their collective identity, more than their individual ones, made national guardsmen recruited into the line army a critical factor in the transition to the modern French state-nation.

It was only after France became a republic that mobilization for war began rapidly to erode communal solidarity. When the fledgling republic resorted to the levy of three hundred thousand in early 1793, community leaders were forced to choose between collective resistance and conscripting unpopular or marginal members of the community. The *levée en masse* of August 1793 completed this rupture between the Revolution and communities. Henceforth, the revolutionary state, experienced directly as coercive military force, took precedence over the democratic institutions of local government. The *levée en masse* was the first universal conscription in European history and

8 Quoted in Denis Woronoff, *The Thermidorian Reaction and the Directory, 1794–1799*, trans. Julian Jackson (Cambridge, 1984), p. 167.
9 Quoted in G. Ellis, *Napoleon* (London, 1997), p. 192.

expanded the standing army to a staggering 750,000 men. However, this was only a one-time requisition of men. Once the influx of recruits peaked, there was no way to make up losses. Therefore, French armies shrank rapidly as a steady stream of deserters returned to their villages. Here they relied on friends and neighbours, and the silence of local officials, to evade the law. The patriotic spirit of fighting to defend liberty, equality and fraternity had been badly tarnished by the harsh realities of military service.

In the absence of an actual conscription law, the Directory's unwillingness to consider a compromise peace forced it to tighten the screws on communities to round up refractory soldiers. Many villages responded by protecting heterogeneous bands of outlaws who attacked purchasers of national property and other accomplices of the republic. Finally, in October 1798, the Jourdan Law provided the basis for routinized conscription. Initially, this procedure met huge resistance. During the first two years of application, over one third of those called up either dodged the draft or deserted on their way to the front. Nonetheless, another 280,000 men were added to the armies by the summer of 1800.[10] This expanded them by eighty-five per cent and gave the Consulate the forces it needed to secure French hegemony over Western Europe. In the process, however, the government learned that it could not rely on patriotic rhetoric or local officials to operate conscription effectively. Therefore, when the Consulate began to replenish the ranks again in 1802, it took conscription out of the hands of community officials and concentrated it in the state apparatus. Thereafter, a myriad of bureaucratic adjustments fine-tuned the process. Another ten years of war under the Empire ensured that Frenchmen became accustomed to the 'blood tax' as a new civic obligation.

The militarization of society was not only a matter of imposing conscription. Newspapers brimmed over with coverage of the campaigns. Every national holiday included a heavy dose of military display and martial rhetoric. War veterans received privileged status and retired officers got generous pensions. The funerals held for Generals Hoche and Joubert were among the most spectacular national ceremonies of the era. The number of generals elected as deputies or named as ambassadors grew every year. The Consulate continued the trend. Finally, in 1802 Bonaparte ensconced the whole process in the Legion of Honour. This rewarded military valour over all other forms of civic virtue. Between 1802 and 1814, ninety-seven per cent of recipients were soldiers. At first, republicans opposed the Legion of Honour as a revival of military nobility, but very few later declined their medals.

10 Calculation based on figures in Hargenvilliers, *Compte générale de la conscription* (Paris, 1808), pp. 51, 68. Other parts of this section owe much to A. Forrest, *Conscripts and Deserters: The Army and French Society during the Revolution and Empire* (New York and Oxford, 1989) and I. Woloch, *The New Regime: Transformations of the French Civic Order, 1789–1820s* (New York, 1994), pp. 380–426.

All of this military spirit would not have developed had France not succeeded brilliantly at war. Ideological arrogance, armed might, and territorial expansion combined to create 'La Grande Nation'. Between 1795 and 1802, France expanded its territory by one-fifth. Belgium was carved into nine French departments in 1795, the Rhineland became four departments in 1798, and Piedmont was annexed as five departments in 1802. Beyond these annexations lay several puppet regimes installed by the victorious French army. The First Republic spread the revolutionary gospel by creating 'sister republics' in its own image. The internal politics of these satellite states mirrored the French republic's volatility, suffering numerous uprisings, coups, and constitutional revisions. They also prolonged the instability of France's international position.

The first sister republic was formed in 1795. After the battle of Fleurus, French troops advanced largely unchecked across the low-countries and easily occupied the United Provinces. A coterie of Dutch 'patriots' acted as a fig leaf of respectability in the creation of the Batavian Republic. However, their treaty of alliance with France exposed them as opportunists running a vassal state. This became the paradigm for future sister republics. Bonaparte's victories in Italy created two more satellites – the Cisalpine Republic (Papal Legations, Ferrara, Modena, and Lombardy)[11] and the Ligurian Republic (Genoa) both formed in 1797. These gave the Directory much needed prestige, but the detrimental effects were more significant and longer lasting. In order to turn the preliminaries of Leoben (April 1797) into the Peace of Campo Formio (October 1797), and thereby retain his precious Cisalpine Republic, Bonaparte had to threaten Austria with renewed attack. This could only be done by stripping southern France of regular army units at a time when royalists were making the most of their election victory that spring. This once again plunged the Midi into factional violence, proving that the Thermidorians and the Constitution of Year III were incapable of restoring stability. Such manifest domestic weakness prevented the Directory from rejecting Campo Formio – essentially a replacement of the Republic's priorities (natural frontiers) by those of Bonaparte (a satrapy in Italy) – and so forced it to live with an inherently unstable international settlement.

The extension of French power beyond the Alps led directly to another two sister republics in 1798. Unlike the other Italian republics, the Roman Republic had virtually no local support, being essentially the civilian branch of the French command there. The Pope's death in captivity the following year gave French Catholics yet another reason to hate their government. The arrogance of French power also inspired the conversion of the Swiss federa-

---

11   To be precise, the first three of these had been constituted as the Cispadane Republic which was soon expanded by the addition of Lombardy and renamed the Cisalpine Republic.

tion into the Helvetic Republic. The 'Grande Nation' had two motives for this blatant transgression, both of which served Bonaparte's interests: to make it easier to protect Milan, the capital of the Cisalpine Republic, and to raid the Berne treasury in order to finance the military expedition to Egypt. The ceaseless expansion of France, including an ill-fated attempt to turn the Kingdom of Naples into the Parthenopean Republic and Bonaparte's gratuitous conquest of Malta, aroused the ire of Austria and Russia. They promptly joined Britain in an offensive alliance against France. Thus, the Directory's system of sister republics and Bonaparte's reckless ambition combined to provoke the war of the second coalition.

The renewal of warfare soon became a national emergency and led directly to the 'Jacobin hundred days'[12] of 1799. Austrian and Russian armies quickly overran the Italian sister republics and invaded the Helvetic Republic. At the same time, an Anglo-Russian force landed on the coast of the Batavian Republic. Remarkably, the Directory stabilized all of these fronts before being eliminated in the Brumaire coup. Unfortunately for its reputation, the Directory's mass mobilization inspired a huge peasant revolt around Toulouse and renewed insurgency in the West. The former was repressed easily using local detachments, but the latter required considerable military force. However, the Consulate reaped the fruits of the Directory's conscription effort, repressed the uprising in Brittany, and launched an offensive into Italy in the spring of 1800. Nonetheless, the new regime remained vulnerable. Another levy of men in March 1800 coincided with the Consulate's complete reorganization of local administration and the judiciary. This made the Consulate's first year as violent and chaotic as the Directory's last. Obviously, winning the war would relax recruiting pressures and help to quell the domestic turmoil.

In the popular mind, the Consulate only became Bonaparte's regime after the French victory at Marengo (14 June 1800). Taking personal command of the campaign of 1800 meant staking his future as First Consul on the outcome. A defeat would have allowed the plotting politicians back in Paris to take over the fledgling regime. News of an initial reverse nearly launched a palace coup. When General Desaix saved the day, Bonaparte issued a victory bulletin extolling the dead hero, but claiming the credit for himself. Who could question his role? Bonaparte had captured the popular imagination with his prodigious Italian campaign of 1796–97 and he did so again in 1800. Before leaving Italy he resurrected the Cisalpine and Ligurian Republics. When he returned to the capital in July, throngs of Parisians turned out to hail the hero. Their cries of 'Long live Bonaparte! Long live the Republic!' fused these entities in the single position of First Consul. Bonaparte's central-

---

12   J.-P. Bertaud, *Bonaparte prend le pouvoir* (Paris, 1987), p. 120.

ity in the consular regime became increasingly obvious during the next six months. He treated his former collaborators more like subordinates and took an outsized place in the festivals celebrating Bastille Day (14 July) and the birth of the Republic (21 September). However, the regime's future was uncertain as long as war continued.

The key to victory over the Austrians lay not in Italy, but in southern Germany. Here General Moreau directed an astute campaign against three times as many troops as Bonaparte had faced in Italy. His encirclement and defeat of the Austrians at Hohenlinden on 3 December 1800, followed by an aggressive pursuit on the road to Vienna, forced Austria to negotiate a peace separate from Britain – the Treaty of Lunéville (February 1801). This basically confirmed Campo Formio and thereby gave France control of Italy and the Rhine. Marengo and Hohenlinden were both crucial victories, but only the latter brought the much-needed peace on the continent. In other words, Bonaparte's victory at Marengo did not consolidate the Consulate, it only consolidated his position within it; Moreau's victory at Hohenlinden ensured the survival of the Consulate as a regime. The failed assassination on Christmas Eve 1800 then allowed Bonaparte to strike down the regime's most intransigent enemies on both the left and right.

Only Britain now stood in the way of achieving peace through victory. Bonaparte considered a cross-channel invasion, but resorted to more indirect methods. A joint Franco-Spanish assault on Portugal took her out of England's orbit and enhanced France's boycott of English goods. Meanwhile, the Russian-led League of Armed Neutrality temporarily closed the Baltic to British commerce. The resulting economic crisis, plus extreme war weariness and a change of prime ministers, brought England to the bargaining table. The subsequent Peace of Amiens (March 1802) gave France more than she could realistically have expected. Above all, the agreement tacitly accepted France's annexation of Belgium and the Rhineland, as well as the statehood of her satellite republics and *de facto* interference in Germany and Spain. In other words, no major power disputed France's hegemony over Western Europe. This was another vital part of creating a post-revolutionary order.

Traditional surveys of the First Republic's foreign affairs have paid little attention to developments in the colonies. However, the years between Thermidor and the Life Consulate also constituted a distinctive period in the history of French colonialism. During these years slavery was legally abolished but the metropole struggled to assert its authority over the colonies.[13] Although French colonies had used plantation slaves for one hundred and

13 The following section is based on S. Peabody, *'There are no Slaves in France': The Political Culture of Race and Slavery in the Ancien Régime* (New York, 1996); P. Pluchon, *Histoire de la colonisation française*, t. I: *La première empire coloniale* (Paris, 1991), pp. 771–1002; F. Gauthier, *Triomphe et mort du droit naturel en Révolution, 1789–1795–1802* (Paris, 1992); Y. Bénot, *La démence coloniale sous Napoléon* (Paris, 1992).

fifty years, in the eighteenth century a principle became firmly established forbidding the presence of slaves in France itself. Despite the universalism inherent in the Declaration of the Rights of Man and Citizen, this existing prohibition on keeping slaves in France was not extended to the colonies during the early years of the Revolution. It took widespread violence in Saint-Domingue and the emergence of the 'republic of virtue' in France to bring about the abolition of slavery in its colonies. The famous decree of 16 Pluviôse II (4 February 1794) applied that part of the Jacobin constitution of 1793 that prohibited owning human beings. This suspended constitution had not included the colonies (unlike the constitutions of 1791 and 1795) and *ipso facto* had not explicitly abolished slavery. However, the abolition of slavery in 1794 took the principle of universal human rights to the colonies. It also opened the prospect of transforming the colonies from subject territories into parts of a larger French federation. Under such a system, the inhabitants, whether white, black or mulatto, would enjoy the full benefits of representative democracy.

The inherent contradiction between extending human rights to slaves and subjugating colonial peoples to the metropole fostered inconsistency and uncertainty for the next seven years. The decree of 16 Pluviôse II was applied in the Caribbean (Saint-Domingue, Guadeloupe, and Guyana), but not in Sénégal or the Indian Ocean (Ile de France, Réunion). Soon after the overthrow of Robespierre, supporters of slavery launched a campaign to repeal the act of abolition. However, they suffered a setback on 13 February 1795 when the Convention amended the Constitution of 1793 to include the colonies. In doing so, it asserted the metropole's authority over them and reaffirmed the decree of abolition at the same time. Six months later, Boissy d'Anglas, the quintessential Thermidorian, outlined France's relationship to its colonies in the light of three issues: great-power rivalry, the superiority of European culture, and physical liberty for all peoples. This was an argument against giving colonies their independence, but also against re-imposing slavery. Despite the efforts of a powerful pro-slavery lobby in 1797, the republic maintained this stance until 1802.

Saint-Domingue was France's most important colony. By 1798, a coalition of former slaves, free blacks, and mulattos had recaptured the major ports from the English. However, this coalition of *gens de couleur* had also sent the Directory's civil commissioners packing. In the absence of a serious external threat from France or its military rivals, Saint-Domingue tore itself apart in a civil war (1799–1800). The free black Toussaint Louverture defeated the mulatto commander Rigaud and quickly extended his authority to Santo Domingo, the Spanish half of the island ceded to France in 1795. Shortly after taking power, Bonaparte promised the blacks of Saint-Domingue that he would not erode their freedom. As long as he was preoccupied by the war in

Europe, he did not even attempt to reassert France's authority over the colony.

As with so many other aspects of the period, however, events in 1802 closed a distinct phase in the history of French colonialism. Being both a racist and an imperialist, the First Consul intended to re-establish the *ancien régime*'s colonial empire, including slavery and the slave trade. All the same, the parlous state of the French navy forced him to wait till peace with England was assured. In the Treaty of Amiens, Britain gave back the Caribbean islands it had seized in 1793 (Tobago, Sainte-Lucie, Martinique). The Consulate then officially confirmed the slave system there, as well as in the Indian Ocean, and re-established the slave trade 'in conformity with the laws and regulations before 1789'. Meanwhile, a large expeditionary force under General Leclerc arrived in Saint-Domingue in February and another, led by General Richepanse, reached Guadaloupe in May. Both were intended first to reassert France's colonial control, then to re-impose slavery. Richepanse met quick success and within a year slave plantations had been restored to Guadaloupe. Saint-Domingue had a different fate. Although Leclerc succeeded in gaining control of the colony, his arrest of Toussaint Louverture provoked a massive rebellion. Like so many of his men, Leclerc died of yellow fever, only to be replaced by the ruthless General Rochambeau and another expeditionary force. This quickly became both a war for freedom from slavery and a war of independence. Under Dessalines' leadership, the now almost entirely black population drove out the French army and proclaimed Haiti's independence in January 1804.

Despite losing Saint-Domingue, Bonaparte returned France to its former status as an imperial power engaged in importing African slaves to its colonies. This phase of French colonialism lasted till 1848, when France again abolished slavery, this time permanently. Thereafter, a century of 'modern colonialism' elaborated on the formula first articulated in 1795 but abandoned in 1802: imperial domination inspired by great power rivalry and justified in the name of a superior culture, now called France's 'civilizing mission', but stripped of the evils of slavery.

Shaping civil society

The post-revolutionary settlement can be viewed in the abstract as the triumphant emergence of civil society from the state tutelage of absolutism and the totalizing ideology of Jacobinism. Civil society as used here means a non-political public sphere consisting of a proliferation of associations outside the family and free of state control. This Hegelian vision of a modern society can help to identify the distinctiveness of revolutionary outcomes. Hegel's model is especially useful for analysing the transitional years between

Robespierre and Napoleon because it draws attention to the articulation between state, civil society, and family. The formation of a definable civil society within the new order remained contested and, in the end, deeply compromised. In order to appreciate the problems inherent in the formation of a civil society, we need to examine developments in three key areas: the economy, religion, and civil law. In each case, the role of politics and the state will be the focus of greatest attention because our overarching purpose in this essay is to trace the emergence of a stable post-revolutionary regime.

A free market economy is paradigmatic for civil society.[14] In Hegel's definition, the spirit of civil society was universal egoism – a shared understanding that individuals participated in commercial exchanges as equals each naturally seeking his own advantage. More than just conceptually, the emergence of a civil society out of the French Revolution depended on the creation of a liberal economy and a class of people shaped by it, the bourgeoisie. Despite the sound and fury of a generation of revisionist historians, the French Revolution remains unarguably a bourgeois revolution. That is, its origins may not lie in a self-conscious bourgeois struggle to destroy those aspects of the *ancien régime* that blocked the bourgeoisie's way to social and economic ascendancy, but its outcomes certainly made that possible. Wealth and talent replaced privilege and status as the organizing principles of the social order. Guilds were abolished, thereby making way for a stricter reliance on wage labour. Seigneurial dues and tithe obligations were either monetized or disappeared altogether. Both internal tariffs restricting the flow of goods and government regulations fixing prices in specific markets were swept away. All of these changes helped to create a liberal economy. But the revolutionaries did not find it any easier to create a free market than had the *ancien régime*. The absolutist state had tried to move in this direction, freeing the grain trade and abolishing guilds, but the resulting local shortages and high prices sparked numerous riots and repeatedly forced a return to government controls. These experiences made it obvious that moving from a traditional controlled economy hampered by a poor distribution system to a market-oriented economy based on wage labour and free trade would be tumultuous at best. A liberal economy is unstable by its nature. How could the revolutionaries, virtually all political and economic neophytes, stabilize such a novel and inherently volatile system? Building and sustaining a civil society as well as a viable post-revolutionary regime depended on finding the answers.

Many of the social and economic policies of the Revolutionary Government (1793–94) were antithetical to the emergence of a bourgeois society and a market-oriented economy. Therefore the triumph of policies

---

14 For a history of the concept of civil society, see C. Taylor, 'Modes of Civil Society', *Public Culture* 3 (1990), pp. 95–118.

favourable to these outcomes must be located in the decade after the overthrow of Robespierre. The Revolutionary Government's unprecedented effort to control the economy was inspired more by war than ideology. The political elite favored liberal economics, but the war effort depended on the *assignat*. Therefore, the Convention closed the stock market to prevent currency speculation, banned the export of capital, and finally adopted the Maximum to prevent price inflation (i.e. currency devaluation). Mass mobilization forced the government to take over arms production, requisition artisans to supply uniforms, shoes, and other equipment, and, above all, to feed the armies and the cities through massive requisitioning. The result was a command economy unsurpassed until the twentieth century. Only when the country was out of danger could the Convention move to create a free market. Just as the experience of East European economies in the 1990s would lead us to expect, the First Republic's progress toward a free market and financial stability happened piecemeal, generated enormous hardship and dislocation, and repeatedly encountered setbacks.

The Convention took its first steps away from state *dirigisme* in the winter of 1794–95, the harshest in France in nearly a century. Repealing the Maximum, ending requisitions on a range of trades, closing most state-run workshops, and lifting the ban on the export of capital (except in specie), all favoured freer markets in goods, labour, and capital. All the same, they combined to throw a stagnant economy into total chaos. The population of cities and towns dropped sharply. Peasants held up grain convoys and pillaged storehouses. Civil servants went unpaid, soldiers deserted, and suicides soared. Despite promises to the contrary, the government continued to supply the army's food and fodder through requisitions, an especially nefarious practice in times of dearth. 1795 was France's black night of the economic soul.

The economy could not be revived and free trade sustained without first stabilizing the currency.[15] This meant coping in rapid succession with the vertiginous inflation of paper money and the shocking deflation provoked by a return to specie. In the last six months of 1794 the *assignat* slipped gently from one-third of its nominal value to one-quarter. However, tax-collection had all but ceased, so the Convention paid its bills by printing more and more *assignats*, rapidly driving them down to less than one-twentieth of their face value by the summer of 1795. To save creditors and the state from instant ruin, the Thermidorians ordered half of farm rents and half of property taxes be paid in grain. This had so little effect that when the Directory took office it resorted to a forced loan on significant property holders, a desperate recourse to fiscal extortion first used during the Terror. In both cases, returns were slow and amounted to only a quarter of the target figure. The Directory

---

15 The following section relies on the magnificent F. Crouzet, *La grande inflation: La monnaie en France de Louis XVI à Napoléon* (Paris, 1993), pp. 380–559.

also slapped a moratorium on sales of 'national property' and private debt repayment across the country. The currency crisis of 1795–96 had brought both the government and the economy to a near standstill. The virtues of a free market remained locked in theory alone.

Early in 1796, the Directory proposed using a syndicate of bankers backed by unsold 'national property' to jump-start the economy. This superbank would serve to withdraw *assignats* and put into circulation massive amounts of specie, banknotes, and bills of exchange. Jacobin lawmakers killed the idea by arguing that the state's currency – or more sentimentally, the Revolution's currency – should not be entrusted to private capitalists. However, without such a stabilizing influence on the market, and without effective tax collection, the National Treasury was at the mercy of speculators and contractors. The government's only significant resource was unsold 'national property'. Therefore, it decided to create an alternative paper currency called *mandats territoriaux* to be accepted as payment for 'national property', henceforth sold at fixed prices rather than by auction. In an act of monumental naiveté, now almost worthless *assignats* were accepted in lieu of the new *mandats* at a rate of thirty to one. Naturally, the *mandat's* value dropped like a stone, inspiring a frenzy of land purchases with devalued currency. This forced the government to stop accepting *mandats* at face value a mere four months after their creation. The Directory then resorted to alarming chicanery to make the final transition to specie. A group of financiers secretly received, in exchange for large amounts of specie, all of the *mandats* paid to the Treasury, but then were given several months to speculate with the *mandats* before they were demonetized in early 1797. Needless to say, the financiers made a hefty profit, as did a horde of land speculators. The whole débâcle cost the state two billion francs in national property and greatly accelerated the concentration of land in the hands of the wealthy.

The return to specie did not immediately revive the economy. Nor was it as irreversible as is usually assumed. Hard currency was scarce, especially in the Treasury, and continued political instability made it difficult to collect taxes. Despite peace treaties with Holland and Spain and the army's ravaging of occupied territory, the republic could not make war pay for itself. Although requisitions had largely ended in 1796, military expenditures continued to consume over half the annual budget. Without adequate revenue the government could not bargain in good faith. Army contractors fixed extortionate prices and cheated on services just to offset the high risks of not being paid. In an effort to gain the upper hand, the Directory restructured army supply into massive conglomerates headed by a questionable mix of politicians, financiers and supply administrators. These were the largest capitalist enterprises of their age. However, the Directory resorted to such dubious expedients to pay them that even the wildest accusations of fraud and mismanagement became perfectly believable. This eroded the regime's credibility and proved the government's weakness in a free market.[16] The crisis in army supply reached such proportions that it began to reverse the ideals of a liberal economy. The Directory resorted to the *ancien régime*'s practice of paying with 'delegations', that is assigning sources of state revenue directly to suppliers. Even this proved so unreliable that requisitions returned in force, paid for with tax vouchers. Lawmakers decreed another forced loan in June 1799 and narrowly defeated a law creating a new paper currency in November. Despite some initial toughness with big contractors, including extorting cash from them before honouring their 'delegations', the Consulate continued to rely on shaky schemes to finance the war. Nonetheless, a concerted effort to remove myriad forms of 'dead paper' from the economy, plus obtaining cash sureties from agents of the fisc, helped to build confidence and stability into state contracting. This was essential to making the market work for the state instead of against it.

The only truly effective means to prevent returning to a controlled economy was to reduce government debt and improve tax collection. The Fructidor coup marked a major turning point in both these matters. However, this new financial authoritarianism alienated a lot of citizens in the process. After the Fructidor coup, the Directory repudiated two-thirds of the national debt by converting it to vouchers which quickly lost most of their value. Although the remaining third was supposed to be as good as gold, it soon fell by fifty per cent. This partial bankruptcy ruined many members of the bourgeoisie, but it proved an important step on the road to a balanced budget. The national debt now stood at less than a tenth of the annual budget, whereas in 1789 it had been more than double.[17] The Consulate restored some of the public's lost confidence in government bonds by paying dividends in hard currency starting at the end of 1800. This only became possible through major improvements in tax collection. The Directory started this process in late 1798 by creating the Agency of Direct Taxes to overcome the dilatoriness of elected officials. When this proved inadequate, the government billeted troops on recalcitrant villagers, a vile practice that lasted till 1801. The Second Directory also introduced a range of indirect taxes, urban customs offices, and a national lottery, all of which the Consulate reinforced and extended using agents whose earnings now came as a cut of their take. These new forms of taxation and techniques of collection owed much to the hated fiscal strategies of the *ancien régime*.

A free market only thrives when capital is available at reasonable rates.

16 L. Bergeron, *Banquiers, négociants, et manufacturiers parisiens du Directoire à l'Empire* (Paris, 1976); H. G. Brown, 'A Discredited Regime: The Directory and Army Contracting', *French History* 4 (1990), pp. 48–76.
17 F. Hincker, *La Révolution française et l'économie: décollage ou catastrophe?* (Paris, 1989), p. 136.

To promote these conditions, the republic's world of high finance also borrowed strategies from the *ancien régime*. When the legislature rejected the creation of a national bank in 1796, the leading financiers in Paris formed the Current Accounts Fund. This strongly resembled Turgot's Discount Fund created twenty years earlier. The purpose was to reduce the rate of interest and facilitate commercial expansion by providing assured returns on promissory notes of all sorts. The Current Accounts Fund prospered, but simply was not big enough or diverse enough to provide sufficient credit for the commercial markets of the day. Therefore, in early 1800, the Consulate restructured the Fund, expanded its capital base six-fold, and renamed it the Bank of France. Although based mainly on private capital, it enjoyed privileges associated with government backing. The new bank helped to control the speculation involved in paying army contractors, lowered interest rates, and facilitated the circulation of specie to the provinces. In 1803, it became the sole bank in Paris authorized to issue bills of exchange, thus adding more stability to capital markets. The Consulate also increased the reliability of everyday commercial activities by fixing the silver and gold value of the *franc*, introduced in 1795 to replace the *livre tournois*. This new 'franc germinal' of 1803 definitively ended the currency crises associated with paper money. Modest interest rates, regular returns on government bonds, balanced budgets, and a stable currency – all absent during the Revolution – now created the basic conditions for a liberal economy.

This does not mean that the Consulate foreswore heavy-handed intervention in the economy. The short harvest of 1801 brought a steep rise in the price of grain. Concern about possible bread riots in Paris induced the government to distribute ration cards to the indigent. The government also tried to keep the price of grain artificially low by using a secret association of merchants and financiers contracted to import and deliver massive amounts of grain to the Paris basin. This mimicked the simulated sales of the *ancien régime*, but on a much larger scale. It also became the basis for a permanent Paris grain reserve paid for by the government and covertly used to keep prices down.[18] Once again the free market was subverted for political purposes. Like other aspects of civil society, the Napoleonic state wanted to appear less involved than it really was.

The role of religion in shaping a civil society separate from the state was a distinctive feature of the years 1794 to 1802. Throne and altar did not always cooperate harmoniously before the French Revolution, but the essence of sovereignty in the *ancien régime* lay in their being mutually reinforcing institutions. The revolutionaries' expropriation of church property and promulgation of the Civil Constitution of the Clergy in 1790 marked a major turning

18   J. A. Miller, *Mastering the Market: The State and the Grain Trade in Northern France, 1700–1860* (Cambridge, 1999), pp. 205–12.

point in the Revolution, but the basic notion of a state church was not that radical. Rather, it was the eight-year interregnum during which church and state were separated that constituted an almost unimaginable development. This made it possible for religion temporarily to become a key part of the new civil society.

The dechristianization campaign of year II and the association of the Festival of the Supreme Being with Robespierre made it almost impossible for Thermidorians to imagine giving state support to any form of religion. Therefore, in September 1794, the Convention officially stopped paying priests their salaries. This critically wounded the Civil Constitution of the Clergy. In March 1795, the Convention fulfilled the logic of the Revolution's Voltairean attitude to Catholicism by decreeing a complete separation of church and state. This came in the guise of proclaiming freedom of worship, but the attendant restrictions had a heavier impact on actual practices. The decree banned all outward displays of religion, including the ringing of church bells (where they had not been melted down for cannons and coins), public processions, clerical vestments, and outdoor services. These displays of piety had long functioned essentially as enactments of community. By prohibiting them, the Convention knowingly subverted the rituals of public life that gave villages and neighbourhoods their sense of collective identity. Local communities had no intention of cooperating in their own evisceration. In the summer of 1795, the demand for Catholic ceremonies and the mounting reaction against republicanism favoured the return of refractory priests to the centre of civil society at the village level. This religious revival was essentially refractory and royalist. The Convention responded by reviving the death penalty for all non-juring priests caught in France. Its very harshness, however, made local officials reluctant to enforce the law. This drove yet another wedge between rural communities and the republic. As far as most Catholics were concerned, freedom of worship equalled an extension of repression.

An outlawed refractory church obviously could not play a stabilizing role in civil society. However, another form of Catholicism remained possible. After the Convention disowned the constitutional church, it was reconstituted as the Gallican Church under the leadership of six 'united bishops'. One might imagine that this national organization of ecclesiastics who had sworn several oaths of loyalty to the Revolution would grow and thrive under years of republican rule. Such was not the case. The Gallican Church confronted enormous obstacles. First, in many regions of France dechristianizers had tormented constitutional priests, forcing them to quit the priesthood and often to marry. Thus, even where the Gallican Church did take shape, and that excluded large parts of central and western France, it could only put a priest in about one out of three parishes. Without enough priests to go around, the Gallican church could not become the norm across the country. Second, many constitutional priests continued to be treated as intruders into local communities and so found themselves in constant rivalry with local refractory priests. Constitutional priests lost their greatest advantage once forced to depend on the community to pay their salaries. In fact, though officially proscribed, refractories seemed to have all the advantages: popular support based on their resistance to the Revolution in defence of the community; better organization in the form of 'roving vicars' and solicitous émigré bishops; and the authenticity of living martyrdom. Third, although ostensibly belonging to the 'legal' church, Gallican priests could not provide the motor of communal life without illegally ringing bells, holding processions, or performing services in public. This erased their only advantage over illegal refractory priests and provoked the hostility of republican officials. For all these reasons, the Gallican Church failed to establish sturdy parish roots.[19]

The difficulties extended upward to the ecclesiastical hierarchy. The important second encyclical issued by the 'united bishops' in late 1795 gained official adherents in only half the dioceses of the country. It took another year and a half to organize a national council. By this time, conservatives had won the elections of 1797 and were creating a more hospitable climate for refractory priests. Many returned from exile and bruising struggles took place over the control of parish churches. This helps to explain why the national Gallican council failed to open a dialogue with the Pope or the refractory church. In any event, the Fructidor coup eliminated any reason for a strategy of reconciliation. Refractory priests were once again exiled under penalty of death. Despite renewed repression of its rivals and the enthusiasm and skillful leadership of Bishop Grégoire, the Gallican Church could not overcome its internal discord and the lack of government support. When the second national council gathered in July 1801, fully one-fifth of all dioceses in France still lacked Gallican bishops. The spottiness of parish implantations and the gaps in ecclesiastical leadership demonstrated just how difficult it was to include Catholicism in a civil society compatible with the secular republic. What progress had been made was at that very moment being exploited by Bonaparte to strengthen his hand in negotiations with Rome over the Concordat.

The Gallican Church's potential role in civil society was also undermined by the Directory's support for secular alternatives. On one hand, La Revellière Lépaux, one of the most anti-clerical members of the Directory, obtained official support for Theophilanthropy. This sterile devotion to nature and civic morality only partly filled the void left by the disappearance

19 C. Lucas, 'L'église constitutionnelle dans la Loire après la Terreur', *Cahiers d'histoire* 30 (1985), pp. 309–39; J.-C. Meyer, *La vie religieuse en Haute-Garonne sous la Révolution (1789–1801)* (Toulouse, 1982), pp. 407–509.

of Festivals of Reason and of the Supreme Being. Although Theophilanthropy found fertile soil in Paris and a handful of provincial locations, it never became a national phenomenon. It was so compatible with the anti-clerical republic that it gradually evolved into a virtual Jacobin sect. In 1799, both its official support and popular appeal steadily waned until the Consulate banned it in 1800. On the other hand, the Directory invested considerable political capital in its *culte décadaire*. After the Fructidor coup, the Directory stepped up enforcement of the republican calendar. In 1798, new laws required local authorities to conduct civic ceremonies every *décadi*. There they would read the latest laws, perform marriages, honour acts of patriotic service, and pronounce republican homilies. The Directory had also developed a full complement of national festivals. François de Neufchâteau, Minister of the Interior, applied his lively imagination to prepare elaborate national festivals. Some of these commemorated key revolutionary events such as 14 July, 10 August and 9 Thermidor. Others exalted youth, marriage and old age. Alternating overtly political celebrations with ones devoted to private virtue and the social order made this programme of festivals a crucial part of the new civil society. It was not enough simply to erode the power of Catholic rituals to shape communal life, they had to be replaced by an entire battery of republican alternatives. But tradition dies hard, and 'this surfeit of festivals risked the evil of banality'.[20] Besides, the festivals had too much theatre and not enough popular participation. Learned allegories based on classical mythology did not resonate with illiterate peasants. The Directory's persecution of the refractory church, ostentatious neglect of the Gallican church, and promotion of secular alternatives shows how important the religious issue was to the new order.

The travails of formal Catholicism and the uninspiring nature of official festivals, all paradoxically helped to foster genuinely popular religious contributions to civil society. The shortage of priests caused by the Revolution exposed strong demand to continue the rituals of Catholicism through lay cults. Many worshippers went beyond simply gathering to sing hymns, recite the rosary, read religious texts, or pray litanies in common – all authorized acts of private worship. Even though deprived of clerical leadership, lay Catholics managed to carry on their traditional public rituals – procession, festivals, vespers, and even mass. Frequently, a lay minister performed a 'white mass' by following the normal liturgy, but without consecrating the bread and wine. Ideally, lay ministers would perform their ceremonies in the parish church, not only because of the holiness of the building itself, but also because of the power of public, communal ritual. If the church doors were securely locked, the faithful would gather on the front steps of the building or

---

20   M. Ackroyd, 'Constitution and Revolution: Political Debate in France, 1795–1800' (D.Phil. Thesis, Oxford University, 1995), p. 215.

in the cemetery. This often required small riots to overpower secular authorities. Women gave these lay cults most of their impetus. Lay worshippers were well aware that the ideology of the Revolution gave their practices a certain legitimacy. The Revolution had validated popular activism and inculcated the notion that people had the right to freedom of expression. Lay ministers peppered their religious ceremonies with political declarations of religious liberty and popular sovereignty.[21] The nature of these lay cults made them significant components of a modern civil society, independent of the republican regime and often critical of it on its own terms. Everything from the Gallican Church to lay cults showed how hard it was for the Directory to let a genuine civil society take shape independently of politics.

Bonaparte had no illusions on this matter. He saw religion strictly in pragmatic terms. He shared the republican conviction that refractory priests gave the popular counter-revolution much of its backbone. He was also convinced that royalism would wither without Catholic resistance to sustain it. Any doubts on this score were clarified by the agitation refractory priests caused when they were allowed to return and reopen parish churches in 1800. However, he did not think either repression or neglect would work. Furthermore, he believed that religion served mainly to foster a moral order that would favour social and political stability. In other words, Bonaparte did not envision religious institutions as part of civil society. This explains the basic features of the Concordat. Catholicism was proclaimed 'the religion of the majority of Frenchmen' in order to inculcate morality and still preserve a secular state and freedom of worship. The French government nominated all bishops while the Pope invested them with spiritual authority. The bishops then appointed all priests, a power they had never had before. The Organic Articles promulgated along with the Concordat at Easter 1802 strengthened the power of the government over the church in France. Clergy were ordained under state auspices and received state salaries; they also wore vestments, conducted ceremonies, and taught catechisms authorized in Paris. They were required to pray for the Republic and read government proclamations at mass. Another set of 'organic articles' also brought the Protestant churches under state tutelage. The government paid pastors' salaries and organized separate consistories for Lutherans and Calvinists. It took until 1807 to formulate a similar arrangement for Jews. This fusion of churches and state greatly diminished the role of religion in constituting a new civil society. Lay cults and a 'petite église' of hardline refractories survived into the nineteenth century, but by and large the Concordat restored religious peace and promoted social stability.

---

21 S. Desan, *Reclaiming the Sacred: Lay Religion and Popular Politics in Revolutionary France* (Ithaca, 1990).

A post-revolutionary settlement had not only to stabilize the relationship between the state and civil society, but to formulate a uniform civil law. This was one of the revolutionaries' great ambitions. The codification of civil law would replace the higgledy-piggledy regional codes and customs of the *ancien régime*. However, the various revolutionary legislatures took a thoroughly unsystematic approach to rationalizing the civil law. Their vast piecemeal effort included thousands of laws, many of them derived from incompatible ideologies. Finally, formulating a uniform civil code became a matter of determining how much of the Revolution, and of the *ancien régime*, would survive. The process began in 1793 when Cambacérès presented the first of three proposals. The revolutionary imaginary had yet to reach its fullest development, so his code appeared premature. Cambacérès' second proposal, presented in 1795, contained a formula which proved basic to the post-revolutionary civil society: 'Three things are necessary for man in society: to be master of his person; to have property to fulfill his needs; to be able to dispose of his person and his property in his own interest. All civil rights amount to the right to liberty, property, and contract.'[22] This was the foundation for a liberal theory of social relations based on possessive individualism.

Thermidorian law-makers agreed on this basic formula, as well as other profound changes wrought by the Revolution: namely, secular marriage, legal divorce, the abolition of feudalism, and the end of primogeniture. All the same, trying to turn agreement on these general principles into the specifics of a uniform code proved impossible until the executive gained the power to initiate and defend legislation. Cambacérès presented a third project in 1796, but by the time it came up for debate it was clear that he lagged behind the reactionary times. Endless and incoherent debates on divorce, succession, and the rights of foundlings demonstrated the inadequacy of the Directorial legislative machinery for adopting a sweeping standardization of civil law. Even the Consular legislative process could not handle such a task until Bonaparte eviscerated it in 1802.

The resulting Civil Code of 1804 stands as a landmark of the post-revolutionary order. The Revolution had destroyed seigneurial systems of land tenure, abolished tithes, flooded the market with expropriated property, threw all contracts and market exchanges into chaos by printing mountains of paper currency, and unilaterally devalued government bonds. With all of this in the recent past, stability could only be restored by confirming the validity of all sales of 'national property' and by making private property legally sacrosanct. The Civil Code did this in its long section on contracts. Hence, its reputation as the foundation of bourgeois society in the nineteenth century.

22 Quoted in J. Goy, 'Code civil', in F. Furet and M. Ozouf (eds), *Dictionnaire critique de la Révolution française* (Paris, 1988), pp. 508–19. On Cambacérès' three projects, see J.-L. Halperin, *L'impossible Code civil* (Paris, 1992).

Defining the legal structure of the family also had great political significance and was essential to a stable society. The Code reinforced patriarchy with a legal vengeance. Husbands gained exclusive control over family property and fathers could imprison their teenage children. Marriage remained secularized, but divorce on demand as adopted in 1792 was limited to specific conditions, including a cruel double standard for adultery. Illegitimate children were deprived of inheritance rights, whereas all legitimate children were assured a portion of the family estate. In sum, the Civil Code was revolutionary on property, reactionary on the family, and compromising on marriage and succession.

Conclusion

The French Revolution has always been associated with high ideals and the violent struggle to realize them. Not enough attention has been paid to the shift away from both of these. Jacobins believed it was possible to create an utterly new society and a new man to go with it; secular salvation would come through civic virtue. This pursuit of regeneration gave way to a period of renovation. Thermidorians abandoned the idea that civic sacrifice alone would save both men and the republic. However, they still hoped that men could be fulfilled by citizenship and the republic consolidated by a constitution. This was captured by the declaration of rights *and duties* of citizens included in the Constitution of 1795. Thereafter, Directorials learned that citizenship and a republican regime were hollow ideals without peace, order, and good government. They found it impossible to achieve these without reverting to authoritarian means. After a decade of revolution, Brumairians were willing to admit that society was harder to change than constitutions and so gave up most democratic practices. Bonaparte proved their point. The post-revolutionary order rested on accommodations with Catholicism, patriarchy and a landed elite, all held in check by an authoritarian state and a cult of the law. The Consulate's pragmatic responses suppressed both revolutionary ideals and the violence that accompanied them.

Both the Directory and the Consulate took steps away from key goals of the Revolution. They both sought a post-revolutionary order and became increasingly reactionary in the process. The ultimate outcome preserved and confirmed important revolutionary changes: the destruction of seigneurialism and artisan guilds, the creation of civil marriage and civil divorce, the consolidation of bourgeois property rights and careers open to talent. And yet, on the other hand, these were so compromised by the elimination of democracy, the re-imposition of censorship, and the reunification of church and state, that calling France 'revolutionary' after 1802 meant more to the rest of Europe than it did to France itself. The transition from the Life Consulate to the Empire was more a matter of style than substance. The genuinely Napoleonic years (1804–14) did not seek to redefine society or politics. This was an age of personal grandeur, an essentially ephemeral period dominated by egomania. After the Legion of Honour, creating an Imperial nobility was the gratuitous indulgence of an insecure usurper. Having consolidated his power in France, Napoleon turned the Bonapartes into a mafia family ruling Europe. However, both his personality and his dynastic dictatorship required perpetual warfare. That made defeat by a coalition of powers utterly inevitable. The Revolution had been over for more than a decade when the allies restored the Bourbon monarchy. This gave old hatreds new life and forced France to undertake a new search for stability, one that lasted another two generations.

2

Family bonds and female citizenship: émigré women under the Directory

Jennifer N. Heuer

In the midst of the Terror, one young woman begged the Revolutionary Government to forgive her for illegally leaving France. Her act of emigration was deemed a crime against the nascent nation for which she could be deprived of her citizenship and even her life. The young woman presented several excuses for her absence. She insisted that her father and husband had acted together to force her to leave home; however, when left to her own devices, she had rushed back to France. She pleaded to know if her forced departure could really count against her: 'Disobeying paternal and marital power, I abandoned them to obey the laws of my country (*pays*) ... I am French and have never stopped being so ... can this quality so precious to my heart be stripped from me?'[1] While insisting on her patriotism, she also suggested that citizenship entailed both different rights and different obligations for men and women, and that her sex was unlikely to harm the 'sovereignty of the people'.

The young émigrée was unusually devoted to the Revolution; she not only documented a repeated struggle to return to France – although she did so under the protective guise of anonymity – but she had also sent her infant son back to her beloved land of liberty a year before she was able to return. The conflicts which she related, however, emerged from a widespread contradiction which had been built into revolutionary culture. After 1789, women and, to a lesser extent, children had a set of potential rights and duties because of their personal status as members of the revolutionary nation. However, their civil, political, and national identity remained legally subordinated to that of the head of the household. This contradiction between independent citizenship status and dependence in the home sparked recurring, if often unexpected, conflicts between family and citizenship rights. When ordi-

1 Archives Nationales (hereafter AN) DIII-238. Other aspects of this case are discussed in J. Heuer and A. Verjus, 'L'invention de la sphère domestique au sortir de la Révolution', *Annales historiques de la Révolution française*, 327 (2002), pp. 1–28.

nary men and women and representatives of the state sought to resolve such conflicts, they were forced to articulate what women's membership in the nation meant, or should mean, and to address competing demands between family bonds and female citizenship.

If this contradiction was embedded from the beginning of the Revolution, the relationship between family and citizenship shifted dramatically throughout the revolutionary era. In the early years of the Revolution – and through the Terror of 1793–94 – French governments often resolved such unexpected conflicts by insisting that women and children not only could, but should, place duty to the country above duty to the family, 'disobeying paternal and marital power' to obey the laws of the revolutionary nation. New laws implicitly defined citizenship as a direct and personal contract with the state, one that pertained to all members of the revolutionary nation. As the violence of the Revolution escalated and as the French nation battled a host of real and imagined enemies, both men and women were expected to demonstrate their patriotism. Women did not vote or hold public office, but they were held accountable for crimes against the nation.

This emphasis on individual citizenship and personal adhesion to the revolutionary nation was reinforced by the relative absence of boundaries between public and private life during the Jacobin republic. As revolutionaries attacked 'despotism' in the state, they also attacked it in the home. They thus limited, although they did not destroy, the powers of the *pater familias*. Legislators instituted liberal divorce laws, including divorce by mutual consent. Although such laws were not explicitly designed to emancipate women, they applied the same principles to men and women and allowed both to dissolve the marriage contract in the same way. Revolutionaries established family councils to limit a father's control over his children, limited paternal control over inheritance, allowed girls to inherit equally with boys, and established a uniform age of majority.[2] They also championed the authority of the 'grand family' of the French nation over literal family bonds, insisting, for example, that the government, rather than individual parents, should decide how French children were to be educated.[3] Such changes encouraged certain people deprived of French citizenship, like our anonymous émigrée, to argue that they had tried to put their duty to the grand family of the nation above loyalty to their personal families, and had only been constrained from doing so by 'paternal and marital tyranny'.

But in the aftermath of the Terror, and especially by the later 1790s,

2 For an overview of changes in family law, see M. Garaud and R. Szramkiewicz, *La Révolution française et la famille* (Paris, 1978).
3 Proponents of public education often argued that children belonged to the general family of the republic before they belonged to individual families. See speeches by Danton and Barère in *Archives parlementaires*, 1ère série, 72:126 and 91:213. The theme of the 'grande famille' was even more prominent in the revoluionary institution of 'national adoption'.

leading republicans sought to avoid a return to the violence and chaos of the radical revolution by establishing a more conservative social order. Wary of completely overturning revolutionary innovations in the family, they nonetheless slowly began to restore the authority of the *pater familias*. By year IV, legislators made primary schooling a matter of voluntary parental choice, suppressed family courts, and proposed a new version of a civil code which would limit the property rights of women; soon afterwards, they challenged divorce by mutual consent, and began to consider restoring paternal control over inheritance.[4]

More importantly, they called into question the principles that had shaped earlier reforms and began to reformulate the relations between family and state.[5] Legislators and intellectuals tried to replace the model of individual rights-bearing citizens, a model that they associated with the intrusive state dictatorship of the Terror, with one of unified and hierarchically organized families as the foundation of society. They increasingly emphasized that the 'citizen' was a being within a network of social relations, especially familial ones.[6] For dependents within the family, especially married women and children, this implied that their relationship to the state was, and should be, mediated by that of the head of household.

At the same time, authorities increasingly redefined and limited the content of French citizenship. Most of the laws of the radical revolution had used 'citizen' as an all-purpose word, one that not only erased social differences but also blurred the distinctions between legal membership in a national community, patriotic duty, and the exercise of political rights.[7] While men and women revived distinctions like 'Monsieur' and 'Madame' to counteract the social levelling of 'citizen', legislators during the Directory also sought to restore a clearer distinction between the legal category of 'French' and the political associations of 'citizen'.[8] They also specifically limited women's political rights and repeatedly insisted that political citizenship was

---

4   L. Hunt, *The Family Romance of the French Revolution* (Berkeley and Los Angeles, 1992) and X. Martin, 'Fonction paternelle et Code Napoléon', *Annales Historiques de la Révolution Française*, 305 (1996), pp. 465–75.

5   S. Desan, 'Reconstituting the Social after the Terror: Family, Property, and the Law in Popular Politics', *Past and Present*, 164 (1999), pp. 81–121.

6   The title of one contemporary tract is particularly revealing of such trends: C.-P.-T. Guiraudet, *De la famille considérée comme l'élément des sociétés* (Paris, 1797).

7   Jurists in the Old Regime had often employed a specific vocabulary to refer to legal membership in the nation, including expressions such as *régnicole* or 'reputed French' (*réputés français*). After 1789, and especially after the declaration of the republic in 1792, revolutionaries often simply used 'citizen' to refer to both political and legal aspects of citizenship or replaced prerevolutionary terms with ambiguous neologisms like 'républicole'.

8   For example, in year V, legislators struggled to make the distinction between the two categories clear when they discussed Protestants who had left France and whose descendants had returned to the country after the start of the Revolution. Legislators proposed treating such Huguenots as legally French, while barring them from political citizenship for at least seven years, the period of time required for other foreigners to become full French citizens.

not relevant to women. After women led an invasion of the National Convention during the Germinal and Prairial uprisings of year III, the Thermidorian government went beyond banning women's political clubs, as they had done in 1793, to forbidding women to attend any political assembly.[9] The Directorial government, which came into power later in 1795, continued these policies, and it voiced growing doubts about the political rights and responsibilities of women.

In this context, one might expect that conflicts between family and national bonds, like those presented by the young émigrée, would cease to present any real challenge to a new order, or that they would be systematically resolved in favour of hierarchical relations within the family. Most recent scholarship on gender and citizenship would seem to confirm such assumptions; historians often present the closing of women's political clubs in the fall of 1793 as the decisive moment in the exclusion of women from the public sphere.[10] Even those who argue that the Revolution created new rights and opportunities for women usually concentrate on the years between 1789 and 1793, occasionally carrying the story through to 1795.[11] From a different perspective, scholars concerned primarily with the institutions of nationality and citizenship often stop with the Terror or leapfrog to the Napoleonic Civil Code, implying that there were few important innovations or struggles in the interim.

But while authorities increasingly attempted to place familial bonds above national ones for dependents within the family, the concept of women's national citizenship also continued to pose challenges to Directorial efforts to create a nation based on unified families. This becomes clear if we consider the consequences of 'Frenchness' as well as political citizenship and move beyond an exclusive focus on political citizenship to consider the consequences of 'Frenchness' by turning from the realm of law-making to its application. The lack of a precise vocabulary for distinguishing between legal membership in a national community and the exercise of political rights had intensified struggles over individual rights and obligations earlier in the Revolution. While legislators attempted to clarify different forms of membership in the nation during the Directory, they were unable to dismiss the morass of previous laws that had used the term 'citizen' ambiguously or to nullify all of the myriad and powerful associations of the word. The most

---

9   D. Godineau, *Citoyennes Tricoteuses: Les femmes du peuple à Paris pendant la Révolution française* (Aix-en-Provence, 1988).

10 J. Landes' interpretation of the importance of 1793 has been especially influential. See J. Landes, *Women and the Public Sphere in the Age of the French Revolution* (Ithaca, 1988).

11 See D. Levy and H. Applewhite, 'Women and Militant Citizenship in Revolutionary Paris', in S. Melzer and L. Rabine (eds), *Rebel Daughters: Women and the French Revolution* (Oxford, 1992), pp. 79–101, or S. E. Roessler, *Out of the Shadows: Women and Politics in the French Revolution, 1789–95* (New York, 1998).

profound consequences of French citizenship status for ordinary men and women also became apparent only when such laws were applied or challenged. Legislators often made it clear whether generic terms of 'French' or 'citizen' applied to one or both sexes and to both adults and children only when forced to do so by the people these measures affected.

Two such questions of interpretation and application of laws from year V are especially revealing: civil court cases and a new consideration of an amnesty for émigrés. Revolutionaries were preoccupied by issues that impinged, often unexpectedly, on family and citizenship status. Legislators sought to develop a new civil code that would work for the emerging post-Terror order. While legislators had changed specific laws, and Cambacérès, the author of several earlier versions of civil codes, had put forward a new incarnation in June 1796, revolutionaries had not ratified it, and continued to try to hammer out a new set of laws. At the same time, many prominent lawyers were involved in trials in which they tried to apply in practice the same visions of social and political order that they debated in the halls of the legislature. One particular *cause célèbre* from late 1796 provides us with an especially revealing window on to these struggles, as it pushed contemporaries to articulate whether or when dependents in the family risked losing citizenship rights in France because of 'paternal and marital power'. Similarly, emigration remained a central problem in year V, but one that was subject to new consideration and passionate debate, as apologists for émigrés not only sent petitions asking for individual exemptions, but also published controversial tracts and importuned the legislature en masse to consider an amnesty. Like our young émigrée, such activists were particularly concerned about whether it was possible for women – and especially for wives and daughters – to have voluntarily 'denationalized' themselves despite the actions of the head of the household and what such 'denationalization' might mean in the world of the late Revolution.

Families and Frenchness in the Parisian courts

In late 1796, M. Hoppé, a young businessman from Hamburg, and the *citoyenne* Anne-Françoise Lange, a well-known actress, appeared before the Parisian courts.[12] Both sought custody of their twenty-one-month-old daughter Palmyre, who had been born out of wedlock. The case was one of a number of short-lived *causes célèbres* which littered the columns of contem-

---

12 Lange was probably best known for her 1793 performances of the role of Pamela in François de Neufchâteau's *Pamela, ou la vertu récompensée*, but she was a prominent actress throughout the Revolutionary period. For an overview of the case, see A. Douarche, *Les tribunaux civils de Paris pendant la révolution, 1791–1800: Documents inédits recueillis avant l'incendie du Palais de Justice de 1871*, 3 vols (Paris, 1905–07), 1:clxxi–clxxiii and 2:357–59.

porary newspapers, and the actress's admirers and critics gossiped avidly over the trial, relishing the lurid tales of sexual and financial scandal that the case revealed.[13] But the struggle between M. Hoppé and the *citoyenne* Lange also opposed familial and national bonds with particular clarity and force. Hoppé's status as a foreigner made the case unusually piquant, but it also encouraged commentators to articulate otherwise implicit assumptions about the nature and significance of French women and children's citizenship.

While lawyers often continued their practices while holding political office, the Hoppé-Lange case also involved an unusual number of prominent figures on both sides of the case who were intimately involved in debating related issues. The *Consultation* for Hoppé was signed by Portalis, Tronson du Coudray, Muraire, and Cambacérès, all important actors in developing a new civil code.[14] All had participated in the recent legislative discussions on the nature of the family and its relation to the state. Cambacérès had proposed a third project for a civil code on 16 Prairial IV (4 June 1796), while Portalis had been appointed to the legislative Commission for revising inheritance laws on 25 Germinal IV (14 April 1796), and had been president of the Council of Elders during a heated discussion on changing inheritance laws, particularly the implications of equal succession for girls and boys. As the case opened in December 1796, legislators were in the midst of discussing whether divorce for mutual incompatibility should be limited, a position which Portalis would passionately support.

Duveyrier, the lawyer for the *citoyenne* Lange, was equally enmeshed in contemporary debates.[15] Indeed, he sent a copy of his brief to the national legislature, claiming that he was compelled to do so after reading an oration in the *Journal de Paris* inspired by legislative discussion over divorce.[16] Duveyrier explicitly contrasted the oration to the opening discourse of Cambacérès' project for a civil code, which decreed that if a father freely acknowledged a child born out of wedlock, the child would be placed in his care. He sought to use the Hoppé-Lange case to demonstrate that granting

13 See Douarche, *Les tribunaux civils*. Crowds filled the courtroom at each stage of the trial, and newspaper columnists for almost all of the contemporary papers covered the case, presenting their views about the respective guilt or innocence of each party.

14 Portalis *et al.*, *Consultation pour M. Hoppé contre la citoyenne Lange, sur une question d'éducation* (Paris, 1797).

15 H. Duveyrier, *Réponse à la Consultation. Faite par M. Hoppé Hambourgeois, et signée Portalis, Tronson du Coudray, Muraire, et Cambacérès* (Paris, n.d.). An incomplete version exists in AN, AD II 34, and a complete version in the Bibliothèque Nationale as 4-Fm-17398. I was unable to verify this definitively, but the author appears to be Honoré Marie-Nicholas Duveyrier, a deputy to the National Assembly and, later, tribune involved in the creation of the Napoleonic civil code.

16 The speaker in question was Siméon, intervening in the legislative debate about divorces based on mutual incompatibility. For further details on this debate, see S. Desan, 'Marriage, Religion and Moral Order: The Catholic Critique of Divorce During the Directory', in R. Waldinger, P. Dawson, and I. Woloch (eds), *The French Revolution and the Meaning of Citizenship* (Westport, Conn., 1993), pp. 201–10.

rights to natural fathers undermined marriage and family as the basis of social order.[17] But to do so, Duveyrier defended the rights of an unwed mother, and a mother, moreover, whose profession as actress made her morals particularly suspect. In order to overcome this possible contradiction, he stressed the civil and political aspects of the mother and child's rights in France.

The two opposing positions were laid out clearly early in the case. Hoppé's champions concentrated on his inalienable, natural rights as a father.[18] Duveyrier's opposing argument rested in part on a defence of the child's inherent Frenchness and the rights which derived from that status: 'The girl whose education is being disputed is born French, of a French mother; our laws owe her protection. She cannot be abandoned to a foreigner without running the risk of being torn from her country and all the advantages which her country guarantees her.'[19]

Such clear-cut conflict between a 'natural father' and a 'French' child could not have taken place in the Old Regime. Following the precedent of Roman law, French law had regulated the 'nationality' of a child born out of wedlock according to the mother's status. An illegitimate child born of a French mother was thus unquestionably French, but the rights associated specifically with such 'Frenchness' were limited.[20] The father – whether French or foreigner – had no official power over the child because of the legal fiction that a bastard child had no father. Since he could not bequeath familial patrimony to illegitimate children, he had no legal claim to control his children's upbringing.[21] Revolutionary legislators transformed laws on inheritance and paternal power, erasing distinctions between children born inside or outside of wedlock. By late summer 1796, as part of the more general rethinking of family relations, authorities – including lawmakers involved in the trial, such as Tronson Ducoudray and Muraire – had overturned some of the most radical of these laws, especially a measure which had allowed illegitimate children to demand retroactively a share of their parents' estates.[22] But the status of bastard children remained murky. The courts had occasionally considered other cases concerning the custody of children born out of wedlock, but there was no law stipulating which parent was ultimately

17 Duveyrier, *Réponse*, p. 1.
18 Portalis, *Consultation pour M. Hoppé*, p. 16.
19 Duveyrier, *Réponse*, p. 50.
20 For Roman law, see Y. Thomas, 'À Rome, pères citoyens et cité des pères (IIe siècle avant J.-C. –II siècle après J.-C.)', in A. Burguière, *et al.* (eds), *Histoire de la famille* (Paris, 1986), pp. 195–239. For French law on this point, see M. Vanel, *Évolution historique de la notion de français d'origine du XVIe siècle au Code civil* (Paris, 1944).
21 On the changing authority of fathers of children born out of wedlock, see J. Mulliez, 'Révolutionnaires, nouveaux pères? Forcement nouveaux pères! Le droit révolutionnaire de la paternité', in *La Révolution et l'ordre juridique privé: rationalité ou scandale* (Paris, 1988).
22 The law of 12 Brumaire II allowed illegitimate children to claim their share of inheritances retroactively. The possibility for retroactive demands was removed on 15 Thermidor IV (1 August 1796).

responsible for the education of such a child, and particularly no law regulating the choice between a foreign father and a French mother in such circumstances.

In Palymre's case, the contest between paternal and maternal citizenship status reflected both the increasing respect granted to the *pater familias* during the Directory and a persistent belief, which Duveyrier invoked strategically, that women and children could, and should, choose the polity to which they belonged. Hoppé's lawyers contended that a father's citizenship status necessarily determined that of the family as a whole. The *citoyenne* Lange had no right to complain if her daughter was taken away from her because she should have known that a father's status always determined his children's fate, and with it, the nation with which they were associated. 'The mother is afraid she will never see her child again. But she exposed herself to this risk by uniting herself with a foreigner. She has only herself to blame. She knew, or should have known, that the father is dominant in deciding the family's fate.'[23] The law, however, was not this clear-cut even for legitimate children, much less for those born out of wedlock. The lawyers' emphasis on the unity of the household and the pre-eminence of the father's status was instead informed by the belief that neither children nor married women could, or should, choose between familial and national bonds. Portalis and his colleagues granted that adults could not renounce citizenship rights in France against their will: 'one can never become a foreigner except by a voluntary abandon of one's domicile'.[24] But the ability to claim or forfeit one's citizenship status was restricted to independent adults and could not be opposed to paternal rights over a minor. A child 'does not and cannot have another country than that of his father, or the country which it will please his father to choose'.[25]

Lange's lawyer, Duveyrier, countered this argument by insisting that children's right to choose their *patrie* over biological bonds should be protected and that Palmyre should not be entrusted to a father who could deprive her of rights as a French citizen because of her position of legal dependence within the family. Since there was no evidence that Hoppé really intended to become French, he might well leave, taking the child with him. This threatened to 'denationalize' her in practice even if not in law. For 'could it not happen that the child, taken to Hamburg, would there forever lose not the right, but the means to recover her country and the rights of her birth?' If his father eventually abandoned the child, died unexpectedly, or remarried, what would become of the child in the cold wastelands of northern Germany? The future was grim: 'Can the child, on this foreign soil, await anything besides abandonment and death?'[26] Such rhetoric tapped a strong view of chauvinism

23 Portalis, *Consultation pour M. Hoppé*, p. 16.
24 *Ibid.*, p. 20.
25 *Ibid.*, p. 18.

in wartime France, but it also testified to a continuing belief that French children should retain the ability to choose and protect their identity as citizens. Contemporary newspapers, such as the *Messager du Soir* and the *Journal de Paris*, which supported Lange's side of the case, singled out this section of Duveyrier's speech as particularly effective. As one columnist observed, Duveyrier 'ended his brilliant discourse with a powerful and infallible argument. The father is a foreigner from Hamburg. The child is French, and as such must participate in the political and civil rights that the laws of her country accord to natural children (a contemporary euphemism for illegitimate offspring); a French child cannot lose these advantages against her will.'[27]

While this argument relied on the gender-neutral term of 'child', Hoppé's lawyers also contended that the value of French citizenship was inherently limited for the child because of her sex. In short, Frenchmen enjoy the 'benefit of living under a government where each citizen is part of the sovereign nation. But this political advantage does not exist for the sex which does not participate in it [the sovereign].'[28] Such claims reflected the emerging vision of a separation of citizenship and 'Frenchness'. While it was widely accepted that women could not vote or hold office, revolutionaries active during the Jacobin and early Thermidorian Convention often believed that women played at least an indirect role in the polity, and the language of the 'sovereign' or the 'citizen' was often remarkably slippery.[29] But by the Directory, legislators and prominent politicians attempted to clarify and limit such terms. Daunou, one of the authors of the Constitution of Year III, the basis for the Directorial Government, thus proposed replacing the term 'people', initially considered to define the sovereign nation, in favour of the 'universality of citizens', arguing that either women or children were not part of the French people or that sovereignty did not reside in the people as a whole.[30] Similarly, in June 1796, when the politician and journalist Roederer protested the use 'increasingly in fashion' of 'Monsieur' instead of 'citizen', his partner retorted that 'Madame' was even more widely used. Roederer considered that a different matter: 'Citizens in the French Republic are members of the State. To be a member of the State is to have political rights. The title of citizen is thus a political title. But a woman is only a member of the family. She has no political right in the State. She must not bear any political title.'[31]

26 Duveyrier, *Réponse*, pp. 54–5.
27 *Messager du Soir ou Gazette Générale de l'Europe*, 29 Frimaire V (19 December 1796), no. 89, pp. 2–3. For almost identical commentary, see *Journal de Paris*, 29 Frimaire V, no. 89, p. 357.
28 Portalis, *Consultation pour M. Hoppé*, p. 19.
29 D. Godineau, 'Femmes en citoyenneté: pratique et politique', *Annales historique de la Révolution française* 300 (1995), pp. 197–207.
30 M. Gauchet, *La Révolution des droits de l'homme* (Paris, 1989), p. 279.

The removal of women from the sovereign nation and the community of citizens, however, was not as easily accomplished as Hoppé's lawyers might have hoped. In this case, Duveyrier argued explicitly that French women did in fact 'participate in the sovereign'. He asserted, first of all, that women were represented politically through their male relatives: 'Do not French women participate in it [the sovereign] through their husbands, their children, their sons, through all of the benefits which the nature of the social contract has placed in common (*en communauté*)?' His argument echoed the theory of familial representation which his contemporary Guiraudet used to argue against rights for women as individuals: 'All of this confusion [over rights] results necessarily from the principle that the nation is only an aggregation of individuals. But when it is considered as a composite of families, represented in each case by the head of the household, there is not one member who does not have his place, not one who can complain about being deprived of his rights.'[32] This form of logic was to become a commonplace in the nineteenth century, and it would be used far more often, as in Guiraudet's treatise, to deny women independent rights such as the vote than to defend maternal custody. Indeed, the concept of women's citizenship through male representation was difficult to sustain in this case, since the women in question were an unmarried mother and her infant daughter.

Duveyrier thus rushed to make a second argument that fundamentally conflated aspects of political and legal citizenship. He contended that women had indirect political rights precisely because of the legal relationship between marriage and national citizenship. 'Do not they [women] moreover participate in it [the sovereign] in the particular power of women to make foreigners into French citizens, without establishing a business or acquiring property?'[33] With this claim, he alluded to an important, if seldom remarked, shift in the relationship between marriage and citizenship. Pre-revolutionary jurists had rarely taken marriage into account in determining the status of a foreigner in France; foreigners could marry in France, but it was the king who created new subjects.[34] The shift of sovereignty to the body of citizens as a whole made familial relationships more important in incorporating outsiders into the polity. The Constitution of 1791 and the Constitutional Act of 1793, and that of year III, all made marriage to a French woman one of the means by which a foreign man could expedite becoming a French citizen.[35] Duveyrier's invocation of the constitution here, however, was potentially

31 Roederer and Corancez, 'Aux auteurs du Journal de Paris', *Journal de Paris*, no. 19 (June 1796). My thanks to Anne Verjus for this example.
32 Duveyrier, *Réponse*, p. 53. Guiraudet, *De la famille*, p. 197.
33 Duveyrier, *Réponse*, p. 54.
34 J.-F. Dubost and P. Sahlins, *Et si on faisait payer les étrangers? Louis XIV, les immigrés, et quelques autres* (Paris, 1999).
35 *La nationalité française: Textes et documents* (Paris, 1985).

subversive. When contemporaries cited these articles, they usually did so to champion the incorporation of foreigners into France.[36] Duveyrier instead contended that French women's membership in the nation was inherently political and that a woman's status could change her husband's, a claim that threatened a vision of social order based in part on patriarchal families.

The courts ultimately decided on a compromise solution. Wary of the intentions of the German businessman, they also suspected the morals of an actress who had given birth out of wedlock. Rather than decide directly between the competing demands of family and national bonds, they ruled that the child should be placed in a state-run institution devoted to girls' education and directed by women whose morals and credentials were recognized by the government. Both parents were to have visiting rights at the school and were required to support their daughter financially.

The very compromise nature of the judgement suggests the difficulty that men and women of the Directory faced when trying to reconcile an increasing emphasis on paternalistic family structures with a lingering belief in the citizenship rights of dependants within the family. More importantly, the case shows us that debate, both implicit and explicit, about whether women were part of the sovereign nation continued to have potential consequences not only for political rights, but also for the application of civil laws. Hoppé's lawyers combined the view that women were not part of the sovereign nation with an emphasis on the pre-eminence of the family. Duveyrier's arguments reflected similar assumptions about the importance of the family as the basis of social order, but he nonetheless portrayed women and children as a political part of the sovereign nation in order to contend that they should retain the right to be able to choose between family and *patrie*. If we turn back to the contemporary issue of emigration – and the issue of whether one could be 'torn from one's country' because of the 'paternal and marital power' of male émigrés – we find a quite different argument. Unlike Duveyrier, and also unlike our young émigrée of the Terror – who insisted on her personal devotion to her *patrie* to justify her return to France – champions of leniency for women and children émigrés during year V would argue precisely for the apolitical nature of their membership in the French nation in order to contend that they should be allowed to come back to France.

36 For one roughly contemporary example, see J.-P. Chazal, *Corps Legislatif, Council des Cinq Cents, Rapport fait Par J. P. Chazal, Deputé du Gard, Au nom d'une Commission spéciale composée des representans du peuple Poullain-Grandprey, Laujacq, et Chazal, sur les effets de l'adoption et l'affaire particulière de la citoyenne Lepeletier, adoptée au nom du peuple français* (Paris, year VI), p. 30.

An amnesty for the innocent? Debates on emigration

Although émigrés were still formally ostracized in year V, more and more returned to France, where they lobbied for a relaxation of the laws against them – especially for women and children. Few scholars have looked at this debate, often tending to view émigrés as counter-revolutionary nobles justly shut out by a republic they had abandoned.[37] But it was a major political issue during the Directory, especially in early 1797. Not only did individuals petition for exceptions or changes to the laws, but the lower house of the legislature, the Council of 500, itself battered the Directory with proposed legislation, while the upper house, the Council of Elders, debated those proposals at length at the precise moments when things were heating up before the elections of March and April 1797. Justifying and instituting laws on emigration forced revolutionary governments to assess repeatedly what it meant to be a member of the revolutionary nation. It also forced them to confront potential conflicts between family and citizenship bonds for dependants within the family.

Men and women who left France after 1789 were declared to be 'civilly dead' and forfeited all their rights and titles as French citizens. But numerous individuals caught by the laws on emigration challenged this exclusion. They argued that losing all titles and rights in France because one left the territory of the revolutionary nation implied that one had been an important member of a community of citizens, membership that did not necessarily apply to women who were incapable of bearing arms or acting politically. They also suggested that dependants within the family had not voluntarily left France but had instead been forced to do so: women followed 'natural duty' by accompanying their spouses or fathers and were not able, or should not be obliged, to choose between family and nation.

In themselves, such arguments were not new in year V. Early revolutionary measures penalizing émigrés had provoked a number of pamphlets, memoirs and individual petitions, many of which were submitted under the relative safety of anonymity. For example, the author of one pamphlet, *Observations d'une femme sur la loi Contre les Émigrés*, argued in late 1792 that women should not be condemned for emigration because their nerves were too delicate for them to witness violence calmly, and because they did not, and could not, exercise political rights: 'the weakness which one attributes to women removes them from public affairs; this same weakness must excuse all the effects it produces when they are not contrary to moral laws'.[38] She made

---

37 Although the inherently incomplete nature of Donald Greer's data and the slipperiness of the term 'Third Estate' mean that figures cannot be regarded as absolute, his statistical overview suggests that large numbers of émigrés were actually commoners. D. Greer, *The Incidence of the Emigration During the French Revolution* (Cambridge, 1951), p. 65.

38 Anon., *Observations d'une femme sur la loi Contre les Emigrés* (Paris, n.d.). Though its publication history remains obscure, the pamphlet enjoyed some popularity, as it exists in at least three versions.

it explicit, moreover, that the law should treat women as a class in this respect; she desired not that 'there be exceptions for some women, but on the contrary, that women in general be excluded from the decree'.[39] Other petitioners, like the author of *Justice, Humanité, les Femmes absentes et les Enfants appelans de la Convention nationale à elle-même*, focused on married women's legal and 'natural' submission in the family. Ducanel contended that women were 'political nonentities'. But the bulk of his plea focused on the priority of familial ties over national ones: 'Long before all the laws on emigration, there existed a more holy law, a law as imperishable as nature from which it emanates; I mean paternal and marital authority.' He called for the severity of the laws on the few women who were conspirators but contended that in general, 'women, like their children, ceded to marital authority in expatriating themselves'; they should thus be exempted from the laws.[40]

The new republican government of the autumn of 1792 briefly considered, but quickly dismissed, the idea of an exception for women as a group, especially those who had left France for neutral territory.[41] The law of 28 March 1793, which established a virtual code of law pertaining to émigrés, explicitly stated that the definition of émigré applied to 'all French of one or the other sex'. Nor did individual pleas during the Terror, like that of the young woman who claimed to have been subordinated to paternal and marital power, convince the republican government. As the *Bureau des Lois* concluded in a retrospective overview of the measures concerning émigrés: 'The laws on emigration placed duty to the country above all other duties. A woman would try in vain to legitimate her absence by invoking the bonds which attached her to an émigré spouse; a child would have no more success invoking the sacred duties of filial piety.'[42] The radical nature of such a policy is especially striking if we compare it to similar measures during the American Revolution. In the United States, a married woman who went over to the enemy to be with her husband was not treated as a traitor, a foreigner or enemy of the republic. She simply needed permission from the sitting legislature or active committee of safety to join her husband, permission that was invariably granted.[43] Except for officially sanctioned cases, no man, woman, or child over the age of fourteen was allowed to leave revolutionary France.[44]

39 Anon., *Observations d'une femme*.
40 Ducanel, *Justice, Humanité, les Femmes absentes et les Enfants appelans de la Convention nationale à elle-même* (Paris, n.d.).
41 *Archives Parlementaires de 1787 à 1960*, 1ère série, 53: 456.
42 AN, F⁷ 4324, 3rd series, dossier 93.
43 L. Kerber, *Women of the Republic: Intellect and Ideology in Revolutionary America* (New York, 1980), p. 123. Kerber notes that this policy freed American revolutionaries from the task of providing for economic dependants and allowed them to gain abandoned property without a struggle – especially as there were often severe restrictions on the supplies and household goods a woman could take with her – but also sanctioned the idea that women had no political obligations to the state.
44 M. Ragon, *La Législation sur les émigrés, 1789–1825* (Paris, 1904).

Apologists for émigrés during the Directory echoed older arguments about the political insignificance of women and the inability of dependants to choose between family and national bonds or the undesirability for them to have to do so. But such claims began to appear with particular frequency after Thermidor, as legislators, philosophers, and writers increasingly sought to portray unified families as the basis of a new social order. By 1797, they had become a common trope among writers trying to locate a domestic haven of innocence, praising women as beings who could neither perform nor witness the violence which had marked France during the Terror.

Lally-Tolendal, an ex-parlementaire, an important member of the National Assembly in 1789, and later a prominent figure in the Restoration, spearheaded the appeal to allow émigrés to return to France and reclaim their rights as French citizens. His *Défense des Émigrés Français* appeared in at least four different editions during the course of 1797 and was ultimately reprinted several times during the Restoration.[45] Many of Lally-Tolendal's arguments were common themes among the apologists of the émigrés. He reviewed the various laws on emigration, arguing that émigrés had not actually ceased to be loyal Frenchmen since the government of the Terror was fundamentally illegitimate and those who had left France had been forced to flee rather than voluntarily abandoning their country. While calling for a general amnesty, however, he also insisted that 'the case of women and children must be treated separately from all others'. The ex-parlementaire justified such special treatment by focusing on women as a distinctive group whose relationship to the French nation was inherently different from that of men. He argued that the government could not place duty to the country above loyalty to the family since 'the country (*patrie*) is born from the family, nature precedes the city (*cité*)'.[46] In his view, émigré husbands and fathers were thus exonerated because they had fled an illegal regime; their daughters and wives were exonerated because they had followed the tender call of familial bonds.

Other pamphleteers echoed Lally-Tolendal's insistence that émigrées had not committed a political act by fleeing France. Exploring the connections between citizenship and gender more deeply, the anonymous author of *Défense des Femmes, des enfans et des vieillards émigrés, Pour faire suite à l'ouvrage de M. de Lally-Tolendal* made one of the strongest pleas for pardoning women for emigration. Her fundamental claim was that 'political impotency is proven for women, and must motivate in favour of their return'.[47] She

45 T.-G. de Lally-Tolendal, *Défense des Émigrés Français, adressée au peuple Français* (Paris, 1797). Other editions include two published in Paris (Cocheris, an VI [1797], and s.l. [1797]), and one published in Hamburg (P. F. Fauche, 1797). Page references here are from the Libraires et Marchands edition.

46 Lally-Tolendal, *Défense des Émigrés*, pp. 29, 35.

47 Anon., *Défense des Femmes, des enfans et des vieillards émigrés, Pour faire suite à l'ouvrage de M. de Lally-Tolendal* (Paris, 1797), p. 77.

called attention to what she saw as the extraordinary actions of the French government during the Revolution: 'No people, ancient or modern, enveloped women in the most vast of political banishments, as if women were, or should be, something in the political order.' Moreover, she argued that to treat women as émigrées was to falsely disguise (*travestir*) 'their persons as political members of the republic'.[48] Here the pamphleteer echoed the claim made by Hoppé's lawyers a few months previously that women did not participate in the sovereign nation. However, rather than argue that their distance from the political sphere meant that the head of the household should choose the nation in which they lived, she argued for a dissociation between political and civil rights precisely to protect women's civil rights and allow them to return home regardless of the actions of the head of the household.

She thus contended that precisely because French women lacked political rights and were now often recognized as lacking those rights, they should not be banished from their homeland and lose their civil rights in France. In her view, the proscription of women was the work of the radical revolution and the laws on emigration themselves had begun to treat French men and French women differently. The Constitution of Year III categorically forbade the return of émigrés to France. But, unlike earlier laws on emigration, it did not specify that this penalty applied to both sexes, suggesting that women might be exempted from its application.

Even those opposed to an amnesty for women used many of the same arguments. In another tract directly inspired by Lally-Tolendal's work, Jean-Jacques Leuliete sought to justify selected measures against those who had left France. He concurred that most émigrées were not guilty of abandoning their country under their own volition but had left instead because of their subordination to their spouses. He acknowledged that 'it is cruel, doubtless, to close the gates of the country (*patrie*) irrevocably to so many women, whose only crime was an overly faithful attachment to the opinions of those mortals dearest to them, to whom they were tied by sacred bonds'.[49] While such logic could conceivably have be applied to other family relations – such as sons over the age of majority who followed their fathers out of France – Leuliete explicitly referred to those who were legally dependent within the family, and were, in his opinion, incapable of acting independently and politically. In his view, women could not be regarded as traitors to France, since they were not, and had never been, opposed to the Republic: 'You plead for an amnesty for women, but I misspeak, one should not say amnesty, since they were never our enemies.' But precisely because their loyalty to the family preceded loyalty to the state, such women would not want to return to France without their spouses, and they should not be allowed to do so. Leuliete portrayed a partial

48   Anon., *Défense des Femmes*, pp. 8, 54.
49   J.-J. Leuliete, *Des Émigrés Français, ou réponse à M de Lally-Tolendal* (Paris, 1797), p. 19.

amnesty as destroying familial unity, for 'what charm could there be for a sensitive woman in a land from which her husband would be eternally banished?' It would be an 'illusory mercy, to misjudge the most noble sentiments of nature, to recall a wife and close the door to her husband'.[50]

The Fructidorian Terror, which was instituted soon after this controversy in September 1797, reactivated and intensified prosecution of émigrés. Nevertheless, the Fructidorians drew implicitly on the preceding reconsiderations of the place of women in the nation as they put together their position on émigrés. The minister of justice suspended the automatic death penalty for female emigrants, suggesting that women and men should be treated differently.[51] The twin ideas that family should take priority over duty to the state for women and that women should not have the duties of citizenship incumbent on men seemed to be vindicated definitively when Napoleon declared a partial amnesty for émigrés on 28 Vendémiaire IX (20 October 1800). It allowed for the legal repatriation of some fifty-two thousand émigrés. The first few categories of people granted amnesty were primarily those who had, in some sense, already been cleared. These included men and women who had already been definitively or provisionally removed from the list of émigrés, foreigners who had been previously allowed to remain in France, manual labourers – the subject of various earlier laws pardoning workers and peasants who had fled during the Terror – and those who had been listed collectively, rather than individually, as émigrés.[52] The 'wives and children' of such émigrés were allowed to return to France with them, as an extension of the amnesty granted to the head of the household.

Article 5, however, aimed specifically at women. It granted amnesty to women who had left France under their husbands' authority. As Fouché, the Minister of Police, explained, certain exceptions 'concerned women under the authority of their husbands or children still under paternal authority or who only left to perfect their education ... (their absence) could not be considered a crime of emigration. A married woman obeyed her husband's orders, she left her country with him without calculating the consequences of the path along which he took her, and without knowing the laws which menaced her.'[53] Women who had left on their own were also exempted from the law, regardless of whether or not their spouses had been cleared of charges of emigration. Although Fouché did not explicitly argue this, it seems clear that this exemption built implicitly on the idea that women were not politi-

---

50 Leuliete, *Des Emigrés Français*, pp. 20, 23.
51 H. G. Brown, 'Mythes et massacres: reconsidérer la Terreur directoriale', *Annales historiques de la Révolution française* 325 (2001), pp. 23–52.
52 Manual workers included 'laboureurs, journaliers, ouvriers, artisans, tous autres exercent une profession mécanique, domestiques et gens âgés, femmes et enfants de tous les individus ci-dessus'.
53 *Rapport du Ministre de la Police Générale et arrêté des consuls concernant les individus sur la liste des émigrés depuis 1789* (Paris, year IX).

cally part of the sovereign nation, and did not thus have political responsibilities to it.

The registers of those who took advantage of this article in the following year record close to thirteen thousand names, or roughly a quarter of all those who took advantage of the amnesty, far more than any other group singled out for a special reprieve.[54] The government did retain the right to deport women whose spouses or children were still considered émigrés if they proved themselves to be dangerous: 'Women whose names were eliminated from the list because of article 5 of the first title, even if their husbands or children remained on the list of émigrés, can be expelled from French territory by an order of the government if they trouble public tranquillity.'[55] This qualification, however, was rarely applied.

The amnesty marks one end to the requirement that women be forced to choose between family and national bonds. But minority voices continued to echo Duveyrier's contention that subordinates in the family retained the ability, if not necessarily the obligation, to do so. The story of Bernard Montagnac, whose struggle to make sense of the categories of French citizenship was widely publicized immediately after the amnesty, reveals the persistence of this belief into the early Napoleonic period. Montagnac, a young veteran, was provisionally, but not yet completely, cleared of charges of emigration and thus potentially still subject to the penalty of civil death. His political and civil 'paralysis' was troubling to him since the twenty-five-year-old soldier was unsure whether he could marry legally, despite having fulfilled all the 'formalities prescribed by the law in order to preserve his *qualité de français* and all his rights of citizenship'.[56] It was a common dilemma in the period. Montagnac's tract, *Sur l'importante question du mariage des prévenus d'émigration,* struck a chord throughout France, going through at least three editions during the course of year IX.[57]

Poirier, the young veteran's lawyer, presented a series of arguments in defence of the lovelorn man. He claimed that Montagnac should be given the benefit of the doubt since he had been provisionally cleared of the charge of emigration, that marriage was too 'natural' and important a phenomenon to be restricted by legalistic quibbles, and that the French population as a whole

---

54 AN, BB[30] 155. Unfortunately, the amount and kind of information required for each woman varies greatly, making it difficult to draw definite statistical conclusions about their marital status and social position. Certainly, there were more women affected by this clause than members of any of the other groups who were singled out for specific status. There are only fifty names on the list of émigrés granted an amnesty since they left before 1789, 74 from Malta, 1,031 deported priests, and only six children.

55 Ragon, *La Législation sur les émigrés.*

56 L. E. Poirer, *Sur l'importante question du mariage des prévenus d'émigration, suivie de la décision affirmative du ministre de l'intérieur* (Paris, 1801), p. 4.

57 The *Catalogue général des Livres imprimés de la Bibliothèque Nationale* lists three editions published in year IX.

would suffer from laws restricting marriage and, in consequence, the birth of new citizens. But Poirier also insisted that such marriages would not harm native French women and children. If women were transformed into foreigners through marriage to an émigré or supposed émigré, they forfeited their membership in the French nation by their free choice; it would be 'by a voluntary abjuration and their personal actions that they would be henceforward foreigners in France'. More importantly, women could always choose to place national ones over familial ones later: 'if a woman prefers her country (*patrie*) over her spouse and children prefer their country to their father, a woman can ask for a divorce and find a new spouse; the children, aided by their mother and her family, can form useful establishments and become excellent citizens'.[58]

Conclusion

The Civil Code of 1804 would go a step further, echoing and expanding on arguments made in passing by Hoppé's lawyers and institutionalized more systematically by the amnesty for émigrés. Legislators proclaimed that dependants in the family no longer had an obligation to place country before their legal and physical subordination within the household, the duty in the words of our young émigrée, to sacrifice 'to it (the patrie) one's father, husband, and all others who must only be dear to us after it'.[59] They also suggested that a married woman should not even face the possibility of considering whether she preferred 'her country (*patrie*) over her spouse'. While acknowledging that a French woman could certainly choose to abandon her country by marrying a foreigner, legislators limited the ability of such women to choose between national and familial bonds after marriage. They made divorce much more difficult to obtain, particularly for women, and proclaimed that a married woman was legally obliged to follow her husband wherever he chose to live.[60] Similarly, they reinforced paternal control over children and emphasized the unity of the household.[61] Napoleonic legislators also rigorously separated civil and political aspects of citizenship, making it clear that Frenchness did not necessarily mean participation in the state, especially not for women and for dependants within the family. They decreed that marriage affected a woman's status but not her husband's and removed earlier articles that

58 Poirer, *Sur l'importante question*, p. 11.
59 'Je me suis dit, les préjugés, l'égoïsme, les loix abusives de notre ancien gouvernement sont changés; on ne devait rien à sa patrie, maintenant comme à Rome, on lui sacrifie son père, son époux, et tous les êtres qui ne doivent nous êtres chers qu'après elle'. AN, DIII 238.
60 Article 214. It did not explicitly state that this obligation applied outside of France, but it also presented no exceptions to the law.
61 See X. Martin, 'Fonction paternelle et Code Napoléon', *Annales historiques de la Révolution française* 305 (1996), pp. 465–75.

expedited a foreign man's access to French citizenship status if he married a French woman, like those which Duveyrier had drawn upon to establish women's participation in the sovereign nation.

Yet the Napoleonic Code did not follow inexorably or automatically from the political debates and clashes of the Terror. Instead, situations as diverse as custody trials and debates over the application of laws mandating residence on French territory reveal that men and women during the Directory continued to test the gendered limits of national citizenship and to rethink the appropriate relationships between family and state. The debates and litigation that accompanied the redefinition of women's place in the polity thus reveal the hidden difficulties and costs of stabilizing post-revolutionary society.

3

The aftermath of the assignat: plaintiffs in the age of property, 1794–1804[1]

Judith A. Miller

But we must finish; we must leave behind these times of calamities; we must forget them even, if possible; and we cannot do so without both sides making sacrifices.[2]

In the late Revolution, a particularly unwieldy legal phrase, the *action en rescision pour lésion d'outre-moitié*, reverberated in both courtrooms and consciences across France. At first glance, this almost undecipherable term would appear likely to trip up even the most silver-tongued lawyer. Indeed, specialists of revolutionary law seem to have retreated before the incomprehensible series of syllables.[3] Yet, no such confusion would have silenced the clamour of barristers, notaries, legislators, all manner of pamphleteers, judges, clerks, and hosts of families gathered in Directorial drawing rooms. They knew that the phrase referred to lawsuits that allowed sellers of immovable goods – homes, shops and land, for instance – to confront their buyers later and demand more money for the property. The term *lésion d'outre-moitié* itself meant 'damage of more than half'.[4] Sellers claimed that they had unwittingly agreed to a price that represented less than half of the property's supposed real value. Now they sought to rectify their error and receive the 'just price', plus interest. If the seller prevailed, the original contract was cancelled and the hapless buyer had to pay up or decamp. Such was the power of that seemingly unintelligible phrase.

At first consideration, suits alleging *lésion* and seeking to undo a sale seem

---

1 This article has benefited from comments at Indiana University's Economic History Workshop, Emory University's Halle Institute, and from Philippe Rosenberg, Robert Chirinko and Leonard Carlson. All translations are mine.
2 L. Barreau (Eure-et-Loire), *Sur les transactions entre particuliers antérieures au 1er janvier 1791*, Council of Elders, 11 Messidor V (29 June 1797).
3 See the comment on the need for work on litigation, F. Crouzet, *La Grande inflation: La monnaie en France de Louis XVI à Napoléon* (Paris, 1993), p. 434.
4 F. Boulanger, 'Le problème de la lésion dans le droit intermédiaire', *Études d'histoire économique et sociale du XVIIIe siècle* (Paris, 1966), pp. 53–94.

inconceivable at best. They upend all that we understand about the sanctity of contract, the inviolability of property and Enlightenment rationality. What was the meaning of one's signature if, months later, one could claim confusion about the property's supposed 'real value' and demand more money? True, Roman law – Justinian's Code, section *'De rescindenda venditione'* – and numerous *coutumes* had established the concept of contract cancellation.[5] Yet, while the great legal minds of the Old Regime such as R. J. Pothier, continued to treat the topic of *lésion* in their volumes on contracts, few lawsuits used it in the last decades of the monarchy.[6] Moreover, reformers such as the physiocrats criticized such lawsuits in the eighteenth century, maintaining that they violated the freedom of contract. The concept fared no better in the first years of the Revolution. The August 1793 draft for a Civil Code proposed abolishing *lésion* as grounds for contesting property sales altogether. Contracts – even if made in error – had to stand, explained Jean-Jacques-Régis Cambacérès, a contributor to this and many of the Revolution's other attempted codes.[7] Two years later, the Thermidorian Convention confirmed that consensus by suspending any suits underway for 'damage of more than half' and forbidding them in the future.[8] Assuredly, the concept seemed destined to disappear, one more remnant of an archaic past of Latin legalisms. Yet, legislation during the Directory allowed an explosion of these suits. Far from expiring unlamented, *lésion d'outre-moitié* was pitched into the pamphlet debates, legislative skirmishes and courtrooms of late revolutionary France.

The rehabilitation of the concept of *lesion d'outre-moitié* under the Directory appears all the more implausible if one considers the regime's commitment to economic liberalism. Had not the Directory – more than any other revolutionary government – upheld the maintenance of property?[9] In his presentation on the Constitution of Year III, Boissy d'Anglas, for instance, had insisted that the time had come to reject the economic egalitarianism of the Terror and instead 'to guarantee finally the property of the rich'.[10] Recent

---

5 H. de Mesmay, 'La nature juridique de la lésion en droit civil français', Thèse de doctorat en droit, Université de Paris II, 1980, pp. 12–13. Early Roman law limited *lésion* claims to contracts made by minors under age 25. Diocletian (C.E. 284–305) and Maximilian extended it to property sales in general. Byzantine Emperor Justinian (C.E. 527–65) codified scattered Roman law in his *Corpus Iuris Civilis*, which became the foundation for much later European law. French law adopted the Roman concept of *laesio enormis*, along with its emphasis on forms, such as contracts, and its concepts of equity. See also Article 1304 in G. Griolet and C. Vergé (eds), *Jurisprudence de MM. Dalloz. Les Codes annotés. Nouveau Code civil* (Paris, 1903), vol. 3, pp. 272–85.

6 *Traité du contrat de vente . . .* (Paris, 1767).

7 Boulanger, 'Le problème de la lésion dans le droit intermédiaire', pp. 60–3.

8 Law of 14 Fructidor III (31 August 1795), *Bulletin des Lois*, Bulletin 175, No. 1061.

9 F. Fortunet, 'Des droits et des devoirs', in J. Bart, *et al.* (eds), *La Constitution de l'an III ou l'ordre républicain* (Dijon, 1998), pp. 17–28. The 'Duties' charge citizens to maintain property in Articles 8 and 9.

10 5 Messidor III (23 June 1795) in *Moniteur*, no. 281, 11 Messidor III (29 June 1795).

scholarship discerns more than mere doctrinaire bourgeois liberalism in the programmes of prominent ministers and representatives – seeing instead a vast national project joining economic regeneration and political pacification.[11] Nonetheless, the Directory, however understood by historians, would appear to endorse unequivocally the principles of freedom of contract and the sanctity of property. Given that background, how does one explain the revival of *lésion* suits by the likes of Cambacérès, Jean-Barthélemy LeCouteulx de Canteleu and Pierre-Samuel Dupont de Nemours?

Any answer must begin by recognizing the particular pressures of that period. The collapse of the Revolution's two forms of paper money – the assignats and then the *mandats territoriaux* – ravaged the country.[12] Once the general price maximums of the Terror had been lifted (24 December 1794), the cost of food skyrocketed. By early 1796, the assignat had fallen to less than .05 per cent of its face value. Death and suicide statistics from the years III and IV attest to the widespread misery accompanying the economic collapse.[13] With a war to fund and a daunting list of state creditors, the representatives tried to avoid any admission that the Revolution's currency could never regain its face value. To abandon it was, in effect, to abandon the Revolution. In early 1796, by issuing a new form of paper currency, the *mandats territoriaux,* backed by the sales of sufficient nationalized property, the Councils hoped to save the Republic's coffers. That money, too, crashed swiftly. The return to hard currency on 16 Pluviôse V (4 February 1797) brought a crushing deflation. By then, the fortunes of debtors and creditors had been tossed hither and yon, commercial and private dealings were in chaos, and from one end of the country to the other came calls for the Councils to act.

Despite the currencies' wrenching fall, French families and businesses had stumbled along, fitfully settling inheritances, signing marriage contracts, buying residences, making loans, and drawing up contracts of every variety.[14] In many cases, inflation had driven them to part with homes, shops and farmlands to pay for food and other necessities. Others, taking advantage of their desperation, had rushed to turn stacks of worthless bills into a suitably elegant Parisian *hôtel* on the rue du Faubourg Honoré, with a rose marble entryway, or, more often, a modest dwelling in disrepair in an outlying town. Sometimes the buyers paid rapidly in cash; in other cases, the sales were attached to *rentes* (annuities) for part of the price, ensuring steady income for the sellers.

---

11 J. Livesey, 'Commercial Republicanism and Agrarian Ideology in the French Revolution', *Past and Present* 157 (1997), pp. 94–121.

12 The standard accounts are S. E. Harris, *The assignats* (Cambridge, Mass., 1930); and Crouzet, *La Grande inflation.*

13 R. Cobb, *Terreur et subsistances* (Paris, 1965).

14 See in particular the work of G. Béaur, including 'Révolution et transmission de la propriété: le marché foncier ordinaire (Lizy-sur-Ourcq et Bar-sur-Seine entre 1789 et 1810)', in *La Révolution française et le monde rural* (Paris, 1989), pp. 271–86.

Those sellers counted on such investments for long-term revenue, as had their pre-revolutionary ancestors. Horrified, they watched as the value of their quarterly payments plummeted. Women and the elderly were particularly vulnerable to those losses.[15] To protect panicked creditors, the Thermidorian Convention finally passed the law of 25 Messidor III (13 July 1795), freezing debt repayment and acknowledging the assignat's crash.[16] However, that law cut off any revenue whatsoever for months on end, ruining creditors.[17] Adding to their woes, the flood of nationalized property placed on the market lowered property values overall. Hard hit by both inflation and the fall in real estate prices, sellers could do little more than mourn their lost properties and vanished hopes. Childhood homes, expected annuities, and once-profitable fields: all had disappeared in the currencies' collapse.

The debtor's fortunes reversed with the end of paper money. The Councils ordered payments to recommence, while promising further instructions to the shaken country. Intoxicated by the idea that they might receive extravagant amounts in silver, creditors waved copies of earlier agreements in the face of their now-defenceless debtors. Buyers who had gambled incorrectly on the return to metal laboured under the unforeseen weight of their debts contracted in assignats. Thus, by 1797, both buyers and sellers had endured many a dark moment, tormented by memories of the miscalculations, desperation and haste that had destroyed their fortunes. Not content to let matters remain as they were, they sought redress through the courts. Clerks wore out quill tips recording tales of leases gone wrong, loans unpaid, and long-lost merchandise. Justices of the peace were soon exhausted by the rush of plaintiffs contesting, enforcing, or denying contracts written during the inflation. Yet, despite the din of opposing parties, the courts had no laws to sort out the wrongs wrought by the disastrous currencies.

Legislative fissures in the wake of hyper-inflation

The solution, or so it seemed, lay in legislation that would permit the recalculation of contracts or even their termination for 'damage of more than half'.

---

15 P. T. Hoffman, G. Postel-Vinay and J.-L. Rosenthal, *Priceless markets: The Political Economy of Credit in Paris, 1660–1870* (Chicago and London, 2000), pp. 177–228.

16 In *Moniteur universel*, no. 300, 30 Messidor III (18 July 1795).

17 There was never-ending legislation regarding debt repayment. On 5 Frimaire IV (26 November 1795), the Councils allowed parties to make contracts in hard currency, although creditors could not refuse to accept paper money. The law of 12 Frimaire IV (3 December 1795) permitted creditors with contracts dated before 1 Vendémiaire IV (23 September 1795) to reject reimbursement until appropriate legislation appeared. Once the *mandats territoriaux* had been voted, the law of 15 Germinal IV (4 April 1796) allowed some payments to resume. The law of 29 Messidor IV (17 July 1796) again suspended payments. The Councils authorized parties to make agreements in the terms and currencies that they wanted 5 Thermidor IV (23 July 1796). The law of 11 Frimaire VI (1 December 1797) permitted debt payments to resume.

Indeed, until the law of 14 Fructidor III abolished *lésion* suits, thousands of lawyers and potential plaintiffs had hastened to use that Old Regime concept to break contracts and demand increased payments.[18] When the Directory opened in late October 1795, the representatives could no longer put off further measures. The regime had promised stability, military victory and a regeneration of commerce. It could not leave creditors destitute, payments suspended and business at a standstill. Deputies sanctimoniously rose to address the question that was – as one representative explained – 'the first one recommended by their constituents'. While on missions, 'along their entire route they were asked solely for a law on transactions', he recounted, and 'arrived in Paris, ceaselessly they heard resounding in their ears the same demand, a law on transactions'.[19] The most illustrious financial and legal minds of the period, such as Jean-Etienne-Marie Portalis, Dupont de Nemours, or Cambacérès, seated in the legislature, could agree that the republic had to act. Nevertheless, they divided on the matter of which actions the country needed.

It took four bitterly contested attempts, from the summer of 1795 until the spring of 1798, to pass comprehensive legislation.[20] At first reading, the Councils' minutes regarding finances impress one most by their tediousness and perpetual recourse to Latin. Yet, beneath the considerable incomprehensible hyperbole were deep cleavages separating conservatives, especially reactionaries and royalists, from republicans, including some former regicides and those supporting the Constitution of Year III and the Directory. As early as 1795, the debates regarding depreciation tables warned of the discord that the question of inflation could provoke. If accepted, tables tracing the rate of depreciation would allow parties to recalculate the figures on their inflated agreements and 'reduce' them to manageable, presumably equivalent, sums in specie.[21] Yet, for two years, each proposed schedule gave way under allegations of inaccuracies and partiality toward either the government or the various parties to transactions. In general, the representatives on the right supported creditors and tables showing sharply plummeting rates. Their opponents upheld the value of paper currency and disparaged creditors' claims. Additional difficulties resulted from the price controls of the Terror. That legacy undermined any attempt to base rate tables on actual prices, for few existed during the maximums, save those of the black market. More

18 M. Marion, *Histoire financière de la France depuis 1715*, 6 vols (Paris, 1914–31), vol. 3, pp. 349–50; Boulanger, 'Le problème de la lésion', pp. 66–7; A. Douarche, *Les tribunaux civils de Paris pendant la Révolution (1791–1800)*, 2 vols. (Paris, 1905–07), vol. 2, pp. 153–4, 192–3.

19 Boirot (de Puy-de-Dôme), Council of Elders, 4 Messidor V (22 June 1797), *Opinion sur la résolution du 30 germinal dernier*.

20 The major initiatives originated in Messidor IV (June–July 1796); Brumaire V (October–November 1796); Floréal V (April–May 1797); and finally, Frimaire VI (November–December 1798).

21 Archives Nationales (hereafter AN), C 489–96.

distressing, any calculations were highly questionable if applied to real estate. Those prices had lagged well behind those for food or other goods. Unable to agree on any uniform table, the Councils then debated abandoning them altogether. Finally, on 5 Messidor V (23 June 1797), failing to settle on any guidelines for judges or baseline rates, the Councils ordered departmental officials to produce tables using local prices and expertise.[22]

Tensions worsened after the spring elections sent a new majority of royalists to the legislature. Their sweeping programme – granting amnesty to émigrés and priests and otherwise negating republican policies – convulsed the Councils. State finances, involving everything from tax collection to the legislature's control over the Treasury, offered a promising springboard for the conservatives' assaults on the legislature's left and the Directory. Many of the members of the Councils' financial commissions, charged with sorting out 'transactions between individuals', were outspoken leaders on the right.[23] They condemned the Revolution and thus its every currency and financial policy. Those representatives demanded laws to allow creditors to collect many debts in full and in specie. They ridiculed past payments made in paper. As for 'immovable' property, they sought means for former owners to obtain more money or even to reclaim their homes and lands. Family patrimony, these legislators and an avid press alleged, had been stolen from their owners, who received mere 'tree bark' in return.[24] The Terror, intoned Charles-François Lebrun in a characteristic year V report, had torn hard metal from the hands of its citizens through the 'terrible effect of these words so oft repeated: *les assignats ou la mort*'.[25] Assignats or death: such were the crimes of the Terror. Now these representatives challenged the Councils to rectify those wrongs. Their adversaries, more committed to the Revolution and its currencies, stalled some of the more excessive resolutions. Some even defended debtors and insisted that the state come to their aid against the arrogance of 'merciless creditors'.[26] Still, whether royalist or republican, few could argue that the state should refuse to confront commercial and familial chaos.

Beyond the political dimensions of the debates loomed significant philosophical and constitutional questions. Could the state rewrite contracts? 'There would be no societies where the legislator would substitute his will for that of the contracting parties', warned one representative, as the Councils

---

22 *Bulletin des lois*, Bulletin 129, no. 1254.
23 They included many who would be sentenced to deportation in the 18 Fructidor V coup d'état, such as Gibert-Desmolières and Barbé-Marbois in the Council of 500, and Tronchet, Tronçon Ducoudray and Laffon-Ladébat in the Council of Elders.
24 [Grenier?], *Encore un mot sur l'action en restitution pour cause de lésion d'outre moitié* (n.p., n.d.).
25 AN C 496, fol. 110, no. 330, Council of Elders, 18 Nivôse V (7 January 1797). Lebrun had opposed the assignat in 1789, predicting that it would cause inflation.
26 Barreau, *Sur les transactions entre particuliers antérieures au 1er janvier 1791*.

tried to sort out the stakes.[27] The lawyers among them would have identified the question of the parties' consent as the fundamental issue. In Old Regime laws, *lésion* resulted from confusion or hardship on the part of one of the parties, and presumably, the eagerness of the other party to profit from it. One had signed a contract willingly, but in ignorance, or out of extreme need. There had been no true consent and the monetary amounts plainly indicated that deficiency.[28] Thus, in the year IV debates, many maintained that the legislator was not 'putting himself in the place of the contracting parties'. Instead, the state was 'repairing the disorder that the assignat's fall' had created and was returning contracts to their 'true value'.[29] That understanding persisted in the year VI. 'The vicissitudes of events have changed the situation of the parties', explained Regnier, reporting on a successful resolution, 'and require them to be returned to the state in which they would have been, if they had contracted in hard currency.'[30] When some feared that such measures would reopen all agreements, even credit with one's baker or cobbler, advocates argued that far greater harm would come from leaving contracts stand as written.[31] It fell to the representatives to provide for a contract's 'repair' when the payments stipulated were insufficient. This understanding followed the broader principles of the Constitution of Year III, namely that the basis for sound government lay not in nature, but in civil society.[32] Property – its limits, definitions and uses – could only be created by the law. Far from an act of questionable constitutionality, then, the Councils were re-establishing justice itself.

The efforts to craft such justice lurched along. In one fleeting, although significant, moment of consensus, the Councils managed to adopt the law of 3 Germinal V (23 March 1797). That legislation briefly allowed the suspended cases for *lésion d'outre-moitié* to recommence. Given the expectations that the return to hard currency would bring stability, the representatives permitted those suits to move forward.[33] Further agreements failed. The

27 AN C 489, fol. 64, no. 239, Council of Elders, 9 Messidor IV (27 June 1796).
28 Eighteenth-century discussions of the parties' 'will' as a necessary component of a contract fall outside the scope of this article. Yet this matter was critical to the evolving legal regimes on both sides of the Atlantic. Within the Anglo-American context, theories of objective value and readily ascertainable prices gave way to an understanding of value as subjective and fluctuating. In the early United States, contract law struggled with a means for seeing the parties' intentions – the 'meeting of minds' – as the key element of an agreement, as opposed to an exchange of equal value. French legal theorists, however, often construed *lésion* primarily as an objective category – discernible from the prices alone and rendering intention largely immaterial. Mesmay, 'La nature juridique de la lésion,' pp. 11–22; M. J. Horowitz, *The Transformation of American Law, 1760–1860* (Cambridge, Mass., 1977), pp. 160–210.
29 See the Messidor IV debates over leases, AN, C 489, fol. 64.
30 AN, C 520, fol. 77, no. 55, Council of Elders, 2 Frimaire VI (22 November 1797).
31 Par un ami de [la justice et de l'humanité], *Question importante incessamment soumise au Conseil des Anciens* (Paris, n.d.).
32 Fortunet, 'Des droits et des devoirs', in *La Constitution de l'an III*, pp. 17–28.
33 *Bulletin des lois*, Bulletin 115, no. 1099.

extremes to which the conservative representatives of the Council of 500 sought to aid creditors, along with the force with which the majority of the Elders rebuffed them, were revealed by spring and summer 1797 resolutions. The 18–19 Floréal V (8–9 May 1797) bill from the Council of 500 offered creditors heartening choices. The seller of 'immovables' could insist that the contract be honoured as written: an inflated contract for ten thousand livres in assignats would be paid with ten thousand livres in specie. If that sum proved overwhelming, the buyer's sole option was to cancel (*résilier*) the agreement, return the property and receive the funds paid, recalculated with the departmental depreciation table. Alternatively, the seller could consult the tables and offer to pay the 'reduced' price in specie with interest. In that case, however, the buyer could not terminate the contract and had to pay up swiftly.[34] The bill left enormous discretion to sellers alone. Crétet, reporting for the Finance Commission of the Elders, declared such measures 'excessive' and 'unjust'. Tilted in the seller's favour, the resolution 'threatened' every contract 'with violent *résiliation* and dangerous lawsuits'. The Elders rejected the resolution and forced the Council of 500 to regroup for one last offensive.[35] That attempt, begun in mid-Thermidor, was debated in the Elders on 14 and 15 Fructidor (31 August–1 September 1797).[36] Vehemently combated, the days' two resulting laws promised creditors that several forms of debts would be reimbursed fully in specie. Debtors had – at most – a year to pay.[37] On the eve of 18 Fructidor, then, creditors would have slept easily, reassured by the tenacity of their supporters in the Council of 500, and dreaming of recovered properties and restored fortunes.

Strained interpretations: The laws of year VI

The coup d'état of 18–19 Fructidor V – which purged the Councils of more than two hundred of the most royalist representatives and even ejected two Directors – dashed the hopes of creditors readying their suits. While the coup did allow the rapid passage of legislation covering contracts, the climate was transformed. Historians know these post-Fructidor months best from Minister of Finance Ramel's bankruptcy of the Two-Thirds (9 Vendémiaire VI –30 September 1797), the Directory's revived persecutions of émigrés and priests

34 AN, C 409, fol. 68, no. 460, Council of 500, 18–19 Floréal V (8–9 May 1797). This consensus contrasts with discussions in the early United States, where such debt recalculation was rejected. D. Paarlberg, *An Analysis and History of Inflation* (Westport, CT, 1993), pp. 34–7.

35 Council of Elders, 29 Messidor V (17 July 1797), Crétet, *Rapport au nom de la commission spéciale* ... ; *Moniteur*, 15 Thermidor V (2 August 1797), no. 315.

36 Council of 500, 18–19 Thermidor V (5–6 August 1797), *Moniteur*, 22–23 Thermidor (9–10 August 1797), nos. 322–3.

37 Laws of 14 and 15 Fructidor V (31 August–1 September 1797), *Moniteur*, 20–21 Fructidor V (6–7 September 1797), nos. 350–1.

and the imposition of a heavily republican culture on a country rent by civil war. In those tumultuous weeks, the representatives returned to the question of the myriad contracts, inheritances, loans and other financial agreements made since 1789. Rid of many outspoken conservative adversaries, including Gibert-Desmolières, Thibaudeau, Laffon-Ladébat and Tronçon Ducoudray, the resulting laws sharply reduced creditors' chances.

Like the resolutions that preceded them, the year VI laws covering transactions presented exhaustingly complicated articles. A rapid reading might have convinced inattentive sellers that the summer's resolutions had survived the coup. Recurrent phrases – reimbursements in specie for some debts and 'reduction' for others, and the possibility of cancellation – gave few indications of any departure from the pre-Fructidor bills. The law of 11 Frimaire VI (1 December 1797) sketched out the basic procedures for many categories of payments and recalculations and promised future guidelines for property sales.[38] Those clarifications appeared in two laws on 16 Nivôse (5 January 1798). That legislation lifted any remaining suspensions of debt repayment. Then, the laws turned to the many forms of agreements made throughout the Revolution. These texts allowed the recalculation of remaining sums due into hard currency for most contracts using departmental depreciation tables. Finally, in articles that would have encouraged impatient creditors, they reopened suits for *lésion d'outre moitié*.[39]

Yet, buried in the familiar language lay barriers to those long-deferred cases. First, the two laws of 16 Nivôse acquitted debtors of any sums already paid, even in worthless paper. Effectively, the Fructidorian Councils were dismissing creditors' assertions that earlier reimbursement in paper constituted completely inadequate remuneration. Then, the law of 19 Floréal VI (8 May 1798) potentially annulled even the most justified *lésion* suits. The relevant articles outlined a new means for estimating the property's value: an apparent technicality, but one on which entire suits depended. The 19 Floréal law utterly overturned Old Regime practices, which had used metallic currency values. Instead, the law ordered that the estimates establish the 'real price in assignats' compared with other 'sales of immovable property of the same nature in the area or the most close neighbourhood at the time of the sale'. In other words, the estimations were to exclude any reference to pre-revolutionary values or calculations in specie. Yet, as the critics rushed to explain, few sellers would be able to find any other local property sales that had sold for an appropriate price in assignats – a problem that would invalidate their claims. According to the law's opponents, who cited Cicero, Seneca, and Rousseau, metallic currency alone offered reliable guides to a

38 *Bulletin des lois*, Bulletin 161, no. 1580.
39 AN, C 519, Council of Elders, 16 Nivôse VI; *Bulletin des lois*, Bulletin 174, nos. 1651 and 1650. (The Council misnumbered the laws, reversing the order in which they voted them.)

property's 'true value'. Using any other standard was 'immoral,' an act of 'pillage' and an attack on both the 'social pact' and on property, alleged one anonymous pamphlet. The law's formula overturned fifteen centuries of practice and resulted from a complete misreading of Roman law and French traditions.[40] The early year VI laws had offered but the illusion of relief, an illusion that the 19 Floréal law destroyed.

Not all was lost for anxious sellers pacing about in judicial antechambers, however. With tantalising ambiguity, the law of 19 Floréal VI also instructed the courts to take into account 'any opportunities or advantages' in the contract that would have favoured either party. Inventive sellers seized upon that phrase. Generally, there was a several-month delay between the signing of a contract and the payment. The assignat's collapse during that period, or during the payment suspensions, had provided unmistakable 'advantages' to the buyer. Revising their cases, sellers clutched at the benefits a favourable interpretation of the law might yield. If their sales prices in assignats did not merit consideration, they reasoned, surely their staggering losses with each delay in payment would persuade the most hardened judge. Thus, despite the intentions of the Councils to rein in plaintiffs, the law's language held means for resourceful sellers to subvert the year VI legislation.[41]

Lésion *lawsuits: contracts in the regime of property*

The *lésion* litigation rush was on, and exaggerated expectations took flight. To believe one critic, 'the almost general rumour' flew that the Councils had broken 'all property contracts made during paper money, and pronounced that none had been made at their just price'. That 'lie' gained credence, 'indirectly accredited by practitioners without delicacy, hungry for lawsuits and discord'.[42] Probably desperate for income themselves, 'practitioners without delicacy' appreciated the possibilities in these suits. One even suggested that potential plaintiffs who had but marginal cases – who nursed 'an illusion' as to the 'fantastic advantages of the law of 19 Floréal' – hire him to negotiate a settlement rather than engage in a long, expensive and unsuccessful case.[43]

40 [Grenier?], *Encore un mot ...*; Council of Elders, 12 Prairial VII (31 May 1799), *Opinion de [Joseph] Cornudet, sur la resolution du 19 germinal an 7.*
41 Even a year after the passage of the legislation, the Councils had failed to define those 'opportunities or advantages', despite challenges to do so. Grenier, Council of 500, 7 Pluviôse VII (26 January 1799), *Second rapport fait ... au nom de plusieurs commissions réunies.*
42 Citoyen Meslier, *La cause de tous les acquéreurs d'immeubles ...* (Paris, Messidor VI).
43 *Affiches, annonces, avis divers de Paris*, Le Citoyen Quesnel, 17 and 19 Prairial VI (5 and 7 June 1798), 5008 and 5056; and 3 Prairial VI (22 May 1798), 4698. I thank Rebecca Spang for these items. Quesnel is the author of *Sur le mode et les effets de la rescision des contrats de vente pour cause de lésion d'outre-moitié* (Paris, [year VI]).

Even prominent jurists such as Auguste-Charles Guichard rushed to publish guides to the new legislation and outline plausible arguments.[44] Lawyers, whether esteemed or disreputable, recognized the powerful aspirations that the words *lésion d'outre-moitié* awoke in their clients.

While the jurists, deputies and pamphleteers debated the finer points of the laws, lawyers chased clients, and plaintiffs jammed the courts. The numbers themselves are telling. In four of seventy-seven *bureaux de paix* (cantonal civil courts) in the department of the Seine-et-Oise, chosen for their extensive records, plaintiffs lodged numerous cases seeking damages or contract cancellation: thirty-five in Germain-en-Laye; seventeen in Meulan; thirty-four in Versailles *intramuros* north; and thirteen in Versailles *intramuros* south. In the Gironde also, in the two rural *bureaux de paix* selected from the seventy in the department, plaintiffs sued to recover in surprising numbers: twenty-five in tiny Civrac-en-Médoc and thirty-three in Saint-Seurin.[45] Names of immediate notoriety appear, especially in the Paris and Versailles records: the divorced wife of Grimaldi, prince de Monaco; the Citoyenne Dervieux, the dancer who married Madame du Barry's architect; and the widow Montmorency Luxembourg, who disputed sales in Meulan.[46] More often, though, both sides came from more middling ranks, from trades devastated by the end of the economy of the court and the capital. Grocers, tanners, butchers, locksmiths, used clothing dealers, cobblers, and innkeepers, joined by formerly more prosperous Old Regime personages – goldsmiths, caterers and military officers – filed into court, often trailing assorted *hommes de loi* and notaries.

Mediation through the *bureaux de paix* was the first step. Occasionally, the defendants agreed that they owed the plaintiffs – most often that a buyer owed a seller – further sums. Repeatedly, however, buyers insisted that they had 'paid in good faith and in full'. Regardless of the rate of the assignat on the day of their last payment, they were quit and the law of 16 Nivôse was on their side. To allegations that the price was too low, they protested that the contract had been falsified to everyone's satisfaction. They had paid much more secretly (as their notaries could attest), they had covered their sellers' debts, they had supplied *pots de vin*, cords of wood, bags of coffee beans, and even gold or silver watches. They would wait for a civil court to rule; they would wait for the estimate; but they would pay nothing more.

Once the case reached the departmental civil courts, judges named two experts, one chosen by each party. That assortment of architects, farmers and

---

44 A.-C. Guichard, *Consultation sur la rescision des ventes et aliénations d'immeubles faites sous le régime du papier-monnaie* (Paris, n.d.); and *Guide des experts, ou instructions et formules sur les expertises et estimations ...* (Paris, year VI).

45 Future research will extend to other *bureaux de paix* in these departments.

46 Douarche, *Les tribunaux civils de Paris*, vol. 2, pp. 621, 625–26; Archives départementales des Yvelines (hereafter ADY), 64L 41, 21 Thermidor VI (8 August 1798).

notaries was dispatched to draw up a detailed estimate. They tramped from room to room, noting still-grand residences, wide staircases and expansive gardens. More often, though, the economic collapse was apparent in the two-room habitations with fallen roofs and broken doors that opened onto flooded alleys. The experts fumbled with the maths, criticizing the absurdity of calcu-lating the value in assignats (or ignorant of that requirement).[47] One diligent pair bought two guides on the recent *lésion* laws for their estimation of seventy-five *perches* of land in Saint-Lô, yet still could not bring their figures into accord.[48] The experts sustained the abuse of the parties who intervened in their supposedly neutral deliberations. Some acquiesced and produced calculations that supported the parties who had chosen them. The more assiduous reminded the participants of their oath of impartiality.[49] When arguments exploded between the two experts, a third intervened. Finally, reports in hand, the courts heard the parties and rendered a judgment. Appeals – as with other civil court appeals – took place in whichever neigh-bouring departmental court the petitioner chose.[50]

At a purely anecdotal level, the cases are rich. One finds the expected purchases made for speculation and that were resold, sometimes at a sharply higher price. For those cases, the suits cascaded from seller to frustrated seller.[51] The declarations reveal the grief of families unable to afford their homes and who had sold them in states of ruin. Their hopes must have reawakened when they realized that they might recover their property after new owners had undertaken the necessary repairs.[52] The accounts of families who had parted with homes to buy food, or of a widower who had retained the right to live in an attic and receive a daily meal of bread and broth, were sadder still. Not all cases were so poignant and the scribes must have exchanged frequent knowing glances. Post-contract gloating cost one foolish seller his case, for instance. He had crowed about the high price he had received for his home in Geneviève-des-Bois, telling all that he had 'taught a young man a good lesson'. (The judge dismissed his claims.)[53] In Fontenay, a

---

47 There was frequent confusion as to the need to calculate the value in assignats. Many experts used pre-1790 and hard currency valuations. ADY, 43L 140, Hue v. Bizet, 12 Frimaire VII (2 December 1798); ADY, 43L 140, Buisson v. Nuntion, 11 Vendémiaire VII (2 October 1798).

48 ADY, 43L 140, Dumont v. Couvains, 21 Nivôse VII (10 January 1799).

49 Expert Pierre Petit complained that those involved 'want to make us defenders of the parties and want to digress from the specific object of our mission'. ADY, 43L 139, Rallet v. Collin, 13 Thermidor VI (31 July 1798).

50 Among the eighteen *lésion* cases judged in the Court of Appeals of the department of the Seine-et-Oise, ten concerned Paris properties. ADY, 43L 86–8.

51 Archives départementales de la Gironde (hereafter ADG), 7L 489, no. 12, Putigny v. Bouchon, 18 Floréal VII (7 May 1799); ADY, 43L 88, no. 131, Roalhac v. Renard and Langlois de Villepaille, 18 Frimaire VIII (9 December 1799).

52 In cases where the sellers retook possession of the home, the law required them to compensate the new owner for the repairs. See ADY, 43L 141, Valtrin v. Heurtant, 2 Thermidor VII (20 July 1799).

53 ADY, 43L 140, Pigeon v. Mourgue, 7 Brumaire VII (28 October 1798).

tavern owner plied the opposing party's witnesses with drink, exasperating the experts who abandoned their mission.[54] A Meulan confrontation ended with a fistfight in court. Instead of noting '*conciliation*' or '*non conciliation*', the clerk scribbled 'lack of respect for the Bureau' as the session's outcome.[55]

Thankfully, thrown punches were a rarity in the *bureaux de paix*. Indeed, the sellers' best chance for additional payments may well have been through mediation, before the high standards for *lésion* came into play. The repetition of phrases by buyers in the *bureaux de paix* who gave in to pressure to settle – 'for form' or 'to avoid a costly and lengthy lawsuit' – suggests that the mediators had found winning formulas. Jean Jarride, for instance, admitted that on reflection, 'an indemnity was necessary, given the discredited value of the assignats' when he purchased arable land in Puy-de-la-Rase (Gironde) for two hundred livres in assignats. He offered sixty livres more in grain and specie.[56] Pierre Mesuret gave Jean, Pierre and François Lacrois 120 livres in specie beyond the three hundred-livre assignat selling price, recognizing 'an indemnity was due'.[57] François Mignot's property, too, 'was worth something more' than he had paid.[58] Indeed, some parties made their way next to a notary's office, declaring that they desired to work out a new contract to save time and money in court.[59]

Once the case reached the departmental court, the seller had to prove that the losses exceeded half the estimated price in assignats. Despite the high standard that had outraged the critics of the law of 19 Floréal, some plaintiffs seemed to have grounds to prevail. In the Seine-et-Oise, sixty cases reached the departmental court.[60] Unfortunately, for forty-four, no judgements appear extant, although many experts – at least those appointed by the sellers – reported that the sales prices had been quite low. Much would depend on how the court applied the concept of 'advantages' and sorted through the botched calculations and experts' disagreements. The sixteen cases whose outcomes can be ascertained ran slightly in the sellers' favour: nine sellers won; seven lost. Likewise in the Gironde, the judgments generally do not appear in the dossiers, although the experts' figures suggest outcomes.[61] At

54 ADY, 43L 139, Rallet v. Collin, 13 Thermidor VI (31 July 1798).
55 ADY, 64L 41, Bain v. Mercier, 11 Brumaire VII (1 November 1798).
56 ADG, 7L 489, no. 3, Widow Lalarme v. Jarride, 26 Vendémiaire VII (17 October 1798).
57 ADG, 7L 489, no. 10, Lacrois v. Mesuret, 6 Frimaire VII (26 November 1798).
58 ADG, 7L 489, no. 6, Nadaux v. Mignot, 26 Floréal VII (15 May 1799).
59 Records of two notaries' *études* in Versailles show a number of such arrangements. Étude Gayot, ADY, 3E 44 (at least eight settlements between 29 Floréal VI and 1 Frimaire VII); and Étude Savouré, ADY, 3E 36 (at least fourteen settlements between 5 Vendémiaire and 12 Fructidor VII).
60 ADY, 43L 46, 55–6, 84–9, 106, 139–41.
61 Given how rarely the experts' reports note the original prices, it seems possible that the departmental court did not disclose that information in order to keep them impartial. In other cases, however, the experts referred to the contract's stipulations throughout the estimation.

Complaints of *lésion d'outre-moitié* in selected *bureaux de paix*

Bureau de paix	Number of complaints	Defendant agrees:			Unknown outcome	No agreement, proceed to civil court
		to relinquish property	to pay more	to allow estimate		
Seine-et-Oise Department						
Meulan	17	1	0	0	1	15 (88%)
St Germain-en-Laye	35	2	3	2	0	28 (80%)
Versailles-intramuros nord	34	0	5	8	0	21 (62%)
Versailles-intramuros sud	13	0	0	1	2	10 (77%)
Gironde Department						
Civrac-en-Médoc	25	0	7	3	0	15 (60%)
Saint-Seurin	33	0	0	1	0	32 (97%)

least twenty-one suits appeared there, and only three judgements are extant.[62] Yet, in each of those cases, the seller prevailed and collected additional sums. In the eighteen other cases, disputes between experts stalled the proceedings. Nonetheless, in seven of those cases, the figures offer credible evidence of the essential 'losses of more than half.'[63] At the level of the appeals in the Seine-et-Oise, sellers fared well. At least seventeen appeals were presented: in seven of the eight cases for which a judgement was recorded, the court ruled that *lésion d'outre moitié* had occurred.[64] Thus, at the level of both the departmental civil courts and at the appeals court, where there are sentences recorded or outcomes discernable from the experts' estimates, they run in favour of the seller.

Did sellers prevail in their belief that the law of 19 Floréal would allow them to incorporate information on payment dates and assignats' rates? They pressed that point and the courts appear to have been receptive. Jean Léonard Desthier and his wife won, asserting that their losses were evident, 'especially if one considers that part of the price was paid only long after the sale' of their home in Saint Germain-en-Laye.[65] Three men from the Lacrois family

62 Later cartons in ADG, 5 L hold more cases. Ongoing research will examine those results.

63 ADG, 5L 184, Tribunal Civil de la Gironde, Sentences arbitrales, Vendémiaire-Frimaire VII; ADG, 5L 199, Rapports d'experts, Vendémiaire-Germinal VII.

64 ADY, 43L 84, 86–9. Many of the cases for which the outcome was unclear had technical problems with their estimations and went back to the departmental court for retrial.

65 ADY, 74L 39, Jean Léonard Desthier v. Géorger, 21 Prairial VI (9 June 1798).

triumphed, noting that their buyer had only paid 'years after the sale'.[66] The Seine-et-Oise court adjusted another assignat contract, explaining that with its insufficient price, 'it could not reflect the true intentions of the parties'.[67] It is possible that the courts proceeded on other occasions to remedy the 'additional advantages' produced by delays in payments.

In all, many of the cases might have been illusory, merely an attempt to harass a buyer into paying more; others might have been well founded. In the absence of sentences, it is hard to judge either the cases' merits or the courts' assessment of their grounds. Yet the sellers' embrace of the laws testified to their determination to wrest what they could from their buyers. As for the new owners, the suits added to their sense of uncertainty, even several years after their purchase. At the least, these suits stirred up resentments, raised anxieties and gave credence to beliefs of the Revolution's crimes. At the most, they could lead to repayments and possible evictions years after the contract had been signed. Property, then, in this late revolutionary regime of property, was far from secure.

Here, one stumbles upon a set of contradictions, however. Certainly, it is not astonishing that sellers wished to undo their perceived damages. Yet, the Councils' willingness to provide such legislation, albeit modest in its intentions, sanctioned grounds that even pre-revolutionary jurists had questioned. Moreover, the courts' apparent openness to a broad interpretation of the so-called 'advantages' article of the law of 19 Floréal further complicates our understanding of the late Revolution's respect for property. One could conclude simply that the Directory wished to compensate former owners – an assortment of bourgeois (both *grand* and *petit*) and notables of the Old Regime and the early Revolution – and even to strip the property from the speculators who had profited from the early months of inflation. Yet, the inconsistencies in such conclusions are troubling: which property owners would benefit from these cases, and which would recoil at the sight of a citation threatening an advantageous year III purchase?

On reflection, one must inquire further about the kinds of property and property-owners susceptible to these suits. The categories of goods excluded from these suits help identify boundaries. Very deliberately, post-Fructidor legislation forbade the use of *lésion* suits for land that had originated as *biens nationaux*. Such property had been seized as backing for state debts and as punishment for crimes against the nation. (Of course, for political reasons the Directory could never have called into question that ownership.)[68] The year VI laws also barred suits if property had been sold by auction. There, some failing – bankruptcy or bad debts – presumably had played a role in the prop-

---

66 ADG, 7L 489, no. 10, Lacrois v. Mesuret, 6 Frimaire VII (26 November 1798).
67 ADY, 43L 124, Veuve Ansous v. Chevalier, 8 Ventôse VII (26 February 1799).
68 The Law of 2 Prairial VII (21 May 1799).

erty's loss.[69] By preventing the former owners of such *biens nationaux* or auctioned property from suing, the legislators focused legal attentions on one particular form of property: patrimonial property that had been lost, supposedly, through no failing, save the unanticipated collapse of the assignat.

Plaintiffs drew on those distinctions. Many who lodged suits directed the court's attention to the property's specifically patrimonial status: most often former residences, others part of long lists of marital property, inheritances and *rentes* running back many decades. The patrimonial dimension of these cases becomes still more obvious in the actions of heirs who initiated suits. Defiant widows and widowers or younger generations with more energy turned to these laws to rebuild their families' fortunes. In the sixty Seine-et-Oise cases, eighteen explicitly involved the heirs' frustration with the earlier sale of family property or another conflict connected to a will.[70] In the *bureaux de paix* examined, also, between one-fourth and one-half of the plaintiffs mentioned that their case sought to recover family property.[71] A Versailles *artiste dramatique*, for example, contested the settlement of his maternal grandfather's estate in which his mother had obtained a share of one-fifth. He objected to the low prices she and the other heirs had received for five properties lining the streets near the château and sought to undo the entire series of sales.[72] In separate cases, two of the Lussac heirs sued Tantantion Delignac to obtain more money from the sales of their family's properties. That the enterprising Delignac had purchased one of the heirs' shares for two thousand livres in assignats, and another for four thousand livres in *écus*, as well other local properties, raised their suspicions.[73] François Amy's heirs felt themselves doubly wronged, losing money first on the sale of the home and later when the buyer paid off the *rente* in a hurry.[74] On other occasions, family councils intervened, attempting to regain patrimony that the deceased or other heirs had sold.[75] Buyers also framed their objections within those patrimonial definitions: the Citizen Bontems tried to negate the case against him by informing the court that his seller had used the proceeds to buy a home in Nangis. Thus there was no loss to the family's estate.[76] From the testimony of these suits, *lésion* litigation emerges indelibly identified with

---

69 Also, sale at auction meant that the property had received its highest possible price. Law of 19 Floréal VI.
70 ADY, 43L 46, 55–6, 84–9, 106, 139–41.
71 In the four Seine-et-Oise *bureaux de paix* examined: Meulan (28%); Saint Germain-en-Laye (26%); Versailles *nord* (41%); Versailles *sud* (46%). In the Gironde: Civrac-en-Médoc (28%); Saint-Seurin (31%).
72 ADY, 80L 9, Boutard v. Monget and Courtillier, 29 Floréal VII (18 May 1799).
73 ADG, 7L 489, no.7, Moreau v. Delignac, 16 Floréal VII (5 May 1799); no. 19, Lussac v. Delignac, 26 Floréal VII (15 May 1799).
74 ADY, 43 L 87, Amy heirs v. Langlier, 27 Prairial VII (14 June 1799).
75 ADY, 43L 87, no. 276, 13 Fructidor VII (30 August 1799).
76 ADY, 43L 141, Saint Arnoulx v. Bontems, 1 Messidor VII (19 June 1799).

the cause of families across France who were desperate to reverse the Revolution's course.

The focus on patrimonial property reveals an important feature of the Directory's commitment to maintaining property. One should not forget that in those same months, the representatives were involved in debates to limit divorce, and to repeal the radical laws ordering equal inheritances between siblings and limited shares for illegitimate children .[77] The deliberations turned on the nature of appropriate familial bonds, bonds constructed by property passing safely from one generation to the next. The sound structure of the state relied on the solid formation of the family. Civil law, then, even suits challenging contracts, became conscripted in the defence of a stable social order.

The sentimental seller of the Civil Code

There is an epilogue to the story of *lésion d'outre moitié*. The concept did not vanish when the last deadlines for initiating these post-inflation suits passed. Instead, contract termination for losses found its way into the Napoleonic Civil Code.[78] With the end of revolutionary currency fluctuations, however, the principal motivation for the Directory's *lésion* laws had vanished. One would not – as one year III pamphlet had grumbled – 'go to sleep with a hundred thousand livres in his purse', and 'awake to find only worthless rags'.[79] Presumably, buyers and sellers could compose agreements that reflected their intentions. Yet the authors of the Civil Code revisited the issue repeatedly over the course of nearly two months. If monetary instability posed no problems in late 1803, then what ordeals was the post-revolutionary economic imagination conjuring that these suits might soothe?

The debates disappoint any search for lofty expositions of legal theory. The committee staggered along, sporadically disputing the laws' Roman origins and pre-revolutionary practices. The expected references to a contract's supposed sanctity – a core tenet of nascent free trade ideology – were rare. The members evinced little acceptance of the idea that prices were driven by markets.[80] Portalis bluntly dismissed any doubts: 'All of 'society' recognized the existence of a 'reasonable price' for property.[81] Given the near

77 *La Révolution et l'ordre juridique privé: Rationalité ou scandale?* (Paris, 1988).
78 Articles 1674–85, *Code civil français, édition originale et seule officielle 1804*, reprint (Glashütten im Taunus and Paris, 1974), pp. 306–30. It remains a part of French contract law to this day, in particular in the accompanying law of 28 November 1949. See also J. J. Anvile N'Goran, 'La lésion dans la vente d'immeubles', Thèse de doctorat en droit, Université de Nancy II, 1991.
79 A. Prunelé, *Fortunes publiques et consolidées ...* (Paris, 16 Prairial III).
80 P. A. Fenet (ed.), *Recueil complet des travaux préparatoires du code civil ...*, 15 vols. (Paris, 1827), vol. 14, pp. 50–1, 55–6.
81 *Travaux préparatoires*, xiv, p. 49.

unanimity of the committee, and its perception of strong public support on this matter, it adopted *lésion* as the grounds for suits.[82] Raising the bar for such claims, the Code required losses of more than seven-twelfths. [83]

Yet, who would sell property for less than five-twelfths of its value and why should the law protect them? The authors could agree that the issue at stake was the lack of the seller's true consent; hence the state should intervene to safeguard the wronged party. But, curiously, the debates focused on jarringly extrajudicial images of wrenching sacrifices and innocence betrayed.[84] The Code's authors' imaginary sellers weep, quiver and moan; their devastated families are ruined by one member's ill-conceived transaction. To the modern reader, these victims' sobs would seem but thin justification for statutes that would challenge the freedom of contract and property rights. Yet, even the least-sophisticated reader seated by an early nineteenth-century fireplace would recognize those shudders, stifled cries and fainting spells. They were drawn from the countless gestures of the period's sentimental and melodramatic narratives.

Briefly, these narrative strategies worked on at least three levels.[85] First, such plots turn on emotions that manifest themselves through a complicated rhetoric of the body. Hands graze and trembling fingertips hint at lovers' mutual turmoil. Language itself fails and characters fall, weeping, to their knees. The body, through its shivers, stammering and even its unconsciousness, reveals the character's heart. Second, the others in the scene, touched, join in the natural language of sentiment. Des Grieux falls mute in his first moments alone with Manon Lescaut: 'A gentle heat spread throughout my veins', he explained. 'I was in a sort of transport, that deprived me for a while of the freedom of my voice, and which only expressed itself through my eyes.' Manon, following novelistic conventions, 'appeared very satisfied' by the 'charms' of his eyes and was equally 'moved'.[86] The opening pages of Rousseau's *Confessions* – his father's 'sighs, his convulsive embraces', and Jean-Jacques' empathetic tears – set the tone for the work.[87] Third, and most

82 *Ibid.*, 54–5.

83 *Ibid.*, 63.

84 See two important collections on law and narrative: *The Moral World of the Law* (Cambridge, 2001); P. Brooks and P. Gewirtz (eds), *Law's stories: Narrative and Rhetoric in the Law* (New Haven and London, 1996).

85 This discussion draws mainly on A. Coudreuse, *Le goût des larmes au XVIIIe siècle* (Paris, 1999); D. J. Denby, *Sentimental narrative and the social order in France, 1760–1820* (New York, 1994); P. Brooks, *Body Work: Objects of Desire in Modern Narrative* (Cambridge and London, 1993); P. Stewart, *Engraven Desire: Eros, Image and Text in the French Eighteenth Century* (Durham, NC, 1992); A. Vincent-Buffault, *The History of Tears: Sensibility and Sentimentality in France*, trans. T. Bridgeman (New York, 1991); D. Marshall, *The Surprising Effects of Sympathy: Marivaux, Diderot, Rousseau and Mary Shelley* (Chicago, 1988).

86 Abbé Prévost, *Histoire du Chevalier des Grieux et de Manon Lescaut*, ed. L. Bovey (Lausanne, 1961), p. 43.

87 J.-J. Rousseau, *The Confessions and Correspondence ...*, trans. C. Kelly, in C. Kelly, R. D. Masters and P. G. Stillman (eds), *The Collected Writings of Rousseau*, vol. 5 (Hanover, NH and London, 1995), p. 7.

critically, the narratives insist on the theatricality or the visual aspects of the characters' actions. Diderot's Suzanne, hearing that her future held only nun's habits, broke into sobs: 'It was another scene of despair', she writes to the marquis de Croismare. 'I would have hardly any others to paint you.'[88] 'Here is only the portrait of a man', begins Jean-Jacques Rousseau's *Confessions*.[89] While the semiotics of such *mises en scène* merit fuller discussion, one important aspect bears emphasis: these narratives transform readers into *voyeurs* of a private moment of emotional transparency. Reinforcing this sense, the narratives often frame the sentimental body, which is seen only through keyholes, bed-curtains, or under arched tree boughs, suggesting further the intimacy that the reader has penetrated. Thus, the language of *pathos* – the body's signs, the other characters' shared and wordless emotions, finally, the intrusion of the reader-viewer into a scene of clandestine rapture or sorrow – give these narratives some part of their power.

Melodrama, which emerged during the Revolution, emphasized sentimental narrative's theatrical and physical elements still further, presenting pantomimes at critical moments, freezing the action on stage.[90] Unlike sentimental narratives, melodrama painted a stark world of innocent victims and cruel villains in the everyday life of household and neighbourhood. The spectator, mesmerized by the *tableaux vivants*, was to respond to the exaggerated travails of the unfortunate characters. The betrayal of familial bonds, the remorse of the unfaithful friend, and the treachery of the oppressive and powerful: such melodramatic elements were communicated by wavering hands, muffled moans and dead swoons. Together, sentimental and melodramatic narratives entreated the reader-audience to interpret the codes of the body and to sympathize with the emotional outpourings of the private dramas.

Such sensibilities would seem far removed from the calculations of depreciation tables that had accompanied the Directorial suits. Indeed, one finds little rhetorical excess in the court records. The documents open with formulaic statements of the parties' identities and property, stating the plaintiffs' belief that *lésion* had occurred. Perhaps weary clerks paraphrased the pleadings, noting only the essentials of the lawsuit. Perhaps the parties and their assistants (notaries and occasionally lawyers) were less attuned to the virtuosity of the Old Regime's *causes célèbres*. Sometimes, the defendant's rebuttal had a few more flourishes, but even those were generally reduced to statements that no damage had occurred. Sentiment and melodrama, then, formed the language of the Code's debates, theatre and novels; they were not the idiom of Directorial litigation.

88 Diderot, *La religieuse*, ed. Gilbert Sigaux (Lausanne, 1960), p. 270.
89 Rousseau, *Confessions*, p. 3.
90 P. Brooks, *The Melodramatic Imagination: Balzac, Henry James, Melodrama and the Mode of Excess* [2nd ed.] (New Haven and London, 1995).

Thus, it is even more curious that the Code's authors largely made their case for the *lésion* articles through imagined parties' heartache and hardship. Tronchet produced several poignant scenarios. First, there was a 'young man of twenty-one, who will have sacrificed his inheritance to the fire of his passions, and of which a greedy buyer will strip him'. Then Tronchet turned to the man 'in misfortune, and whom necessity will force to sell'. How could anyone say a hasty sale had improved his situation? 'What? Because having no resources ... he sacrificed his property to save his honour and to shield himself from the pursuit of his creditors, his situation would be improved!' Next, the fairer sex: 'It will be a wife, not in charge of her estate, who will not know the value of the property that she had to sell.'[91] Portalis, too, depicted the agonies of 'a young man of twenty-one despoiled by a contract of sale ...' The law now defined him as an adult (*majeur*), but nature distributed maturity unevenly. One must leave property uncertain for a few years, rather than sanction the losses that might come with a reckless agreement. His arguments even equated being 'fooled' (*trompé*) with being 'oppressed', a charged word in the rhetoric of revolution and melodrama.[92] For Cambacérès, also, the twenty-one-year-old man provoked concern: 'What father would not tremble for his son, if a young man ... still the prey of passions, and ready to sacrifice all for the enjoyment (*jouissance*) of a moment, could by an indiscreet signature irrevocably despoil himself of his fortune.[93] Napoleon, too, demanded laws to intercede if 'the seduction of passions or hardship determine a property owner to cede his [goods] for nothing'. Owners were but trustees, handing property from one generation to the next. What society would allow 'an individual in a moment of madness [to] sacrifice the inheritance from his father and the patrimony of his children to the heat of his passion?' Fear of a *lésion* suit also might deter the 'rich man' who would otherwise to take advantage of 'the poor man, oppressed', who was forced 'to yield his fortune' out of 'need'.[94] Even Berlier, who had his doubts about these suits, constructed his objections as melodrama: These suits would 'threaten' the great number of buyers 'of good faith' in the effort 'to wrest' the sums 'that they would sacrifice for their tranquillity'.[95]

Lest one be swept away by these scenarios, one must return them to a less literary context. There were, after all, actual social referents for these dramas: the Revolution had lowered the age of majority from twenty-five to twenty-one; and since 1794, women's control over property had come under steady assault.[96] Only six years had passed since the end of paper currency. Yet,

91 *Travaux préparatoires*, vol. 14, pp. 68–9.
92 *Ibid.*, pp. 40, 43, 48–9.
93 *Ibid.*, p. 43.
94 *Ibid.*, pp. 57–8.
95 *Ibid.*, pp. 51, 59.
96 S. Desan, 'The War Between Brothers and Sisters: Inheritance Law and Gender Politics in Revolutionary France', *French Historical Studies* 20 (1997).

there is an odd silence in the Consular discussions. Neither the searing revolutionary inflation, nor the use of *lésion d'outre-moitié* in the late Directory received attention. Certainly, the vignettes focus on the same patrimonial property that the *lésion* laws of 1797–98 had protected. The property of the Code's debates is not that of commerce or even of individuals. It belongs to a 'father', 'wife' or 'son'; it constitutes an 'inheritance', a 'fortune' or protects a family's 'honour'. (Despite the complaints of the Code's conservative opponents that its articles allowing divorce and imposing equal inheritance had destabilized the family, the Code nonetheless placed property within a structure of patriarchy and generational transfers.) The images suggest the limits of rationality in the French economic imagination of the early nineteenth century. The surefooted, reasoning 'economic man' of the Enlightenment had no place in these tales. Young men, mature men, widows and wives: all were defenceless against the ravages of lost love, damaged honour, or one frightful miscalculation. The intimacy of the settings painted by Tronchet and the others make the functioning of such images clearer still. As in sentimental narratives, the viewer intrudes upon the private, even shameful, grief of families. The scenarios whisper of wayward sons, imprudent wives and fathers, and not of the recent counter-revolution, coups and war, or even of sellers hell-bent on recovering lost fortunes.

Jean Carbonnier has suggested that the Civil Code pointed toward a future, and that its authors wished 'not to rivet the Civil Code to a commonplace of time, threatened with ageing'. The Code announces 'a history to accomplish'.[97] Certainly, the Code's authors directed eyes toward the future. Yet it is worth pausing briefly to look for additional themes and even structures in their language, especially the other ways in which those discourses further depoliticized the Code. Not surprisingly, the use of sentimental and melodramatic narratives in the discussions of *lésion* laws was no rarity. Introducing the Code more generally, in but one instance, Portalis fashioned images of the Code's origins in a centuries-long legacy of law, of 'generations [that], by succeeding each other, blend, intertwine and merge' without conflict.[98] Marriage, in his discussion of one of the most debated sections of the Code, joined 'reasonable and sensitive beings', by 'mutual consideration' in a 'commitment that must be reciprocal'. The wife's 'fecundity' brings 'a new instinct', and with it 'a new order of pleasure and virtue'. 'Together', parents watch over the child's 'first crises of the heart', and 'quell or guide the first appearances of passions ... protecting [the heart] against all the forms of seduction that surround it'.[99] Redolent with images of the communion of

97 'Le Code civil,' in P. Nora (ed.), *Les Lieux de mémoire*, 3 vols (Paris, 1984–92), vol. 1, pp. 1333, 1349.
98 F. Ewald, *Naissance du Code Civil: La raison du législateur* (Paris, 1989), pp. 52ff. The original is still more fluid: 'Les générations, en se succédant, se mêlent, s'entrelacent et se confondent.'
99 *Naissance du Code Civil*, pp. 54–5.

natural emotions, of tender generational ties, of the hazards of passions, such language throughout the crafting of the Code performed acts of narrative legerdemain. It subtly severed law from its past, from the world of its creation.

It is ironic – but certainly not coincidental – that as Tronchet, Cambacérès and others created their ahistorical *tableaux vivants* of heart-rending decisions, they facilitated Bonaparte's 1803 purge of the opposition in Tribunate, the one body that debated bills.[100] The world of revolutionary politics was vanishing, and with great speed. In every assault on the legislature, on the press and in every effort to conscript civil society, one discerns the 'precocious solidity' of the coming Empire.[101] The intimate passions of the Code's sentimental scenarios did their part, helping to chill the fierce storms of the late Revolution. They imperceptibly, but powerfully, ushered in the frozen, apolitical world of Napoleonic France.

100 I. Woloch, *Napoleon and his Collaborators: The Making of a Dictatorship* (New York, 2001), pp. 86–9.
101 *Ibid.*, p. xii.

4

Science and memory: the stakes of the expedition to Egypt (1798–1801)[1]

Marie-Noëlle Bourguet

11 Messidor: I am worried about my trip to Egypt, not understanding very well what good a geometrician is on such an expedition.[2]

These concerns, which the young *polytechnicien* Édouard Devilliers confided to his journal when, upon leaving Malta, he learned the squadron's true objective, deserve to be taken seriously. How do we understand Bonaparte deciding to send off to the Orient some 160 savants and engineers along with the thirty-five thousand men from the army? What meaning do we give his undertaking? Was it an ostentatious gesture, simply a mask for a man's mad ambition? Or, on the contrary, was the expedition an essential tool of a political project that calls for a careful inquiry into the relationships between science, travel, and politics at the end of the eighteenth century?

The historiography of the expedition has scarcely broached the question formulated in this way. Specialists in colonial history and historians of Egypt view Bonaparte's undertaking as one aspect of European expansion, an example of the domination exerted by the West upon the world. Historians of the arts and sciences see the expedition, because of the yield of its fieldwork and its discoveries, as part of the prehistory of disciplines such as archaeology, Egyptology, and more generally, the history of travel and geographic exploration. But the question of the relationship between these two aspects – the political and the scholarly – remains obscure. Even before the knotty

1 I am most grateful to Judith Miller for her help with revisions to this translation. This piece has adapted material from my article, 'Des savants à la conquête de l'Égypte? Science, voyage, et politique au temps de l'expédition française' in P. Bret (ed.), *L'expédition d'Égypte, une entreprise des Lumières 1798–1801* (Paris, 1999), pp. 21–36. For a fuller development of certain themes and analyses discussed here, see my 'Missions savantes au siècle des Lumières: Du voyage à l'expédition', in Y. Laissus (ed.), *Il y a 200 ans, les savants en Égypte* (Paris, 1998), pp. 38–67; and 'De la Méditerranée,' in M.-N. Bourguet, B. Lepetit, D. Nordman and M. Sinarellis (eds), *L'Invention scientifique de la Méditerranée, Égypte, Algérie, Morée* (Paris, 1998), pp. 7–29.
2 É. de Villiers du Terrage, *Journal et souvenirs sur l'expédition d'Égypte (1798–1801)*, ed. baron Marc de Villiers du Terrage (Paris, 1899), p. 39.

controversies surrounding the bicentennial celebration of the expedition had demonstrated the difficulty historians have in freeing themselves from univocal categories – those of denunciation or celebration – when attempting a comprehensive approach to their topics, understanding the links between the political and the scholarly dimensions of the expedition appeared complicated. Since then, it has seemed even more necessary to identify and explicate those connections more fully.

And yet, it is precisely the expedition's dual dimension, both military and scientific, that gave Bonaparte's enterprise its singular historical status and thus provoked Devilliers' concern. The project's twofold pretension of making science operate under the aegis of war and of associating the growth of knowledge with territorial conquest distinguished it from earlier undertakings. In order to help us understand the origins and the objectives, we must first clarify what elements came from earlier times, that is, from the tradition of scientific travel in the eighteenth century. Then we turn to an analysis of the institutional conditions and practical considerations of scholarly activity in Egypt. Finally, we consider the operational methods deployed by the expedition, and the forms of knowledge that were thus constructed.

From voyage to expedition: the Baconian tradition[3]

In fact, it is not the scholars' presence aboard an expedition that would have provoked the surprise of the young *polytechnicien*. The practice arose from an already long tradition, one that went back to the beginnings of modern empirical science, for which Francis Bacon had formulated the programme in his *New Atlantis* (1627). His vision united travel, science and expansion, in order to describe the activity of knowing as one of exploration and discovery. Under the aegis of a prince and a learned assembly, travellers from his fictional island paradise set off regularly on secret missions around the world. 'We have twelve that sail into foreign countries, under the names of other nations ... who bring us the books, and abstracts, and patterns, and experiments of all other parts', explained one inhabitant. 'These, we call Merchants of Light.'[4] Thus, the philosopher identified the function that the early modern era attributed to travel: to be, par excellence, an instrument of learned investigation.

In fact, the desire to use travellers to advance knowledge was affirmed gradually in Europe over the course of the seventeenth and eighteenth centuries. This aspiration shows up in the growing number of instruction

---

3   E. C. Spary, 'L'Invention de l'"expédition scientifique': L'histoire naturelle, Bonaparte et l'Égypte', in Bourguet *et al.* (eds), *L'Invention scientifique de la Méditerranée*, pp. 119–38.

4   J. Spedding, R. L. Ellis and D. D. Heath (eds), *The works of Francis Bacon*, 15 vols (Boston, 1860–64; reprinted St. Clair, Michigan, c. 1969) vol. 5, p. 409.

manuals intended to guide the eyes and activities of those who went far off and visited unknown lands or seas. In France, one can find further evidence of this ambition in the appearance of certificates or titles such as 'botanist of the King' at the end of the seventeenth century or 'correspondent of the Academy of Sciences' in the eighteenth century. These certificates, given to travellers or inhabitants of the colonies, charged them with gathering observations and specimens and sending them back to Paris. Finally, the second third of the eighteenth century provides further evidence on the form of the first official expeditions organized for scientific purposes. The two academic missions sent in 1735 and 1736 by Louis XV to Peru and Lapland to establish the length of the earth's meridian marked the beginning of this new era, when scientific activity became an indispensable asset for the glory of princes and the prominence of states on the international stage.[5]

The race for discovery first played itself out at sea with the great voyages of circumnavigation in the second half of the eighteenth century. These efforts completed the reconnaissance of the oceans, brought more accuracy to the mapping of islands and landmasses, and finally resolved the enigma of the *Terra Australis*. Expeditions whose heroes were Bougainville, Cook, La Pérouse, and Malaspina, as well as the savants embarking with them, busily observed and measured the sky, described the lands and the people they encountered, all the while collecting, drawing, and classifying the flora and fauna. The crew – a veritable small scholarly community – that La Pérouse gathered in 1785 to sail the world on *L'Astrolabe* and *La Boussole* gives a sense of the range of talents needed for these undertakings: two astronomers, a botanist, a few naturalists, a gardener, a painter, two artists, a watchmaker, and an interpreter.

The heroic epics of these navigators paralleled the tales of less-publicized adventurers who plunged into interior regions alone or in small groups to explore hitherto uncharted territories – Central America, Siberia, and soon after, Africa – and to complete the inventory of the world, such as the so-called 'apostles' whom Linnaeus sent to collect plants from the four corners of the earth. Alexander von Humboldt is a quasi-emblematic figure of these scholarly travellers in the Enlightenment. Having completed his training as a mining engineer, Humboldt left Germany intending 'to travel the world as a vagabond physicist'. He first wanted to visit Egypt, but news of the departure of the French fleet diverted him to other horizons. Equipped with an extraordinary array of instruments – chronometers, sextants, telescopes, thermometers, barometers – he instead explored the New World for four years in the company of the botanist Aimé Bonpland. From the Amazon to Chimborazo, he dedicated himself to observing nature in its most diverse and extreme

5 M. L. Pratt, *Imperial Eyes: Travel Writing and Acculturation* (London and New York, 1992), especially pp. 15–37.

manifestations. His collections and measurements constructed the vision of science as capable of appropriating and understanding the world by means of an encyclopedic cartography of its phenomena.[6]

From those descriptions of eighteenth-century missions, it should be apparent that if Bonaparte and the Directory developed a new model in their plans for the 1798 Egyptian expedition, they did so less in the concept of a scientific mission, or in their chosen destination, than in the *form* they adopted. Until the mission to Egypt, land exploration had been undertaken by individual travellers, such as Volney's mission to Syria and Egypt from 1783 to 1785, or Mungo Park's to Africa in 1795. At most, these undertakings had small teams of men, including several scholars and their guides, such as the Danish expedition launched towards *Arabia Felix* in 1761. As for Bonaparte, however, he embraced a *dispositif* previously reserved for maritime exploration: scholarly efforts launched under the state's supervision and the patronage of scientific institutions. Conducted on the ground by a group of savants recruited for that purpose and working under the army's protection, often with its direct collaboration, the seagoing model thus was transformed to fit the Bonapartist adventure overland.

Geopolitics, orientalism and revolution: the genesis of an expedition

During the crossing to Egypt in 1798, savants and officers spent time reading Herodotus and the ancient geographers, as well as Savary, Niebuhr, Volney or any of the five hundred volumes dedicated to the East – travel narratives, learned works, and political memoirs – that constituted the library with which the commander-in-chief had taken care to equip the expedition. In fact, far from being the invention of Bonaparte, the Egyptian dream had long existed in French political and cultural life.[7] Already in Richelieu's day, the idea of a passage to the Red Sea had emerged. During Louis XIV's reign, Leibniz suggested to the monarch resuming the tradition of the Crusades and seizing Egypt. Finally, two series of factors came together in the last decades of the eighteenth century to give these plans a renewed relevance. To the east, the decline of the Ottoman state compromised the political balance and threatened France's presence in ports around the Mediterranean, notably in Egypt where its merchants were the object of constant humiliation by local beys. To

---

6 M.-N. Bourguet, 'La République des instruments. Voyage, mesure et science de la nature chez Alexandre de Humboldt', in M.-C. Hoock-Demarle, É. François, M. Werner (eds), *Marianne–Germania. Deutsch-französischer Kulturtransfer im europäischen Kontext* (Leipzig, 1998), pp. 405–36.

7 On the political origins and cultural context of the expedition, see: F. Charles-Roux, *Les Origines de l'expédition d'Égypte* (Paris, 1910); H. Laurens, *Les Origines intellectuelles de l'expédition d'Égypte: L'Orientalisme islamisant en France (1698–1798)* (Istanbul and Paris, 1987); H. Laurens (ed.), *L'Expédition d'Égypte (1798–1801)* (Paris, 1989), especially ch. 1.

the west, the closing of the North Atlantic after the independence of the American colonies, and, for revolutionary France, the loss of its sugar islands, together transformed the geopolitical situation. England and France thus were forced to turn their eyes and their rivalries toward other horizons: the Indian Ocean, the Pacific, and the South Seas.[8] The Mediterranean too warranted interest anew.

It is in this context that the plan for an Egyptian conquest took shape in the years 1770–80. The Baron de Tott first suggested the undertaking after his mission to the East. The idea was then defended by the merchant Magallon, who was set up in Egypt, and supported by other observers. Finally, the idea was taken up again at the highest level of the state by ministers such as Choiseul, and later Sartine and Talleyrand, and by ambassadors such as Saint-Priest and Choiseul Gouffier. Certainly, these plans did not generate unanimity, notably in the Ministry of Foreign Affairs. Although Vergennes, comforted by Volney's analysis in *Voyage en Syrie et en Égypte* (1787), also believed that the ruin of Ottoman power was inescapable, he countered the supporters of foreign intervention with an innovative strategy: corps comprised of officers, engineers and workers sent to help the Sublime Porte reform itself, eventually regaining control of its empire (starting with Egypt) and finally embarking on the path of progress.

The French monarchy, paralysed by its internal difficulties and the first revolutionary troubles, left these plans unfulfilled. Ten years had to pass before they reappeared during the Directory. This expansionist ambition is at first surprising, coming from a government born of the Revolution. Yet, the project powerfully reveals the way in which images of the East could acquire a new resonance and force from the universalist and emancipatory ideology of the French Revolution.

The idea of the East's supposed 'despotism', in particular, resonated in the eighteenth-century imagination. As Montesquieu had defined it in his 1748 *L'Esprit des lois*, despotism was a fundamental characteristic of countries with immense lands and extreme climates. They were subject to the will of a single, arbitrary ruler, who governed by fear and who had no institutional counterweight other than religion. The philosopher qualified these political regimes as essentially 'eastern'. Even if this model turned out to be largely discredited by the studies conducted on the ground in the1760s by James Porter in Turkey and by Abraham-Hyacinthe Anquetil-Duperron in India, the idea that the East suffered from decay and was incapable of undertaking its own reform remained part of European assumptions. Diplomats and travellers saw these expectations of Eastern decline confirmed by the political, military, economic and social crisis that cut across the Ottoman Empire at the

---

8   One can invoke, for example, the expedition of Captain Baudin towards the South Seas, planned in 1798 and launched in October 1800.

end of the century. The Egypt that Volney visited in 1783, and that Bonaparte's Frenchmen would see fifteen years later, fully supported such conceptions: the land was bled white, its commerce and craft industry in decline, part of its territory abandoned, and at least a third of the population eliminated by famines and plagues.[9] This crisis occurred, moreover, at the very time Europe was emerging from its own long-term demographic stagnation and becoming aware of its own development, of its superiority. Reinforced, then, by what was perceived thereafter as the East's 'backwardness', the civilizing mission of the 'Occident' – a term Condorcet introduced in its modern usage – gained legitimacy. After Egypt, after Greece and Rome, after the Arabs, the successive relays of civilization, it fell to Europe – most particularly to Enlightenment France – to open a new period in the history of humanity. That era, founded upon reason and liberty, would regenerate a subjugated and decadent East. And, at last, France would return the sciences and arts to Egypt, a fitting restoration to the land that once had been the cradle of those riches and that centuries of despotism had caused it to forget.

One can see how, from such premises, the ideals of 1789 could have appeared to give this vision of history a political reality and thus have justified the liberating mission of the Revolution's successive governments. From 1795, the French Republic conducted an expansionist war in the name of 'natural frontiers' and people's liberty. It launched revolutionary armies into Belgium and Holland, across the Rhine, towards Italy, the Ionian islands, and finally beyond the Mediterranean into Egypt. In that flight forward, the Ottoman Turks were designated as the counterpart of the feudal aristocracies of Europe and the peoples subject to their despotic tyranny as a sort of 'eastern Third-Estate'.[10] This encounter between the image of a decaying East and a universalist notion of history formed the cultural and ideological background of the expedition to Egypt. Emphasizing the role of cultural and political representations does not minimize the importance of the economic stakes and the colonial aims of an enterprise in which false expectations also played a part. Talleyrand evoked them explicitly before the Directory in February 1798: through its soil, which was supposed to be immensely fertile, and its geographic position, considered the 'natural centre of commerce for three of the world's four parts', Egypt would be an ideal substitute for the lost islands. Once conquered and regenerated, Egypt would furnish France with the most valuable products – wheat and rice, cotton, sugar, indigo – at the same time as it would allow France to threaten the English rival as far away as

9   On the economic and social situation in eighteenth-century Egypt, see: A. Raymond, *Artisans et commerçants au Caire au XVIIIᵉ siècle*, 2 vols (Damas, 1973–74); and 'Les Effets négatifs de la pénétration commerciale européenne sur l'économie du Caire après 1750', in R. Ilbert and P. Joutard (eds), *Le Miroir égyptien* (Marseille, 1984), pp. 101–8.

10   Laurens, 'L'Expédition', in Laurens (ed.), *L'Expédition d'Égypte*, pp. 21–2.

India.[11] Nor should we ignore the role of ambition and political calculation that, after his victory of Campo Formio, pushed the young commander-in-chief to offer his services to the Directory. Bonaparte, a reader of Maurigny, the Baron de Tott, and Volney, advocated a distant expedition into an Egypt made familiar by books, to that country in decay, where everything needed to be built anew. His imagination led him to envision Egypt as a laboratory ready for activity and a grandiose theatre where, far from the national stage, his glory would be enacted. The intention here is different: to suggest how representations of the East and the West, confronting each other, formed a grid on which such projects could be laid out, combining dream and utility, ambition and utopia. It is by rendering the expedition of Egypt thinkable, even legitimate, in the eyes of contemporary actors that these representations forged the conditions of its very possibility.

Savants in the land of Egypt

Barely arrived in Egypt, Bonaparte announced the creation of an 'Institute for the Sciences and the Arts'. A replica of the one in Paris, it consisted of four sections, mathematics, physics, political economy, and literature and the arts, and brought together the most prestigious savants of the expedition – Monge, Berthollet, Fourier, and Bonaparte himself, all already members of the *Institut national*, as well as Geoffroy Saint-Hilaire, professor at the Museum of Natural History. Set up in a Cairo palace equipped with a garden and a library, a laboratory, an astronomical observatory and a printing press, its operations had to serve a three-fold purpose. First, it would aid 'the progress and propagation of the Enlightenment in Egypt', thanks to publications such as the *Décade égyptienne*. Second, it would develop 'the research, study, and publication of the natural, industrial and historical statistics of Egypt' for the use of European savants. Finally, to accompany the conquest, it would offer 'its advice on different questions on which it would be consulted by the government' – from making beer or gunpowder to research on agriculture, hydrography or Egyptian legislation.

As ostentatious and forceful as it may have been, this creation was nonetheless remarkable. In wanting to transplant to Egypt the institutions and forms of sociability that had encouraged the development of scientific life in Europe and to 'naturalize' them, according to the term of the time, Bonaparte affirmed the universality of science and the possibility of

---

11 C. L. Lokke and G. Debien, 'L'Expédition d'Égypte et les projets de cultures coloniales', *Bulletin de la Société royale de géographie d'Égypte* 20 (1939), pp. 337–56; P. Bret, 'Le Réseau des jardins coloniaux: Hypolite Nectoux (1759–1836) et la botanique tropicale, de la mer des Caraïbes aux bords du Nil', in Y. Laissus (ed.), *Les Naturalistes français en Amérique du Sud, XVIe–XIXe siècles, 118e Congrès national des sociétés savantes, Pau 1994* (Paris, 1995), pp. 185–216 (especially pp. 196–208).

de-centring its practice. In its daily operations, the new Institute of Egypt had to take its place in the network of a universal republic of letters. 'I assure you that these meetings are at least as interesting as those at the Institute of France', the young naturalist Étienne Geoffroy Saint-Hilaire wrote, enthusiastic, to Georges Cuvier, his colleague at the Museum.[12] There, one heard, in fact, Monge explaining the 'mirages' soldiers experienced during desert marches by the laws of optics, Berthollet setting out his theory on 'the laws of chemical affinity' based on observations made at the Natron lakes, and the young physicist Malus, his research on the polarization of light.[13]

The forced isolation into which the savants were thrown after the defeat of Abukir Bay (August 1798), cutting their ties with the learned community of Europe; the harassing urgency of accomplishing tasks according to the ups and downs of the conquest; an overly strict subordination *vis-à-vis* Bonaparte's imperious authority; finally, increasing insecurity could not fail to introduce discouragement, homesickness and exasperation. As one example, we know of the altercation between the army's head doctor, Desgenettes, and General Bonaparte once they were back from Syria in July 1799, concerning the plague that had ravaged the army. Or the attitude of the mineralogist Dolomieu: frustrated at having to conduct his observations in such precarious conditions, disappointed at not being able to satisfy his expectations of volcanoes and mountains in Egypt, little concerned about pleasing his superiors – his memoir on agriculture in the Nile Delta denounces the conquerors for sustaining illusions about the richness of Egyptian soil – the scholar preferred to give up. He received permission to leave Egypt in March 1799.[14]

Without going into more detail as to the conditions of scholarly work in Egypt, one point deserves special emphasis here. The observations and comments made by savants and engineers during their Egyptian sojourn raise the question of the universality of science: To what extent does science depend on the place where it is practised? We can see the framework of an unequal, asymmetric discourse emerge from the contrast that the French established between the science they practiced in Egypt and the science they knew in the metropole. The former – and, in general, science practised outside Europe in colonized lands or countries recently opened to Western

12 Letter from 29 Vendémiaire VII (20 October 1798), É. Geoffroy Saint-Hilaire, *Lettres écrites d'Égypte*, ed. É.-T. Hamy (Paris, 1901), p. 97.

13 J.-É. Goby, *Premier Institut d'Égypte: Restitution des comptes rendus des séances. Mémoires de l'Académie des inscriptions et belles-lettres, nouv. sér.* VII (Paris, 1987), pp. 6–7, 42, 53. On the activities of the Institute, see also: C. C. Gillispie, 'Aspects scientifiques de l'expédition d'Égypte', in Laurens (ed.), *L'Expédition d'Égypte*, pp. 370–96; N. and J. Dhombres, *Naissance d'un nouveau pouvoir: Sciences et savants en France, 1793–1824* (Paris, 1989), ch. 2.

14 Goby, *Premier Institut d'Égypte*, passim, especially pp. 38, 46–7; A. Cooper, 'From the Alps to Egypt (and back again): Dolomieu, Scientific Voyaging, and the Construction of the Field in Eighteenth-Century Natural History', in C. Smith and J. Agar (eds), *Making Space for Science: Territorial Themes in the Shaping of Knowledge* (London, 1998), pp. 39–63.

influence – was shaped by the obstacles which, from the exterior, hindered its progress. In other words, for the French savants, the construction of knowledge in Egypt was a result of the social, cultural and material conditions of its production and shared the limitations of that colonial context. Science in the metropole, however, liberated from the bounds of its context, envisioned itself as contained fully within a linear history of the progress of knowledge. That narrative described science as developing freely, moving from discovery to discovery according to an internal dynamic. Thus, the representational system that framed the remarks made by Bonaparte's savants about their Egyptian experience prepared the grounds for the debate over the meaning of 'colonial science', laden with an epistemological, cultural and political significance, that grew throughout the nineteenth and twentieth centuries.[15]

As for their relationship to Egyptian society, it played itself out in an asymmetrical, uneven mode. Whereas the French savants continued to look to Paris, hoping to establish their reputations – and their future careers – through the work they were doing in Egypt, the Egyptians remained excluded from these activities and bodies of knowledge. Certain learned Egyptians showed themselves to be curious about the techniques and instruments brought by the French, such as Abd al-Rahmân al-Jabarti, who chronicled his astonishment at the power of the astronomical telescopes of Nouet's observatory, at Conté's forge and metal furnace, and at the engineers' windmills and bridges. But the general population expressed indifference, if not hostility, to the French activities. During the revolt of October 1798, the people of Cairo pillaged General Caffarelli's residence where the instruments were kept. As for the *ulemas*, guardians of a traditional science based on religion, they were at once impressed by the books brought from France and shocked by the agnosticism displayed by the French. The exhibitions – the release of hot-air balloons or chemical experiments – by which the French expected to demonstrate the greater efficacy of their science provoked only misunderstanding and contempt on the part of the Egyptians. 'They performed for us even more experiments just as extraordinary as the first, which intellects such as ours

15 On the notion of colonial science, see the classic article of G. Basalla, 'The Spread of Western Science', *Science* 156 (1967), pp. 611–22, and the wealth of literature dedicated during the past twenty years to the question of scientific and technological exchange and the modernization of science. In particular, see: N. Reingold and M. Rothenberg (eds), *Scientific Colonialism: A Cross-Cultural Comparison* (Washington, D.C., 1987); X. Polanco, 'Une science-monde: La mondialisation de la science européenne et la création de traditions scientifiques locales', in X. Polanco, *Naissance et développement de la science-monde* (Paris, 1990), pp. 10–52; P. Petitjean, C. Jami, and A.-M. Moulin (eds), *Sciences and Empires: Historical Studies about Scientific Development and European Expansion. Boston Studies in the Philosophy of Science*, 136 (Boston and London, 1992); A. Lafuente, A. Elena and M. L. Ortega (eds), *Mundialización de la ciencia y cultura nacional, Actas del Congreso Internacional 'Ciencia, descubimiento y mundo colonial'* (Aranjuez, 1993); A. Lafuente and L. Lopez-Ocon, 'Le Transfert des pratiques scientifiques et techniques dans le contexte de la science-monde', in I. Gouzevitch and P. Bret (eds), *Naissance d'une communauté internationale d'ingénieurs (première moitié du XIXe siècle)* (Paris, 1997), pp. 7–19.

could not manage to grasp', recounted Jabarti in a tone of derisive humility.[16] Whatever the case, the *Décade égyptienne*, a newspaper intended to diffuse knowledge of the West in Egypt, appeared in French, not Arabic. Condescension from the ones, proud of their rationalism and experimental science; a defensive withdrawal by the others, faced by forms of knowledge to which no entryway had been opened. For the brief time of the French expedition, an encounter between western science and a different culture, between tradition and a system of knowledge, played itself out in this unequal confrontation.

Surveying Egypt

For all that, for the French scientists, the essential part of their activities was conducted outside the city of Cairo, on journeys, reconnaissance missions and explorations. 'The commander-in-chief seemed to want the members of the Institute and the different members of the Commission to spread out to different parts of Egypt to examine the interesting things they could find there', wrote one engineer.[17] In fact, the meetings of the Institute, with almost two-thirds of the topics dedicated to cartography, ancient or modern geography, Egypt's monuments and peoples, the Nile's flooding, mineralogy, flora and fauna, attest to the savants' exploratory activity during their thirty-eight-month Egyptian sojourn. Their dependence on the army's movements for their travels and investigation, however, raises directly the question of the relationship between science and war, particularly when it comes to the methods for learning about space.[18]

One geographic difference is immediately evident. In the region of Cairo and the Delta, where most French troops were concentrated, scholarly exploration was carried out very informally and a simple escort sufficed. From the beginning to the end of the campaign, members of the Commission for Arts and Sciences made 'frequent trips' across Lower Egypt. The engineer Jomard spent two months visiting Cairo to create a map of the city and observe its population, investigating house by house. The mineralogist Dolomieu methodically criss-crossed Alexandria and the surrounding area: 'I visited, I could almost say foot by foot, the entire land covered by the ancient city and its different districts, as well as all the new alluvial deposits that added to the continent all of the terrain occupied by the modern city.' Geoffroy-Saint-Hilaire increased his zoological excursions: 'I had the good fortune to be

16 Cited by A. Louca, 'De la *Description* au dialogue', in Laissus (ed.), *Il y a 200 ans*, p. 108.
17 Prosper Jollois, *Journal d'un ingénieur attaché à l'expédition d'Égypte (1798–1802)*, ed. P. Lefèvre-Pontalis (Paris, 1904), p. 84.
18 B. Lepetit, 'Missions scientifiques et expéditions militaires: des modalités de leur articulation en Égypte', in Bourguet *et al.* (eds), *L'Invention scientifique de la Méditerranée*, pp. 97–110.

encouraged and protected by General Menou, who commanded the province of Rosetta. He gave me an escort to penetrate into the delta and to go hunting there in security.'[19]

The voyages into Upper Egypt took place under entirely different conditions, however. We know how Vivant Denon, seizing the opportunity presented by General Desaix's pursuit of Mourad Bey, was the first to explore the upper Nile: 'I am going to open, so to speak, a new country, ... to tread upon a land ... closed to all Europeans for two thousand years'. But while the war opened up previously inaccessible areas, it also imposed constraints, forcing the scholar-travellers to submit to incessant troop movements and to be satisfied with 'surveys made in haste' and sketches drawn without even dismounting. On his return, and despite a portfolio full of drawings, Denon still lamented: 'Of this I remain most convinced: when one has observations to make or objects to draw, one must not travel with soldiers, who, always active and anxious, want constantly to get going or to get there.' [20] Even the commissions of savants and engineers sent later, directed by Fourier, Girard and Costaz and sent into Upper Egypt, notably in the spring and summer of 1799, would need the army's intervention to sustain them: 'We can travel only when escorted by a battalion .... At the time, we were very exposed with [only] our six garrison men fifteen leagues from any French-occupied town .... During the day, everyone rushed around his area with one or two soldiers.' In this case, scholarly exploration hardly differed from military reconnaissance missions. Making rapid incursions through an unknown and threatening territory gave travellers a sense of urgency and a heightened consciousness of working for posterity. 'We felt a certain pleasure to think that we were going to transport the products of the Egyptians' ancient science and industry to our own country: it was a veritable conquest we were going to attempt in the name of the arts.'[21]

The Egyptian territory, between topography and history

If the ties between the military operations' *dispositif* and the scholarly missions' fieldwork were so tight, it is because they had the same object: the territory, its material as well as its intellectual appropriation. This spatial

19 A. Lacroix and G. Daressy, *Dolomieu en Égypte (30 juin 1798–10 mars 1800)* (Cairo, 1922), p. 55; É. Geoffroy Saint-Hilaire, *Lettres*, p. 66 (letter to Antoine-Laurent de Jussieu, 25 Thermidor VI [12 August 1798]). On the links between military reconnaissance and geographical exploration, see M.-N. Bourguet, 'The Explorer', in M. Vovelle (ed.), *Enlightenment Portraits* (English ed., Chicago, 1997), pp. 257–315.

20 D. Vivant Denon, *Voyage dans la Basse et la Haute Égypte pendant les campagnes du général Bonaparte*, 2 vols (Paris, 1802; reprint, Cairo, 1989), vol. 1, pp. 87, 218.

21 É. de Villiers, *Journal*, pp. 115, 181–2.

dimension is essential in accounting for the intentions that guided the expedition. In fact, it is remarkable that in order to study Egypt, to understand the reasons for its recent state and to find ways to regenerate it, Bonaparte had not deemed it necessary to surround himself with specialists of the language, history and law of the Orient (Dupuis and Langlès were asked, but refused). Instead, besides a few interpreters, only two members of the Commission, Venture de Paradis and Marcel, could really be described as Orientalists. The majority of his team was composed of naturalists, mineralogists, topographers, mining engineers, and civil engineers (including about forty young *polytechniciens*). These were the men he asked to study Egypt through investigative and exploratory missions. Everything unfolded as if Bonaparte from the start had established the principle that the observational capacities and technical know-how of these savants, naturalists and engineers would be ultimately more useful for knowing the country and transforming it than an erudite knowledge of its laws, traditions, or even history.

By the privilege accorded to the study of soil, geography, and territory, the Egyptian expedition was an offspring of the Enlightenment. The cognitive model it deployed had dominated the century, making the study of places and the survey of terrain – topography, climate, soil, flora and fauna – the empirical base of all knowledge and the obligatory path to a full understanding of natural and human phenomena. For all the enlightened minds of the time, from Montesquieu to Humboldt by way of Volney, voyage and local observation were a privileged route to discovering the relationship between these phenomena, and toward a comprehensive analysis of the complex unity of the world. The epistemological importance these approaches accorded to geography, the common object of all knowledge, explains why travelling and surveying seemed at the time to be an obligatory and superior form of scientific practice. Seen from this angle, the Egyptian expedition was the counterpart, in a colonial context, of the 'medical topography' survey conducted in France at the end of the Old Regime under the patronage of the Royal Medical Society, or of the 'departmental statistics' launched early in the Consulate. All of these established the study of topography and the descriptive survey of territory as indispensable prerequisites for political action. '[The monuments of Egypt] were little known, no more than the soil upon which they rested ... It was reserved for France to describe them', recalled the geographical engineer Jacotin, responsible along with Le Père for the vast territorial inquiry launched by Kléber in November 1799 'to gather all the information necessary for making known the modern condition of Egypt'.[22] The knowledge of

22 P. Jacotin, 'Mémoire sur la construction de la carte d'Égypte', *Description de l'Égypte, ou Recueil des observations et des recherches qui ont été faites en Égypte pendant l'expédition de l'armée française, publié par les ordres de Sa Majesté l'empereur Napoléon le Grand*, 9 vols in fol. and 11 vols pl. (Paris, 1809–28),

society came through the knowledge of the space it occupied; its reform through territorial improvements and the spatial regulation of its development.

Even the 'passion for ruins' that seized many of the expedition's savants, particularly on the missions sent to Upper Egypt, deserves to be reconsidered from this perspective. As a matter of fact, Pharaonic antiquity was not established as a priority for scholarly investigation at the time of departure from France: if all the members of the Commission of Arts and Sciences had a solid classical education, none of them had been chosen for his taste or special competence in matters of Egyptian antiquity such as one found in the works of Bernard de Montfaucon and the Count de Caylus. On site, no section of the Institute was specifically devoted to antiquity and the antiquarian project never appeared to be an end in itself for the teams dispatched throughout the country. Even for those who undertook to travel up the Nile to explore Upper Egypt, antiquity was but one object of study among all those making up the material of a territorial inquiry. 'We were forming', explained the engineer Jollois, 'a commission charged ... with gathering all the information on Upper Egypt that one could want, as much about commerce, agriculture, and the arts as about natural history and antiquities'. Rather than the result of any pre-established plan, the passionately archaeological orientation acquired by certain missions was largely the product of circumstances and, above all, of the enthusiastic and energetic personalities of some of their members, often engineers such as Jomard and Chabrol de Volvic, or their young colleagues Jollois and Devilliers. Thus Devilliers told how, having barely finished their professional tasks – surveying, topographic and geodesic readings in the Nile valley – Jollois and he would devote themselves to visiting historical sites methodically. They even took off in pursuit of new discoveries, much to the irritation of the chief engineer Girard, one of these 'bored', uninterested types that the civilians – like the military – counted in their ranks. On one of their escapades the two young men found the site of the tomb of Amenophis III, already forgotten in Strabon's time. 'One day, during our research in the Valley of the Kings, while coming over the crest of the western slope', Devilliers recounted, 'Jollois and I were led into a secondary valley where we found a tomb which had not been indicated by any of the voyagers who preceded us.'

État moderne, 2:2 (1822), pp. 1–2. On this topographical and etiological approach in the voyages and investigations at the end of the eighteenth century and the beginning of the nineteenth century, see: M.-N. Bourguet, *Déchiffrer la France: La statistique départementale à l'époque napoléonienne* (Paris, 1988) and 'Voyage, enquête, statistique: les polytechniciens et la construction de l'espace au début du XIXe siècle', in B. Belhoste, A. Dahan Dalmonico, D. Pestre, A. Picon (eds), *La France des X: Deux siècles d'histoire* (Paris, 1994), pp. 215–30. On the cartographic work of engineers and topographers, see A. Godlewska, 'The Napoleonic Survey of Egypt: A Masterpiece of Cartographic Compilation and Early Nineteenth-Century Fieldwork', *Cartographica* 25:1–2 (1988).

It is not irrelevant for the science to which their enthusiastic discovery was to lead, that it was largely the work of engineers. Where a traditional traveller, a simple amateur of antiquities such as Vivant Denon, may have been satisfied collecting 'sketches and views', the novice archaeologists were concerned with 'measuring and drawing' all the monuments they explored. Equipped when possible with rulers, compasses, and theodolites – even though in their desert outings they contented themselves with calculating distances by the strides of their camel (a 'veritable animal pendulum') – they undertook detailed descriptions according to the principles of architecture and descriptive geometry learned at the *École polytechnique*, endeavouring to link their measurements together in order to get a comprehensive vision of a site's lay-out. 'It is by considering [these amazing constructions] in their details, by making frequent comparisons, that one can acquire some general rules on the arrangement of edifices, and that one can encounter some of the ideas of the people who constructed them.' Above all, in studying the location of ancient monuments in relation to the topographic and hydrographic environment, notably in relation to the course of the Nile, they sought indices that would allow them to put an end to the debates and speculation on its ancient level – lower or higher: 'What further demonstrates incontestably that the soil has risen is the Greek inscription found on the pedestal of the northern colossus: it is buried at about 0.65 metres.' This was a concern of the engineers and topographers, of course, who dreamt of future territorial improvements and who worried about being able to restore canals or dig a passage through the Red Sea. But beyond a technical and utilitarian preoccupation, their measures and calculations also sought to link clearly the long history of pharaonic civilization to the history of the earth. At the same time as they made studying Egypt's past the prerequisite for any plan to administer the territory, they invented Egyptology as a historical discipline, at the intersection of geology, architecture, and geometry.[23]

From the expedition to the Description: *the stakes of memory*

When the evacuation of Egypt began, following the surrender signed by Menou on 30 August 1801, the savants refused to hand over to the English as the spoils of war the scientific papers and collections amassed during the expedition. Étienne Geoffroy Saint-Hilaire successfully demanded that these materials, with the exception of art objects and antiquities, remain the savants' possessions. The scene is emblematic of the contrasting destinies that

23 P. Jollois, *Journal d'un ingénieur*, p. 9; É de Villiers, *Journal*, pp. 194–6, 199–201; M. A. Lancret, 'Description générale de l'île de Philae', in *Description de l'Égypte. Antiquités, Descriptions* (1808), vol. 1, p. 28. Cf. A. Forgeau, 'Le Repérage des sites de l'Égypte pharaonique par les membres de la Commission des sciences et des arts,' in Bourguet *et al.* (eds), *L'Invention scientifique de la Méditerranée*, pp. 33–52.

divide the expedition's military failure and the extraordinary posterity of its scientific and artistic work. The naturalist himself had a premonition that he confided to Cuvier at the end of 1799: 'It will come to pass that the work of the Commission of Arts will be excused in the eyes of posterity for the frivolity with which our nation cast itself, so to speak, into the East.'[24] Nevertheless, the contrast is intriguing. It invites an interrogation of the trace left by this scientific-military adventure, and poses questions about the role it could have played in the construction of identities and imaginations on both sides of the Mediterranean.

The idea of a publication that would gather the result of their explorations and investigations into a vast collective work weighed on the savants throughout their sojourn in Egypt, especially after the discovery of the upper valley of the Nile. Kléber gave the project official backing when the Commission for Information on Modern Egypt (*Commission des renseignements sur l'Égypte moderne*) was formed in November 1799. It was only after defeat and return to France, however, that the lengthy task of elaboration, compilation and illustration began under government auspices. This resulted in the *Description de l'Égypte*, a monumental collective publication whose first edition (in-folio) appeared in instalments from the Empire to the Restoration (1809–22), followed by a more manageable series (in-octavo), published by the editor Panckoucke between 1821 and 1829.[25] The project's continuity itself already indicates that the work was, from the start, at the time of the expedition, conceived for the exclusive benefit of a European public. 'We strongly sensed the importance of the unique opportunity we had been given: we considered ourselves accountable to Europe *savante* for what we would make of it', explained the engineer Costaz, referring to the exploration of Upper Egypt.[26] Yet, military defeat and the subsequent abandonment of the conquest made that scholarly publication all the more essential, while also modifying its status and significance. Leaving aside a detailed textual analysis of the *Description* itself, we can discern from its publishing history alone a few signs of these transformations and of the issues at stake.

Let us begin with the title. For the account that he hastened to publish once back in France, Vivant Denon chose the title *Voyage dans la Basse et la Haute Égypte*, thus indicating the itinerary that constituted his adventure, a suggestion that the annexed map reinforced, pointing out the movements of Desaix's division with a dotted line, a delicate track across the Egyptian desert. The title *Description de l'Égypte* indicated an entirely different choice: copied on the expedition's geopolitical framework, sliding from travelogue to

24 1 Nivôse VIII (22 December 1799), É. Geoffroy Saint-Hilaire, *Lettres*, p. 147.
25 M. W. Albin, 'Napoléon's *Description de l'Égypte*: Problems of Corporate Authorship', *Publishing History* 8 (1980), pp. 65–85.
26 L. Costaz, 'Description des tombeaux des rois', *Description de l'Égypte: Antiquités, Descriptions*, vol. 1, pp. 393–414.

description, from line to surface, it induces a level of generalization (it deals with the entire region) and constructs a spatial unity that, as we have seen, the savants' methods hardly composed, for their outings and reconnaissance missions had covered the country only very unevenly.

The order chosen for the series would accentuate this discrepancy further. Following a logic in keeping with the work's geographic and encyclopedic ambitions, four topics were initially envisioned: topography, antiquities, the modern state and natural history. But, under the Empire, the imperatives of military security drove Napoleon in October 1808 to declare the map of Egypt that had been meticulously compiled by the topographical and geographical engineers a state secret. The Emperor thereby prohibited its publication (it would not appear until 1818). The first section suppressed, the geographical memoirs were redistributed to other sections, notably into that on the modern state. Thus, the original objective was obscured – to compose a portrait of Egypt in the form of an inventory based on a topographical map – whereas antiquity found itself, in fact, placed in the foreground.

Quantitatively, also, it took the first place. In effect, ancient Egypt alone occupied four of the nine volumes of text and five of the ten volumes of plates in the folio edition. As we have seen, this weight must not create a retrospective illusion about the place accorded to pharaonic times in the initial project. The same savants and engineers who had been enthused by seeing Thebes and Dendera, who made good use of their abilities in drawing and geometry, were the principal authors of the plates and memoirs, thereby increasing antiquity's portion in the published work and especially its visual representation. Jomard and Chabrol de Volvic alone signed more than a hundred drawings dedicated to ancient monuments. But this predominance also needs to be understood in terms of the political and cultural context in which the *Description de l'Égypte* took shape in the early years of the nineteenth century. In this respect, the circumstances recall those that presided over Bougainville's publication of his *Voyage autour du monde* (1771). In that case, the thin geographical and commercial results of his circumnavigation led the sailor to revise the text of his travel log to give the episode of his Tahitian sojourn a central place. Those changes offered him a means both to alter the voyage's significance and to take part in contemporary debates over the nature of man and the origins of society. Similarly, in the case of the Egyptian expedition, the failure of the military and colonial operation transformed the savants' labour into a printed work, turned toward an exaltation of the past: a mirror for an incomplete conquest, the *Description de l'Égypte* also spoke of the desire to overtake and reorient, if not to rehabilitate, Egypt. From that, the illustration that served as a frontispiece takes on its full meaning: whereas imposing ancient monuments spread across the surface of the image, the recent history of Egypt and its current situation were only depicted in the battle scenes between the Mamelukes and the French, running in a frieze around the central painting. The conquest of Egypt and the submission of its inhabitants were evoked here only as the opportunity, or the pretext, for the discovery of pharaonic antiquity.

At the time, this 'pharaonic Egypt' – image of a civilization where science and religion merged in the study of nature; the model of an elitist and hierarchical society, subject to the undivided power of a monarch – was of use in the West alone. In France, it offered first a flattering mirror to the Napoleonic regime's authoritarian ideology, while feeding the public's fascination with mystery. A generation later, it would serve as a grandiose background for the scientific and technical utopia that the Saint-Simonians imagined establishing in Egypt. But the Egyptians themselves were unaware of that image and resolutely remained outsiders to the *Description*. One example is significant: sojourning in Paris at the moment when the last volumes of the *Description* came out, and a close friend of the geographical engineer Jomard, who was its editor, the Egyptian Rifâ'a al-Tahtâwi, member of the scholarly mission sent by Mohammed Ali in 1826, made no mention of this work in the account of his trip. Moreover, Tahtâwi did not feel the need to bring a copy with him when he returned to Egypt. Written in French, the *Description* remained inaccessible, and its contribution, with the exception of the maps in the atlas, barely useful to Egypt.[27]

At the time, Egypt retained another memory of the expedition, that of its sombre side, of its disastrous effects – plague, famine, destruction – linked with three years of occupation and the ravages of the final battles against the Anglo-Ottoman forces. The French presence was too brief, punctuated by violence and extortion, for the projects of reform and development, that were, after all, imposed, to have borne fruit, even under the government of Menou, the only one seriously to consider Egypt a land of French colonization. Circumstances other than military occupation would have been necessary for the influence to have been felt. The period of conquest having past, the relationships of domination and subordination would need to have given way to ties, built little by little on a mutual esteem, on exchange, on reciprocity.[28] It was this emerging dialogue that generated, from the late 1820s, the

27 C. Traunecker, 'L'Égypte antique dans la *Description*', in Laurens (ed.), *L'Expédition d'Égypte*, pp. 351–70; A. Godlewska, 'Map, Text and Image: The Mentality of the Enlightened Conquerors: A New Look at the *Description de l'Égypte*', *Transactions of the Institute of British Geographers* (1995), pp. 5–24. On the role of the *Description* in the construction of an Orientalist discourse that perpetuated the domination of the West over the East through art and erudition, see E. Said, *Orientalism* (New York, 1978) and *Culture and Imperialism* (New York, 1993). On the use of the atlas of the *Description* in nineteenth-century Egypt, see: G. Alleaume, 'Entre l'inventaire du territoire et la construction de la mémoire: L'Œuvre cartographique de l'expédition d'Égypte' in Bret (ed.), *L'Expédition d'Égypte, une entreprise des Lumières*, pp. 279–94.

28 A.L. al-Sayyid Marsot, 'Social and political changes after the French occupation', UCLA colloquium Napoléon Bonaparte's expedition to Egypt: Considering the effects, 10 May 1997; A.

friendship between Jomard and Tahtâwi: a true dialogue, constructive, in that it allowed the young sheik to sustain a two-fold ambition. He sought to affirm the cultural specificity of his country at the same time as he acclimatized western science and technology in the East, the very 'seeds of improvement' that the savants and engineers of the French expedition had come to plant in Egyptian soil.

Yet, while these re-knit exchanges were giving the Egyptian elite of the first half of the nineteenth century a way to appropriate and, this time, to bring to fruition those 'seeds' of modernity – printing and newspapers, administrative reform and the development of technology and science enabling the mastery of space and development of land – the pharaonic times, that paper legacy constructed by the *Description*, were strangely still absent. On this point also, the personality and itinerary of Tahtâwi marked – even though isolated – an interesting rupture. The Egyptian was still living in France when he learned about the discovery of Champollion who, by deciphering hieroglyphics, had finally made the language of the ancient Egyptians accessible. By becoming henceforth aware of the pharaonic roots of Egypt, Tahtâwi discovered or recovered, beyond the Islamic past, a lost dimension of the culture and collective identity of the Egyptians. In pharaonic antiquity, where the Arab historians wanted to see only idolatry and superstition, the learned youth recognized the inaugural period of a civilization, a constitutive element of the national identity of Egypt. This new awareness even pushed him to protest boldly against Mohammed Ali's prodigality in giving the Luxor obelisk to Louis-Philippe. In a memoir addressed to the pasha in 1835, Tahtâwi pleaded for the preservation of Egypt's antiquities, a patrimony whose aesthetic value and cultural importance he already perceived. His forceful demand proudly affirmed how, on the basis of the knowledge generated by the French expedition, an Egyptian national consciousness could arise, integrating the diversity and multiplicity of the past, as far back as its most ancient roots.

Louca, 'Rifâ'a al-Tahtâwi et la science occidentale (1801–1873)' in *D'un Orient l'autre: Les métamorphoses successives des perceptions et connaissances*, 2 vols (Paris, 1991), vol. 2, pp. 201–17, and 'De la *Description* au dialogue', in Laissus (ed.), *Il y a 200 ans*, pp. 94–125; R. Solé, *L'Égypte, passion française* (Paris, 1997).

5

The frivolous French: 'liberty of pleasure' and the end of luxury

Rebecca L. Spang

The philosophy which preaches enjoyment is as old in Europe as the Cyrenaic school. Just as in antiquity it was the *Greeks* who were the protagonists of this philosophy, so in modern times it is the *French*, and indeed for the same reason, because their temperament and their society make them most capable of enjoyment.[1]

Pleasure gained more from the Revolution than did science.[2]

> E'en nations have their playthings; right or wrong,
> Or bless'd, or scourg'd, all ends in dance and song.
> See France, long held in hoodwink'd bondage fast,
> Rouse from her lethargy of ages past ....
> Kings, Priests and Nobles sweeps to general doom,
> Like worn-out lumber from a filthy room.
> Ten dreadful years she heaves convulsive throes,
> The fev'rish crisis of a nation's woes ....[3]

'Paris became gay again': so noted Jules Michelet in one of the final paragraphs of his monumental *History of the French Revolution* (1853). With Robespierre and Saint Just dead and the word 'citoyen' sullied, the great Republican historian brought his Revolution to a fittingly sombre close – but not before he had alerted his readers to the rebirth of pleasure that began on 10 Thermidor II. For this was a favourite image among nineteenth-century historians of the Revolution, and few chose to omit it completely. The brothers Edmond and Jules Goncourt were perhaps especially lavish in describing

I am grateful to Patrice Higonnet, Donald Sutherland, Suzanne Desan, Josh Cole, Judith Miller and Howard Brown for their helpful comments on the original version of this paper.

1 K. Marx and F. Engels, *The German Ideology*, trans. Clemens Dutt, in K. Marx and F. Engels, *Collected Works*, 49 vols (London, 1976), vol. 5, p. 417.
2 E. and J. Goncourt, *Histoire de la société française pendant le Directoire*, 4th ed. (Paris, 1879), p. 14.
3 T. Touch'em, *The Age of Frivolity: a poem addressed to the fashionable, the busy, and the religious world*, 2nd ed. (London, 1807), p. 2.

coffeehouses, fashion plates, fireworks and ice creams, but other authors also delighted in adding details to this generally lascivious picture.[4] Some gasped in astonishment, most shivered in righteous horror: Thomas Carlyle's references to 'saloons' and 'soupers not fraternal' seems almost generous in comparison to Amédée Gabourd's 'hideous saturnalias' and Hippolyte Taine's 'conclave of sovereign bellies'.[5]

Recent scholarship has not completely departed from this imagery.[6] Historians may have endeavoured to treat this period with the seriousness it deserves, but the figures of the *incroyable* and the *merveilleuse* remain easily the era's most familiar representations.[7] Indeed, few figures in the history of French fashion are so immediately recognizable as those scantily dressed icons of the Directory. Clad in revealingly fitted or daringly sheer clothes, they flit through the pages and illustrations of costume histories and cultural studies, reminding us that the period after Thermidor is almost exclusively known – by all but a handful of specialist scholars – as a time of idleness and pleasure-seeking.

This era's reputation for idle enjoyments and its status as a legitimate topic of research have been inversely proportional. Scholars who appreciate the importance of the economic and political policies formulated in the period after Thermidor have had generally little patience with the Goncourtian collage of dancing, gambling and 'women – undressed, half naked, naked', while those who wax lyrical about Madame Tallien's beauty have only a few harsh words for the political cabals and greedy peculations of the period. For culturally conservative commentators of all ideologies – from royalists to communists – the Directory's ballrooms and diaphanous dresses offer eloquent testimony to the moral bankruptcy of that particular republican experiment. If *dansomanes* and strawberry ices are not as terrifying as the guillotines and revolutionary tribunals of year II, they have nonetheless been considered just as damning.

How is it that this period has so often been portrayed as one of almost mad

4   E. and J. Goncourt, *Histoire de la société française pendant le Directoire*.
5   T. Carlyle, *The French Revolution* (London, 1837), book 9, chs 1–2; A. Gabourd, *Histoire de Paris depuis les temps les plus reculés jusqu'à nos jours* (Paris, 1865), vol. 4, p. 477; H. Taine, *The Revolution*, trans. J. Durand (London, n. d.), vol. 3, p. 419.
6   'Impétueusement, et malgré la poursuite de la guerre, la gaieté et le goût des divertissements reprirent leurs droits', F. Furet and D. Richet, *La Révolution française* (Paris, 1973), p. 278; see also R. Sennett, *The Fall of Public Man* (London, 1986), pp. 184–7. For a brief overview of this trend in the historiography, see M. Lyons, *France under the Directory* (Cambridge, 1975), pp. 1–4.
7   On these figures in particular, and on social caricature more generally, see S. Siegfried, *The Art of Louis-Léopold Boilly* (New Haven and London, 1995), pp. 70–84; on fashion in this period, see A. Ribeiro, *Fashion in the French Revolution* (London, 1988); L. Hunt, 'Freedom of Dress in Revolutionary France', in S. Melzer and K. Norberg (eds), *From the Royal to the Republican Body* (Berkeley, 1998), pp. 224–50; M. Delpierre, *et al.*, *Modes et révolutions, 1780–1804* (Paris, 1989), and E. Lajer-Burcharth, 'The *Muscadins* and the *Merveilleuses*: Body and Fashion in Public Space under the Directory', in C. Coates (ed.), *Repression and Expression: Literary and Social Coding in Nineteenth-Century France* (New York, 1996), pp. 137–46.

light-heartedness, of frivolousness verging on folly? After all, as a growing body of scholarship indicates, political elites during the Directory were as concerned with finding a workable form of republican government as their predecessors had been, and few French men and women would have said at the time that the Revolution had conclusively ended in summer 1794.[8] Moreover, recent historiography is nearly unanimous in insisting that extreme hardship characterized many French lives in the second half of the 1790s. Shortages and near famine conditions – not silks and restaurant suppers – seem to have been almost the norm.[9] Yet taking this era seriously cannot be a matter of simply rejecting the frivolous as inconsequential or even of dismissing this characterization as a grossly inaccurate fantasy, unsubstantiated by archival materials. Rather, we need to ask how 'frivolity' became central to so many depictions of these years and how we can relate it to the other transformations – realized, attempted or imagined – that also distinguish this period.[10]

Writing about one famous (and almost certainly fictional) episode – the notorious *bal des victimes*, where relatives of the guillotined supposedly gathered to dance away the night – Ron Schechter has argued that the common picture of Directorial giddiness is largely a construction of nineteenth-century Romanticism. A creation of the 1820s literary culture of the fantastic, the victims' ball became a convenient shorthand for a period that historians otherwise 'tend to ignore'. As an image shared by Romantics and Robespierrists, Communists and Orleanists, the *bal des victimes* was, in Schechter's words, 'a means of escaping politics'.[11] Undoubtedly, this has been one important function served by this invented memory, but it has not been the only one. Remembering the Directory as a period of wanton self indulgence, rather than as a period of economic and social reconfiguration, has also made it possible to overlook the ways in which the very idea of the self (indulged or not) and its relation to others was reconceived in the political and, especially, the socio-economic ideologies of this era. Entrance to the fantasmatic Victims' Dance may have depended on familial proximity to the guillotine, but access to the actual balls of the period was most commonly regulated by the price of admission.[12]

8   For arguments especially relevant to this paper, see J. Livesey, 'Agrarian Ideology and Commercial Republicanism in the French Revolution', *Past and Present* 157 (1997), pp. 94–121; J. A. Miller, *Mastering the Market* (Cambridge, 1999), ch. 7.

9   R. Cobb, *Terreur et subsistances* (Paris, 1965), especially chapter 8; W. Doyle, *The Oxford History of the French Revolution* (Oxford, 1989), pp. 288–95, 322–5.

10 A few other papers have attempted something of this kind, see R. Schechter, 'Gothic Thermidor: The *Bals des victimes*, the Fantastic, and the Production of Historical Knowledge in Post-Terror France', *Representations* 61 (1998), pp. 78–94 and E. Lajer-Burcharth, 'David's *Sabine Women*: Body, Gender and Republican Culture under the Directory', *Art History* 14 (1991), pp. 397–430. See also, R. L. Spang, *The Invention of the Restaurant: Paris and Modern Gastronomic Culture* (Cambridge, Mass., 2000), chs 5–6.

11 Schechter, 'Gothic Thermidor', pp. 86–9.

12 See announcements in *Affiches, annonces, avis divers de Paris* (hereafter, AAAD), 2 Prairial IV, p. 4508; 3 Prairial IV, p. 4520; 4 Prairial IV, p. 4540; 8 Brumaire V, p. 584; 9 Brumaire V, p. 604.

Scholars have long recognized this period as crucial for the formation and consolidation of the structures of modern France. Centralized administration, legal codification, compulsory military service: these features of the modern state have attracted historians' careful attention.[13] But this period also witnessed the redefinition of less overtly regulated, but equally important, realms of modern life. Legal codes and bureaucratic protocols were clearly all part of the effort to forge a coherent society but they were also strategies for defining the very individuals who would make up that society. In other words, 'society' and 'the individual' both had to be (re)created in this period, as responses to the apparent failure of communitarian politics under the radical republic. If France was not to be a single virtuous will, then some other, more stable, form of civil society would have to underpin political life.[14]

Yet even as we consider the particular ways in which the 1790s witnessed the individuation of civil society, we must also attend to the much longer-term developments and broader chronologies of which this process was a part. Reliance on 'the Thermidorian Convention' and 'the Directory' as our chief categories of analysis implicitly confines interpretation to questions of the state and seems to assume that changes in state structure drive and define all others. But the individuation of civil society that we can see taking shape in this period was neither dependent upon, nor mirrored in, a triumph of Liberalism within state structures or popular consciousness.

This is not to say that lawmakers played no role in the renaissance of French pleasure-seeking. Far from it. Had the General Maximum remained in force after 1794, or had the war effort been drastically reduced, frivolity might have developed in very different ways. Nor are such ahistorical counterfactuals the only way of pointing to the role played by the state. In March 1800, for instance, the new Prefect of the Paris Police, Louis-Nicolas Dubois, and his secretary general, Antoine Piis, issued a decree that formally guaranteed 'liberty of pleasure' (along with freedom of dress and religion) to all 'good citizens'.[15] According to the Paris Police, state mechanisms of repression would not, henceforth, attempt to limit 'pleasure'. But neither would they open all the brothels nor even guarantee that wine poured from the city's fountains (except on special occasions such as the December 1804 coronation of Napoleon as Emperor).[16] What, then, could be the significance of promising liberty of pleasure?

13 For a recent comprehensive treatment, see I. Woloch, *The New Regime: Transformations of the French Civic Order* (New York and London, 1994).

14 S. Desan, 'Reconstructing the Social after the Terror: Family, Property and the Law in Popular Politics', *Past and Present* 164 (1999), pp. 81–121.

15 24 Ventôse VIII, reported in *Journal des Débats*, 27 Ventôse VIII; reproduced in A. Aulard, *Paris sous le Consulat*, 4 vols (Paris, 1903–09), vol. 1, p. 212.

16 For accounts of the coronation festivities, see P. M. Saunier, *Tableau historique des cérémonies du sacre et du couronnement* (Paris, 1805), p. 97; J. Dusaulchoy, *Histoire du couronnement ou relation des cérémonies religieuses, politiques et militaires* (Paris, 1805), pp. 283–4.

It is the argument of this paper that the Prefect's remarkable letter needs to be seen as part of a long-term transformation in French society and culture that made '*plaisir*' into a commodity. If the period 1795–1800 was a time of continued food shortages, credit failures and personal tragedies, then the accompanying revived insistence on French *légèreté* cannot be seen simply as a natural response to the 'puritan repression' of 1793–94.[17] Rather, it needs to be understood as an active construction that actually helped to resolve the tensions and difficulties generated by the first five years of revolution. In appeals to a familiar stereotype, a major change in economic attitudes was masked as the continuity of national character. For, in the specific forms it took during the later 1790s, French 'frivolity' expressed itself almost entirely in the shops of Paris.[18]

The French – as any reader of Edmund Burke's *Letters on a Regicide Peace* (1796) knows full well – are a frivolous lot. They change governments as easily as hairstyles and readily confuse whim for reason, luxury for necessity. They are effeminate, suggestible and incapable of chivalry. With 'paltry blurred shreds of paper' where their innards ought to be, it is hardly surprising that the French should have brought chaos to European politics and champagne to European tables.[19]

Burke was hardly the only observer to comment on the apparently mad changeability of French national character during the Revolution. *The Gentleman's Magazine* felt certain that this was so because '[the French] never had any *real* character; their polished, servile, courteous appearance was a mask', while John Moore worried that 'the same levity and vivacity of character which proved a consolation to them in the gloom of despotism, may prove pernicious in the sunshine of liberty'.[20] The association of light-hearted novelty-seeking with Frenchness was not necessarily British: Frederick Meyer, a Hamburg lawyer, found in 1798 that Paris under the Republic was much like Paris during the Old Regime, for an 'insatiable fondness for perpetual change in all varieties of voluptuousness' continued to structure Paris life.[21]

---

17 Many historians have been content to understand post-Terror pleasure seeking as a simple return of the repressed. For example, see Furet and Richet, *La Révolution française*, p. 449.
18 The Goncourt brothers also saw commercial frenzy as a distinctive quality of the Directory, a period they evoked as 'What a strange spectacle! Half of Paris is selling the other half!' *Histoire de la société française pendant le Directoire*, p. 4.
19 The *Oxford English Dictionary* offers a sentence from Burke's *Letters on the Regicide Peace* as an example of how the word 'frivolity' has been used ('When frivolity and effeminacy had been ... acknowledged as their [the French] national character ...'); the claim that French 'gut feelings' had been replaced with 'shreds of paper about the rights of men' is from his *Reflections on the Revolution in France* (1790).
20 *The Gentleman's Magazine and Historical Chronicle* (London, 1792), vol. 62, p. 645; J. Moore, *A Journal during a Residence in France*, 2 vols (London, 1794), vol. 1, p. 36; see also J. Pinkerton, *Recollections of Paris, 1802–1805*, 2 vols (London, 1806), vol. 1, pp. 44–8.
21 F. Meyer, *Fragments sur Paris* (Hambourg, 1798), p. 264.

A well-established tradition existed of characterizing the French as superficial (much as there was of considering the Spanish obsessed with honour and the Germans prone to dreaminess). At the end of the eighteenth century there was neither anything especially innovative about accusing the French people of a congenital lack of seriousness, nor any widespread agreement on how to respond to this caricature. Already in 1725, a professor of rhetoric at the Paris college of Louis-le-Grand had felt compelled to argue in defence of his countrymen that the French were only frivolous when it came to frivolous things. Constant in their faith, their system of government and their military successes, they were changeable in fashion, architecture and language only insofar as those changes were improvements. By narrating them diachronically, Porée could turn instances of seemingly idle behaviour into the chief elements in a tale of progress.[22] Thirty years later, the Marquis de Mirabeau responded to an apparently identical accusation in a very different fashion, arguing in the founding work of physiocracy that only a tiny percentage of the French population was actually as 'frivolous' as was widely believed. Defining the question in terms of 'those personal interests of the moment that are known as enjoyments [*jouissances*]', Mirabeau could only have turned their prevalence into a tale of national advancement by espousing a Mandeville-like doctrine of private vices and public benefits. Rejecting such an analysis, he instead argued for the statistical irrelevance of French pleasure-seeking. Common, perhaps, in certain parts of Paris, it was, he argued, all but nonexistent in 'entire provinces'.[23]

On reflection, it is indeed difficult to imagine how the overwhelmingly rural population of eighteenth-century France could have struck anyone as much giddier than the average Western European peasantry. It is likely that the stereotype referred primarily to urban elites, and that the peasants had yet to be made into typically light-hearted Frenchmen. Yet whether the caricature had any basis in truth or not, it proved remarkably tenacious and even a decade of revolutionary upheaval did little to disturb it. Instead, the events of the 1790s in many ways served to re-inforce this picture and to inflect it with a new and powerful meaning. The changeability of French tastes and the delights of Gallic repartée came quickly to be linked – at least in the eyes of some observers – to the radical changes occurring in French politics. Edmund Burke was certainly expounding this model when he identified the recent vogue for reading philosophical works as one of the causes of the French Revolution. Stephen Weston followed suit, when he wrote that arrival in Paris had brought him to 'the emporium of novelty, in laws, manners and

---

22 P. Porée, *Discours sur la question 'Est-ce avec fondement, ou non, qu'on accuse les français de légèreté?'* (1723) in *Mélanges de litterature, de morale, et de physique*, vol. 7 (Amsterdam, 1775), pp. 103–63.
23 Marquis de Mirabeau, *L'Ami des hommes* (Avignon, 1756), pp. 140–2.

religion'.[24] The appeal of this construction for visiting Britons is obvious: by associating political and social change with character traits for which the French – and the French alone – were notorious, anxious foreigners could contain the threat of revolution.

French writers, even those ostensibly supportive of the Revolution, were also happy to exploit this trope. The *Journal de la mode et du goût français* cited the Revolution's 'inconceivable rapidity' as the motive force behind the quickly changing styles that it chronicled. In the early 1790s, numerous tradesmen advertized their new products as made desirable by changes to the political system. From *bleu-blanc-rouge* liqueurs and national bonbons to Republican snuffboxes and patriotic wallpapers, the French Revolution witnessed the production of an extraordinary range of new goods.[25] This should not surprise us, for the revolutionary culture of sensibility (like all 'sensibility') was a deeply materialist philosophy in which the physical world, as perceived by human sense organs, actually shaped the soul and formed the spirit. Goods, from tricolour cockades to republican dinner plates, were not merely symbolic of already existing inner states. Rather, they helped to create those states.[26]

The Jacobins and the revolutionary tribunals, though both more often depicted in terms of their austerity or brutality than with reference to their superficiality, hence scrutinized dress, diet and décor with an attentiveness that verged on the obsessional. In 1793, the Commune of Paris suggested that 'men who wear checked clothes' should not be trusted; meanwhile, section militants carefully inspected pastries for telltale signs of monarchist sympathies.[27] They observed tailoring and trends with a careful eye, but the revolutionaries of year II did so as part of a world-view in which frivolousness was, effectively, logically impossible. Since all patriotic individuals were, by definition, transparently virtuous, details were not mere preferences of the moment but coded signs and portents.[28] The Terror, that is, made changing politics

---

24   S. Weston, *Letters from Paris During the Summer of 1791*, 2 vols (London, 1791), vol. 1, p. 44; he also noted that the Palais Royal was the centre for 'extravagance' in both 'politics and pleasure' (p. 117).

25   *Journal de la mode et du goût français*, 5 September 1790, p. 1; AAAD, 1 January 1790, p. 6; 19 June 1790, p. 1766; 31 October 1792, p. 4547; 25 April 1793, p. 1759.

26   Condorcet's *Esquisse d'un tableau historique des progrès de l'esprit humain* begins with the statement, 'Man is born with the ability to perceive, to receive sensations ... This ability develops based on the actions of external objects.' J.-A.-N. Caritat, marquis de Condorcet, *Esquisse d'un tableau historique des progrès de l'esprit humain* (first published, 1793; re-published, Paris, 1988), p. 79. See P. Higonnet, *Class, Ideology and the Rights of Nobles during the French Revolution* (Oxford, 1981), pp. 194–6.

27   *Chronique de Paris*, 29 July 1793 cited in D. Roche, *The Culture of Clothing*, trans. J. Birrell (Cambridge, 1994), p. 149; Archives Nationales, F⁷ 4610 (dossier Bouchon, 18 Nivôse II) details the examination of a suspicious cake.

28   The notion of transparent virtue owed much, obviously, to Rousseau; see the classic J. Strobinski, *Jean-Jacques Rousseau: La transparence et l'obstacle* (Paris, 1957) and C. Blum, *Rousseau and the Republic of Virtue* (Ithaca, 1986). See also P. Higonnet, *Goodness beyond Virtue* (Cambridge, Mass., 1998), pp. 225–9.

and changing styles necessarily dependent on each other, but did so in the name of high seriousness and patriotic solemnity. Morality took a particularly weighty material form.

It is striking, then, that both French and foreign authors revived the typi-fication of the French as frivolous with special force and vigour in the period immediately after Thermidor. In the Anglophone context, this was largely a matter of extending the Burkean analogy and reassuring conservative readers that political upheaval in France, though unfortunate, was not likely to have international consequences. The very seriousness with which revolutionaries had interrogated fashions and confiscated pastries was read as a sure sign of delirium. When John Carr wrote of the French that they 'at present (in 1803) work, walk, eat, drink and sleep in tranquillity, and what is of more conse-quence to them, they dance in security', he made it clear to his British readers that revolutionary challenges to the established order had been a brief-lived infatuation.[29]

Within France itself, however, this revival served a different function. For some authors, such as the disappointed republican Louis Sébastien Mercier, sketching a picture of Parisian pleasures was a way of indicating just how disastrously wrong the Revolution had gone. When Mercier (a favourite source for later generations of culinary and cultural historians) wrote of the 'Palais Egalité, ci-devant Palais Royal', that 'partridge patés, beautiful cher-ries, fresh new peas and heads of wild boar' were the diet of the thousands who ate, lived and strolled within its borders, he was not praising the easy availability of scrumptious morsels but describing a scene of the most grotesque debauch.[30] In chronicling the failures of equality in the revolution-ary capital, Mercier found the restaurants and gourmet shops of central Paris an especially apt target, for they made the conflict between the 'haves' and the 'have nots' visible in an especially material, even corporeal, fashion. As a satirist, he was working within a politically charged language of 'fat and lean' that had been central to revolutionary caricature and rhetoric. Yet by 1798, this language was quickly losing its efficacy and later generations would miss the satire's barb almost completely.[31]

Mercier's Le Nouveau Paris, like the reports of British travellers, inter-preted the consumption of delicacies and the seeking of pleasures as revela-tory of a failure of social and political seriousness in the Directory's revolutionary project. Mercier despaired and John Carr was comforted, but neither's image of properly revolutionary activity really went beyond the Jacobin solemnity of 1793–94.[32] This is perhaps hardly surprising (given the

29 J. Carr, The Stranger in France, or a Tour from Devonshire to Paris (London, 1803), p. 116.
30 L. S. Mercier, Le Nouveau Paris (Paris, 1798), ch. 91.
31 For more on mis-appropriations of Mercier, see my The Invention of the Restaurant, chs 5 and 7.
32 Higonnet, Goodness beyond Virtue, pp. 197 and passim; see too, J.-P. Gross, Fair Shares for All: Jacobin Egalitarianism in Practice (Cambridge, 1997).

extent to which the events of the Terror haunted everyone of this generation), but a major change in the logic and language of *enjoyment* was actually
underway in the late 1790s. Contemporaneous accounts of Directorial frivolity were intimately entwined with descriptions of buying and selling and
largely silent on matters amatory or conversational. Mercier and Carr spent
hours in the Palais Royal, that early example of a public promenade *cum* shop-
ping mall and Weston, after all, had called Paris 'the *emporium* of novelty in
laws, manners...' (emphasis added). French light-heartedness, that is, seemingly no longer manifested itself in witty retorts or dangerous liaisons. Instead,
it described a relationship between people and goods. The skin-tight fashions
of the day may have hinted at the stimulation of a host of appetites, but the
dresses and trousers had first to be purchased.[33]

To make sense of the stereotype's transmutation (and of the *ordinance*
promising 'liberty of pleasure'), we need to recall that throughout the first five
years of the Revolution, much economic and social discourse had operated
within a framework set by the binary terms of 'luxury' and 'necessity.' Heated
political debate over subsistence was driven by a continued concern with
provisioning cities (especially Paris) and by efforts to transform Old Regime
charity and poor relief. Revolution-era advocates of a public welfare system
often spoke of the 'right to subsistence' (and some even argued that it should
be included in the *Declaration of the Rights of Man*) but others, such as the
Jacobin Félix LePeletier, intimated that regenerated French society would see
'equality of enjoyment' as well.[34] One measure proposed to the Convention in
summer 1793 had even gone so far as to advocate the introduction of a tax on
all 'refined pleasures' (*jouissances recherchées*) to be levied on riding horses,
porcelains, fine art and worked pieces of gold and silver. (The proceeds were
to go toward funding new schools for the training of artillery officers.)[35]

The proposed tax on 'pleasures' never became law, but it is worth pausing
to emphasize that it would have applied neither to theatre attendance nor to
concert patronage but to goods more commonly referred to at the time as
'luxuries'.[36] Old Regime definitions of *plaisir* often stressed the ephemeral
nature of that sensation, but there was nothing fleeting or spontaneous about
the list of *jouissances* adumbrated by the petitioners of 1793. The literature of

33 For a lengthy advertisement of the new fashions, see *AAAD* 26 Ventôse VI, pp. 3242–4.
34 L. DiCaprio, 'Women Workers, State-Sponsored Work, and the Right to Subsistence during the
    French Revolution', *Journal of Modern History* 71 (1999), pp. 519–51, especially p. 524. F.
    LePeletier, cited in Higonnet, *Goodness beyond Virtue*, p. 121.
35 Foudras and Créquy Montmorency, *Pétition à la Convention Nationale* (4 August 1793), pp.
    11–15.
36 For an analysis of the moral and social connotations of 'luxury' in Old-Regime France, see S.
    Maza, 'Luxury, Morality, and Social Change: Why there was no Middle-Class Consciousness in
    Pre-revolutionary France', *Journal of Modern History* 69 (1997), pp. 200–29. Many of the *cahiers
    de doléances* had called for renewed enforcement of sumptuary taxation, for examples see
    Archives parlementaires, vol. 2, pp. 336, 341, 360, 377, 405.

libertinage was full of random moments of enjoyment, furtively seized, but such ecstatic episodes could be of little use to tax collectors.[37] In suggesting 'pleasures' as a revenue source for the state, the authors of the proposal were building on the familiar notion of a luxury tax even as they struggled to give it a new and workable form.

Rejecting 'luxury', like denouncing 'counter-revolutionaries', was easily done, but that did not mean that people readily agreed on a definition of what was luxurious. The dramatic eighteenth-century expansion of available consumer goods had subtly, and repeatedly, changed the definition of luxury.[38] Condillac noted in the 1750s that 'linen is no longer a luxury' and sales of mirrors more than quadrupled during the century.[39] It is perhaps not surprising that Diderot, defining the purpose of his *Encyclopédie* (1751), chose 'luxury' as his example of a word that was daily 'abused' – used to refer to so many objects that the word itself had no real meaning.[40] The definition of necessity proved equally slippery. (A blue coat, lined in white and trimmed in scarlet, was, after all, a necessity for anyone joining the National Guard.[41]) Sugar and coffee may both have been exotic novelties in 1690 but, by 1790, they had become necessities – at least for some people.[42] Revolution-era legislators therefore unwittingly undertook a Sisyphean task when they tried to use the structuring opposition between 'necessity' and 'luxury' as a basis for economic policy.

In ordinary usage, 'luxury' was the opposite of 'necessity', but this simple semiotic binary was inadequate as the basis of any sort of coherent state practice. It was no easier for lawmakers to define 'luxury' than it had been for Diderot, and 'necessity', too, suffered from the absence of fixed referents. Indeed, revolutionary efforts at precise definition may actually have interrogated the category of 'necessity' so thoroughly as to make it almost meaning-

---

37 Several recent works have stressed that Old-Regime libertinage had its own temporality, characterised by an emphasis on the 'here and now' to the exclusion of either the past or the future, see: C. Cusset, *No Tomorrow: The Ethics of Pleasure in the French Enlightenment* (Charlottesville, 1999); T. Kavanagh, 'The Libertine Moment,' in C. Cusset (ed.), *Libertinage and Modernity (Yale French Studies* 94), pp. 79–100.

38 Consider, for instance, the development of thriving industries specialized in the production of imitation luxury goods. See C. Fairchilds, 'The Production and Marketing of Populuxe Goods in Eighteenth-Century Paris', in J. Brewer and R. Porter (eds), *Consumption and the World of Goods* (London, 1993), pp. 228–48.

39 Condillac, *Oeuvres complètes*, vol. IV, pp. 208–9, cited in Roche, *Culture of Clothing*, p. 514; D. Roche, *The People of Paris*, trans. M. Evans and G. Lewis (Leamington Spa, 1987), p. 153.

40 Diderot, article 'Encyclopédie,' cited in K. Baker, *Condorcet: From Natural Philosophy to Social Mathematics* (Chicago, 1975), p. 19.

41 Roche, *Culture of Clothing*, pp. 148, 254–5; see also D. L. Clifford, 'Can the Uniform Make the Citizen? Paris, 1789–1791', *Eighteenth-Century Studies* 34 (2001), pp. 363–82.

42 C. Jones and R. Spang, 'Sans-culottes, *sans café, sans tabac*: Shifting Realms of Necessity and Luxury in Eighteenth-Century France', in M. Berg and H. Clifford (eds), *Consumers and Luxury* (Manchester and New York, 1999), pp. 37–62; see also Higonnet, *Goodness beyond Virtue*, pp. 197–8.

less. What emerges most strikingly from all the debates is how expansive the definition of 'necessity' became (in the General Maximum, for instance, it covered anchovies, figs and twenty-four different sorts of paper) and how nebulous was that of 'luxury'. Efforts to stabilize or universalize the terms of the luxury-necessity binary cost the Legislative Assembly and the National Convention countless hours of committee work but yielded little in terms of either general rulings or easily applied laws.[43]

In the period after Thermidor, arguments couched in the language of necessity were further tainted by their resemblance to what William Sewell has called 'the sans-culotte rhetoric of subsistence'.[44] Since popular agitation over issues of subsistence (which included sugar, coffee and chocolate, as well as bread and wine) in 1793–94 was intimately linked to denunciation of all those 'enemies of the people' who were trying to 'starve' the Republic into submission, later demands that goods of 'prime necessity' be made readily available almost automatically brought with them the spectre of militant *sans-culottisme*. During the winter of 1795–96, single women and aged *rentiers* were perhaps among the groups most likely to be living in dire want, but theirs were not the images conjured by arguments for state provisioning. Commitment to such policies was taken to indicate not humanitarian fellow feeling but dangerous radicalism.[45]

Thermidorian efforts to end the Terror led to the abolition of the General Maximum as well as the closing of the Jacobin Clubs. For most contemporaries, the economic and political aspects of Terror were intimately linked. In revoking the Maximum, lawmakers turned a deaf ear to urban popular demands and allowed inflation to skyrocket (hence guaranteeing the *assignat*'s demise). But they did more than that. They also implied that identifying necessities and setting fixed prices were inherently terroristic acts, inevitably accompanied by brutal repression. During the debate that preceded its abolition, one *conventionnel* described the Maximum as among the 'violations of principles and acts of arbitrariness' that were the Revolution's greatest errors.[46]

Throughout the 1790s, and under a host of different pressures, the project of designating some goods as necessities and others as luxuries had first intensified, then dissipated. By the end of the decade, both terms, though

43 C. Brinton long ago commented on the practical difficulties of the Maximum, see his *A Decade of Revolution* (first published, 1934; re-published, New York, 1963), pp. 135–6; see also R. L. Spang, 'What is Rum? The Politics of Consumption in the French Revolution', in M. Daunton and M. Hilton (eds), *The Politics of Consumption: Material Culture and Citizenship in Europe and America* (Oxford, 2001), pp. 33–50.

44 W. Sewell, 'The Sans-Culotte Rhetoric of Subsistence', in K. Baker (ed.), *The Terror*, vol. 4 of *The French Revolution and the Creation of Modern Political Culture* (Oxford, 1994), pp. 249–70.

45 Gross, *Fair Shares for All*, pp. 91–2.

46 Beffroy, during the debate on the Maximum (3 Nivôse III), reported in *Le Moniteur*, 6 Nivôse III, pp. 398–9.

not completely abandoned, had lost much of their explanatory efficacy. Efforts, official and otherwise, to theorize the relationship between people and the world of goods were left grasping for a new vocabulary.[47]

Faced with socio-economic turbulence and a conceptual semi-void, numerous authors relied on the notion of 'character' (both national and individual) to explain events.[48] The construction's appeal for conservative Britons has already been noted but it was also employed in French texts, where it helped articulate a certain vision of the relationship between polity and economy. We can see this happening as early as the December 1794 debate on the Maximum, in which one of its antagonists argued that it was not the nature of goods themselves, but the character of those who consumed them, that made luxuries a threat to some republican governments. France however, he noted, was summoned by Nature herself to a commercial lifestyle; it had been laziness (rather than prosperity) that caused the fall of Rome.[49] Several years later, Jean-Baptiste Pujoulx made a similar point, asserting that it would be wrong to introduce extravagant consumption into a country 'where business, industry and the existence of an immense population were not founded on luxury' – but such was not the situation in France. 'To try to change the customs and the character of a people', argued Pujoulx, 'and return it abruptly to the simple tastes of some northern nation' would be like trying to force a river to flow back into its source.[50] Each nation, every people, had its own customs, habits, usages; what was true for Sparta or for Schleswig could not be so for France after 1789.

Pujoulx was hardly the only writer of the late 1790s to put emphasis on the uniquely national parameters of French consumption. A parable offered by the *Journal des dames et des modes* suggested that any benefits to be gained from the rejection of extravagance and fashion would be more than undercut by the forced emigration of thousands of workers. A sudden move to frugality would have more dire consequences for the French economy than had the revocation of the Edict of Nantes.[51] The 1799 thesis of a Montpellier medical student began from very different premises, but it too linked fashion to the definition of national character and decried the current tendency to borrow styles 'from our rivals and our enemies'. Dressing like a Newmarket jockey (or even like a Roman republican matron) implied that France lacked either the ability or the taste necessary for forming its own styles. Yet since skilled workers and good taste were known to abound there, it had instead to be a

---

47 For an introduction to economic theory in this period see Miller, *Mastering the Market*, pp. 164–8 and Livesey, 'Agrarian Ideology and Commercial Republicanism'.
48 For a fascinating analysis of this concept in the context of English literary life, see D. Lynch, *The Economy of Character* (Chicago, 1998).
49 Eschasseriaux, reported in *Le Moniteur*, 5 Nivôse III, p. 393.
50 J. B. Pujoulx, *Paris à la fin du XVIIIe siècle* (Paris, 1801), p. 183.
51 *Journal des dames et des modes*, 3:59 (15 Thermidor VII), pp. 321–4.

more worrying shortfall – a failure of 'national spirit' – that prompted this behaviour both unpatriotic and health-destroying.[52] In terms that recalled Montesquieu, Jacques Joseph Lemoine's 1808 prize-winning answer to the question posed by the Académie de Dijon ('Does the French nation deserve the reputation for fickleness that it has with foreigners?' 'La nation française mérite-t-elle le reproche de légèreté qui lui font les nations étrangères?') also linked fashion, frivolity and national character.[53] Lemoine argued that any tendency to changeability and light-heartedness on the part of his compatriots was a product neither of state institutions nor of innate flaws but of local climate and natural conditions. Given where they lived and what the land was like, the French were neither fickle nor frivolous; rather, they had proven remarkably constant in that they were always true to their environment.

A fashion magazine, a medical dissertation and the learned Dijon Academy (whose essay prize had been won by Rousseau's 'Discourse on the Arts and Sciences' in 1750): these disparate sources all highlight how quickly 'frivolous' consumption had shifted from being the moral failing of an individual to an economic imperative for the nation. Products that had been catalogued in 1793–94 as idle luxuries suited to effeminate counter-revolutionaries were now valued items of French national production. As early as the final day of year II, Robert Lindet (who had himself been responsible for much subsistence policy during the Terror) did not hesitate to blame Robespierre's 'destructive genius' for both fostering a climate of suspicion and ruining the national silk industry.[54]

Lawmakers and administrators increasingly perceived goods as something to be treated neither as moral absolutes nor as lessons of history, but as elements in an economic system to be measured and managed. Even if goods were novelty items and objects of feminine adornment – 'frivolities', in other words – their production and sale were signs of a reinvigorated economy and, as such, had to be watched with a wary eye. By the early years of the Consulate, lace and ribbons were policed as rigorously as they had been in year II, but they were no longer interpreted as serious indicators of political sympathies. Rather, they were imports or exports, quantities and values to be converted into numbers and entered into charts.[55] The secret police's daily

---

52 J. J. Brunet, *Essai sur l'influence des modes et les habillemens sur la santé des hommes* (Montpellier, VII), pp. 13–14.

53 J. J. Lemoine, *Les Français justifiés du reproche de légèreté* (Paris, 1815).

54 B. Baczko, *Comment sortir de la Terreur* (Paris, 1989), pp. 165–6. Baczko also describes Babeuf's macabre understanding of the link between economic policy and political repression: the latter, Babeuf argued, was the result of Robespierre's Malthusian perception that France could not support its entire population. Since production could not be increased, war and terror would have to be utilized to reduce the population, pp. 250–3.

55 On the quantification of social life in this period, see A. Desrosières, *The Politics of Large Numbers: A History of Statistical Reasoning*, trans. C. Naish (Cambridge, Mass.,1998), especially pp. 31–46.

memoranda to the Minister of the Interior and to Napoleon reported on the condition of all industries, regardless of the use-value of the objects produced. 'The fake pearl manufacturers are in a slight decline', noted Prefect of Police Dubois in his daily report for 14 April 1805, before commenting on rumours about planned troop movements.[56] Even regular theatre attendance – often cited by scandalized British and American visitors as evidence of the French preference for spectacle over substance – was an indicator of economic upswings. In the words of one police report, the fully sold-out performances of the Théâtre du Vaudeville could only mean that the 'rumour of a money shortage is really a royalist plot'.[57]

In guaranteeing 'liberty of pleasure' to each loyal citizen, therefore, Dubois and Piis's decree of March 1800 affirmed the new regime's commitment to a depoliticized understanding of consumption (now depicted as an important domain of individual expression and enjoyment).[58] Never elaborating a fuller account of the freedoms granted, they implied that the state had no interest in meddling in the private affairs of its citizens.[59] Yet, as we know, some forms of pleasure were actively condemned by the regime.[60] For all that Dubois and Piis had promised liberty of pleasure to each loyal citizen, Napoleon's police state tracked those enjoyments very carefully. The police decree intimated that 'pleasure, dress and religion' were personal freedoms, but it also made these liberties the properties of 'all loyal citizens' alone. These freedoms were also far from being absolute: the right to dress as one pleased, for example, did not extend to women dressing as men (or men as women) and cross-dressing was repeatedly criminalized in nineteenth- and twentieth-century France.[61] Nevertheless, pleasures of a certain orderly variety started to become almost compulsory; a failure of enjoyment, if not tantamount to treason, nonetheless marked the priest, the poor man and the Jacobin as suspect.[62]

Writing of objects as *plaisirs* and *jouissances*, authors of the early nine-

---

56 A.N. F⁷ 3833 (25 Germinal XIII). The police also kept Napoleon notified of conditions in the fan industry, the wine-export business, and the embroidery trades. See the daily police reports dated 23 Messidor, 28 Brumaire, and 28 Pluviôse X, A.N. F⁷ 3830.

57 A.N. F⁷ 3491 (23 Germinal VII).

58 On the relation between consumption and Romantic notions of the individual, see C. Campbell, *The Romantic Ethic and the Spirit of Modern Consumerism* (Oxford, 1987).

59 Only the sketchiest historiography of pleasure is available, see *Formations of Pleasure* (London, 1983); C. Dean, *The Self and its Pleasures* (Ithaca, 1992); and the works cited on libertinage. It might be argued that Foucault's *History of Sexuality* constitutes one step in the direction of writing the political history of pleasure.

60 M. Sibalis, 'The Regulation of Male Homosexuality in Revolutionary and Napoleonic France, 1789–1815', in J. Merrick and B. T. Ragan (eds), *Homosexuality in Modern France* (Oxford, 1996), pp. 80–101; V. Rosario, *The Erotic Imagination: French Histories of Perversion* (Oxford, 1997).

61 See Hunt, 'Freedom of Dress' and Rosario, *The Erotic Imagination*, pp. 69, 76–7, 193.

62 For an analysis of ideological structures as the 'obscene imposition of enjoyment', see S. Zizek, *For They Know Not What They Do: Enjoyment as a Political Factor* (London and New York, 1991).

teenth century hinted at the libidinal outlets afforded by buying and selling. For one symptomatic account, we might look to the volumes of Jacques Peuchet's *Bibliothèque commerciale*. Like so many other administrators of the Napoleonic period, Peuchet seems to have little to recommend him. Like Antoine Piis, Peuchet belongs to a group of dramatists, press censors, police officers and minor administrative figures who are now known, if at all, mainly by the dismissive term of *girouette* ('pinwheel').[63] Political changeability has become their defining character trait; a 'frivolous' (or, self-preserving) failure of ideological commitment their one claim to historical memory. Though their histories may have little of the grand drama afforded by suicide or exile, their lives and works are relevant here. Their writings are significant more by their quantity than their quality; we should not expect to find daring new ideas, or a critical perception as sharp as Say's or Lavoisier's. By definition, a *girouette*, who turns with the prevailing winds, cannot be a 'founder of discourse'.[64]

James Livesey has reminded us that many political economists of the Directory envisioned France as an agrarian commercial republic and analyzed city life as a necessary component in the regular circulation of wealth. Increased agricultural production would be stimulated by scientific discoveries made in cities and by the demand of the many consumers who lived in them.[65] Peuchet's perspective, however, was somewhat different, for he concentrated on cities as places of production and concluded that goods manufactured in an urban environment would also have to be consumed there. No matter what the agronomists might say, 'never will they convince the ploughmen of Picardy, of Normandy, or of Alsace ... to buy clocks, mirrors or fine metal goods'. No matter how affluent those peasants might become, Peuchet argued, they would always prefer to hoard their profits, for they had no 'taste for these pleasures [*jouissances*]'.

In the first volume of his *Bibliothèque commerciale*, Peuchet gravely observed that while French spending on 'social pleasures' (*jouissances de société*) was still unfortunately in decline, 'purely animalistic consumption' (*consommation purement animale*) had never been greater.[66] Among Paris-based writers, this had been a common refrain throughout the second half of the 1790s, often supported with reference to statistics that compared the number of pastrycooks to the number of publishers.[67] Mercier and

63 On Piis, see L. Mason, *Singing the French Revolution* (Ithaca, 1996), pp. 86–9, 118; J. Tulard, J. F. Fayard and A. Fierro, *Histoire et dictionnaire de la révolution française* (Paris, 1987), pp. 1031–2.
64 I borrow the term 'founder of discourse' from M. Foucault, 'What is an Author?', in his *Language, Counter-Memory, Practice*, trans. D. Bouchard and S. Simon (Ithaca, 1977), pp. 113–38.
65 Livesey, 'Agrarian Ideology and Commercial Republicanism'.
66 J. Peuchet, *Bibliothèque commerciale*, 1:1 (Germinal X/March 1802), pp. 370–2.
67 P. Villiers, *Manuel du voyageur à Paris* (Paris, year X), p. 155; L. Prudhomme, *Miroir de l'ancien et du nouveau Paris* (Paris, year XIII), p. 221; A. J. N. de Rosny, *Le Censeur ou voyage sentimental autour du Palais Royal* (Paris, 1802), p. 89.

Prudhomme, one-time republicans turned authors of officially innocuous social description, offered this comparison as a way of implying that Paris's newly rich were the most vulgar of gluttons, incapable of valuing anything they could not literally consume. Such descriptions gave the political rhetoric of 'fat' and 'lean' an especially literal content, but they also – by labelling food an 'animalistic' pleasure – further weakened any link between daily material existence and 'necessity' of a distinctly human variety. In Peuchet's account, enjoyment was cleansed of its animal associations by becoming sociable. Social pleasures, however light-hearted, were nonetheless *social* and civilized. Pleasures – of the appropriate sort – could be the building blocks of society.

The shift this paper describes cannot be conclusively traced to a single intellectual heritage nor explained by specific administrative reforms. And yet it happened. As a category of legal and economic analysis, 'luxury' gradually dropped from use, to be replaced by the personalized category of 'pleasure'.[68] Throughout the eighteenth-century debates on the subject, luxury had always been defined within a specific social context. It was either a threat to social differentiation or an exaggeration of it but, in either case, luxury was understood to have ramifications that extended far beyond those who indulged in it. After 1794, however, artworks, jewellery, lace and silks (like turkeys, truffles, bonbons and sturgeon) were increasingly perceived as personal pleasures. The transition from luxury to pleasure made individual desires the basis (rather than the bane) of social organization.

By the middle of the nineteenth century, luxury was of analytic usefulness for those interested in studying medieval sumptuary laws or cataloguing the books collected by connoisseurs (*éditions de luxe*).[69] In the eighteenth century, numerous factors, ranging from the growing importance of empirical medicine to the rise of classified advertisements and the desperate idiosyncrasy of Rousseau's autobiography, had laid the groundwork for an increasingly differentiated understanding of human necessity.[70] Different individuals had different needs. In the period after Thermidor, we may be witnessing a much more radical individualization of the category of desire. With the growing scepticism toward a politics based on the General Will, individual wants, desires, pleasures and preferences became paramount – at least for some individuals (white, male, propertied) and in certain domains of daily life.

68 For an analysis of how the Revolution made it possible to solve the previously insoluble question of luxury, see Higonnet, *Class, Ideology, and the Rights of Nobles*, especially pp. 12–14.
69 The 1835 dictionary of the Académie Française was the first edition to offer 'Cet ouvrage est imprimé avec un grand luxe typographique' as a sample usage of the word 'luxe'.
70 For a more extended discussion of this point, see Jones and Spang, 'Sans-culottes, *sans café, sans sucre*'; Spang, *Invention of the Restaurant*, chs 2–3; C. Jones, 'The Great Chain of Buying: Medical Advertisement, the Bourgeois Public Sphere and the Origins of the French Revolution', *American Historical Review* 103 (1996), pp. 13–40.

6

The social contours of meritocracy in the Napoleonic officer corps

Rafe Blaufarb

One of the most tenacious myths about Napoleon concerns his relationship to the meritocratic legacy of the French Revolution. Despite significant caveats offered by revisionist research, the notion that Napoleon was dedicated to ferreting out merit in the lower, plebeian reaches of the army and raising it to prominence in dramatic battlefield promotions remains stubbornly fixed in the popular historical imagination. To be sure, there is something to this view. One can hardly ignore the meteoric ascent of Augereau, son of a domestic servant and fruitseller, who reached the rank of general by the age of thirty-six before rising still further to that of Marshal of the Empire. Or the even more fulgurant career of Augereau's peer in the Marshalate, Jean Lannes, an apprentice dyer, who became a general at the age of twenty-seven. But are these examples representative of Napoleon's officers in general, or even of his generals, in particular? Surely Jean-Toussaint Arrighi de Casanova was more typical of this latter species. Son of a Corsican deputy to the French legislature, a graduate of the royal military school at Rebais (and therefore a *gentilhomme* of proven ancestry), Arrighi de Casanova owed his promotion to the rank of general at the age of twenty-nine not merely to these qualifications and whatever military capacity he possessed, but also to the fact that he was Napoleon's cousin by marriage. Another young man who became a general before the age of thirty, Raymond-Aimery-Philippe-Joseph de Montesquieu-Fezensac, had enough blue blood running in his veins to dispense with the need for formal military schooling and marital ties to the Bonaparte family – how degrading such an alliance would have been for one of such illustrious lineage as he! The Aboville brothers are representative of another kind of Napoleonic general. Sons of an Old Regime general and graduates of the demanding royal artillery school at Chalons, Augustin-Gabriel and Augustin-Marie – generals at thirty-six and thirty-three, respectively – were able to parlay their fine education and familial tradition of royal military service into brilliant careers under the Revolution, Consulate, and Empire. Of course, not all of Napoleon's generals were members of his clan, courtly aristocrats, or military nobles. Some were new men whose lack of nobility and military antecedents would have excluded them from the officer corps before the opening of careers to talent in 1789. One of these was Gilbert-Désiré-Joseph Bachelu, son of a *conseiller maître* in the *Cour des Comptes* of Dôle, a young man of solid, even stolid, *bourgeois* stock. Graduate of the rigorous *École de Génie* of Metz, he rose rapidly through the corps of military engineers, becoming a general in 1809 at the age of thirty-two.

While suggestive, the careers of generals do not provide the best insight into the unspoken social parameters of Napoleonic military meritocracy. Many of Napoleon's generals, like Augereau and Lannes, had already been elevated to that rank before Brumaire. Their careers thus tell us more about revolutionary than Napoleonic notions of merit. Moreover, generals are necessarily unrepresentative of the officer corps as a whole. Occupying the sensitive frontier between the army and the government, they are political animals whose careers reflect a much broader range of factors than those purely military. And even as military men, they are no more representative. Simply put, the ordinary social barriers to promotion are often lifted for military genius, particularly in wartime. Rather than among the generals, the place where underlying conceptions of merit emerge most clearly is at the lower echelons of the officer corps, particularly at the points in the hierarchy where young aspirants leave the civilian world for the army. If we leave aside the generals and turn our attention instead to the military school graduates, new *sous-lieutenants*, and other subaltern officers, a different picture of military meritocracy emerges. What we find in the case of the French army after Brumaire is that, without ever breaking openly with the ideal of the career open to talents, Napoleon sought to raise the social level of the officer corps by recruiting young men from good families (but especially those with military traditions) and forge within the crucible of military service a new elite bound to the regime.

Proclaiming an end to the tyranny of mediocrity, demagogy, and indiscriminate social levelling which they claimed had been imposed on France by nearly a decade of republican rule, the Brumairians moved quickly to restore meritocracy, in their view one of the founding principles of the Revolution. By empowering the state to grant pensions to the families of soldiers, decorations to military heroes, and prizes for accomplishment in the arts and sciences, the Consular constitution gave the new regime a powerful means of honouring public service and superior talents. In the army, this supposed revival of meritocracy took on a social dimension as it metamorphosed into a tightly orchestrated campaign to improve the poor composition of the officer corps, which the Brumairians believed had been compromised by the dubious recruitment policies of the republic. Soon after the seizure of power,

Pierre-Antoine-Noël-Brune Daru, an Old Regime *commissaire des guerres* and political survivor whose career in the war ministry had continued to prosper under the Directory, recommended to Bonaparte that the only way to achieve a 'degree of perfection' in the army was to cashier those officers 'who corrupt it by their immorality and compromise it by their ignorance'.[1] Baraguey d'Hilliers, an inspector-general who had entered the army directly as an officer during the Old Regime, was one of many influential officers who supported Daru's call for a purge. Concluding a review of the four military divisions under his inspection, he warned that the government 'could not move too quickly' to remove the officers 'that the Revolution, error, or luck' had placed in the army.[2] These appeals found a receptive audience and warm advocate in the person of the First Consul. Painfully aware of the penury of 'well-educated young men' in the military, Bonaparte was already interested in the idea of combing-out the officer corps.[3] The conclusion of peace with Austria in early 1801 provided him with the moment of respite he needed to carry out this operation.

After nearly a decade of grinding warfare, any regime would have found itself forced to refurbish its military establishment and rejuvenate its personnel. The tough campaigns of the revolutionary wars had taken their toll. Already in year IV, the Directory had recognized the problem and taken steps to address it. Understrength units were consolidated, allowing the government to retire the aged, infirm, and war-weary.[4] In year VI, it reinforced these efforts by creating permanent depot companies where the older officers could wind down their careers instructing new recruits and carrying out administrative tasks in support of the front-line troops.[5] But the threat of invasion in year VII interfered with these reforms and even forced the government to resort to slapdash methods of officer recruitment – including the democratic election of officers by the groups of conscripts preparing to leave for the frontier. Only with the signature of the Peace of Lunéville and the end of war on the continent was it possible for the French government to return to the task of repairing its military machine.

In army-wide reviews, officers whose age and infirmities prevented them from continuing active service were granted retirement, often with substantial pensions. This culling-out fell disproportionately on those officers, typically of undistinguished social origins, who had begun their careers as soldiers

1 Archives Nationales (hereafter AN), 138 AP 15, Daru, 'Mémoire sur l'infanterie', VIII.
2 AN, AF IV 1116, Baraguey d'Hilliers, 'Mémoire au premier consul: rapport de l'inspection de l'an XI dans les 9ème, 10ème, 11ème, et 20ème divisions militaires', 1 Floréal XI.
3 Quoted in A. Dansette (ed.), *Napoléon: pensées politiques et sociales* (Paris, 1969), p. 288.
4 On these efforts, as well as on the larger issues raised in this paper, see chs 5 and 6 of my forthcoming book, *The French Army, 1750–1820: Careers, Talent, Merit*, (Manchester, 2002).
5 On these operations, in which the seemingly omnipresent revolutionary military reformer Dubois-Crancé once again played a prominent role, see the documents in Archives de la Guerre (hereafter AG) X^b129 and GD 58 (Dubois-Crancé's personnel file).

during the Old Regime.[6] This not only accelerated the generational shift in the army which had already begun to emerge under the Directory, but also reinforced the government's complementary efforts to draw young men from more elevated social backgrounds into the military profession.

As well as proposing geriatric officers for retirement, the inspectors also evaluated the officers' level of instruction, which had suffered during the Revolution from the abolition of formal military schooling, the haphazard recruitment of officers, and, above all, the unrelenting pace of warfare. The inspectors sought to inculcate in the officer corps a greater level of technical competence, sustained by a more rigorous work ethic. In unit after unit, they ordered officers to attend classes on tactics and spend more time manoeuvring the troops.[7] The inspectors also sought to do something about the officers' shaky grasp of military legislation – perhaps a pardonable shortcoming given the rate at which successive legislatures changed the laws! They ordered the officers to memorize regulations on civil-military relations, discipline, advancement, military justice, and unit accounting.[8]

The inspectors also prepared reports on each officer individually. These documents enable us to detail the personal and professional qualities the inspectors believed were necessary for military excellence. One quality which figured prominently in the inspectors' notes was technical mastery. Officers who 'understood manoeuvres and fulfilled their duties with zeal', 'possessed knowledge of mathematics', or simply 'knew their *métier*' were nearly always marked for promotion. Those spectacularly deprived of these qualities, however, were designated for reprimands or worse.[9] Yet, close analysis of the individual notes shows that technical proficiency and even basic instruction, however dear to the professionalizing hearts of the inspectors, did not constitute the essential factors in promotion decisions. If counterbalanced by seriousness, application, and a will to succeed, even ignorance was not fatal to one's prospects in the Napoleonic army. Although Captain Pradez of the 39th demi-brigade had but 'little knowledge', he 'made up for it by his great zeal'. His sheer bull-headed persistence ultimately won him the Legion of Honour.[10] Although knowledge of the military art was valued and technical mastery rewarded, Napoleon's inspectors esteemed certain intangible qualities of character more highly than formal instruction.

6   In the 32nd demi-brigade, for example, ten of the thirteen officers awarded retirement were veterans of the royal army. These were all middle-aged men, forty-five to fifty-five, who had joined the army as teenagers as much as three decades earlier. AG, X^b 253, 'Etat nominatif des officiers de la 32ème demi-brigade qui se sont trouvés sans emploi' (24 Pluviôse XI).

7   AG, X^c 253, General d'Hautpoul, 'Revue d'inspection, 8ème hussards' (1 Germinal X); and X^c 135, General Laboissière, 'Livret de revue, 2ème dragons' (10 Floréal X).

8   For an example, taken from the 8th Hussars, see AG, X^c 253, General d'Hautpoul, 'Ordre du clôture' (12 Germinal X).

9   AG, X^b 431, General Schauenbourg, 'Revue, 43ème demi-brigade' (30 Vendémiaire XIII).

10   AG, X^b 425, Général Vilatte, 'Etat nominatif des officiers' (13 Vendémiaire XIII).

What interested the inspectors particularly were described by one as 'social qualities', those personal attributes that gave bearing, suggested morality, and commanded respect.[11] Officers noted for their '*moeurs*', 'probity', or '*belle tenue*' could expect to be put forward for promotion.[12] But those officers in whom these qualities were conspicuously absent received little indulgence from the inspectors. Officers noted as failing to uphold 'the dignity of their *état*' or lacking in 'the appropriate sentiments' were summarily dismissed.[13]

Especially abhorrent to the inspectors were officers addicted to what was generally called 'crapulous' behavior. Usually indicating the 'habitual debauchery of women or wine', the term 'crapulous' could be used in a more general sense to denote anything '*vilain*'. Signifying the 'dirty, dishonourable, impure, miserable, [or] infamous', the word '*vilain*' had originally carried a social meaning, designating peasants, *roturiers*, and all other 'men of nothing'.[14] These unflattering social connotations suggest why the inspectors took such a dim view of tippling, games of chance, and fornication, activities which had always been part of military culture. In their eyes, the problem with the crapulous officer was not his pursuit of these vices *per se*, but rather their pursuit in public ways which compromised his dignity, blurred hierarchical relations, and engendered shameful social promiscuity.

The purge of crapulous officers from the 2nd dragoons brings out this nuance.[15] *Sous-lieutenant* Bazin, who had entered the royal army as a common soldier, was dismissed not only because he 'got drunk every day', but, more crucially, because he undermined his authority by drinking 'indistinctly with his subordinates and the most degenerate civilians provided that they paid'. One of his comrades in this particularly ill-behaved regiment, *sous-lieutenant* Delcot, was cashiered for 'getting publicly intoxicated in a café with a prostitute from the dregs of the people'. Another colleague, Lieutenant Nicot, was drummed out of the army for 'borrowing indiscriminately from his subordinates and the bourgeoisie'. Yet another, Lieutenant Colliquet, was removed for consorting with a prostitute, 'a crapulous girl from the gutter with whom he has often had scandalous scenes in the middle of the street'. Villette, still another lieutenant in the regiment, was purged for contracting a 'marriage unworthy of an officer'. By marrying a prostitute, he had forfeited the 'esteem of his comrades who tried everything to dissuade him from entering into this dishonourable union'. These examples suggest that, as much as the vice itself,

11 AG, X^b 134, 'Rapport de la 3ème division au ministère de la guerre' (25 Thermidor X).
12 AG, X^c 100, General Oudinot, 'Etat nominatif des officiers du 4ème cuirassiers' (13 Messidor XI).
13 AG, X^b 425, General Suchet, 'Rapport au ministre,' (1 Frimaire XII).
14 *Encyclopédie*, vol. 4, p. 435; and *Dictionnaire de l'Académie française*, 4th ed. (Paris, 1762), vol. 1, p. 236, and vol. 2, pp. 938–9.
15 The following is taken from two letters written by the regiment's commander, Colonel Pryvé, to the minister of war. AG, X^c 134, 15 Frimaire and 10 Prairial XII.

it was the public manner in which it was pursued that provoked the inspectors' wrath.

The inspectors' determination to remove officers whose misbehaviour compromised their hierarchical authority and personal dignity reflected the government's resolution to raise the prestige and social standing of the military profession. Although soldiers of modest social origin might eventually overcome their 'old *sous-officier* habits', the regime preferred to recruit officers directly from higher social strata.[16] As one superior officer of Old Regime *bourgeois* background put it, young men from good families were simply more 'capable of learning', while plebeian veterans were often set in their common ways. Efforts to improve these old warhorses, he pronounced, were hopeless, as futile as trying to 'scrub the colour from the face of a nigger'.[17]

Napoleon shared this assumption. A pragmatist who had long ago shed whatever revolutionary idealism he had once possessed, he put little store in the government's capacity to effect dramatic social transformations. Rather than try to mould new military elites from common social clay, he believed that the state's resources could be put to better use by 'taking existing fortunes and employing them in its service'.[18] Although he never reinstituted formal social exclusions, like the system of noble proofs which had limited access to the royal officer corps before 1789, Napoleon's constant penchant for officers from distinguished backgrounds reflected his conviction that useable talents were rare indeed at the lower echelons of society.[19]

This emerging social bias in the recruitment of the Napoleonic officer corps was reinforced by the growing emphasis on '*éducation*' as a requirement for promotion. Officers with a 'distinguished education' or 'a spirit cultivated by education' were singled out by the inspectors as likely candidates for superior rank.[20] Since no French citizen was legally barred from the new *lycées*, this emphasis on education formally respected the ideal of revolutionary meritocracy. In practice, however, secondary schooling was too costly for most families to afford. That, coupled with the failure of revolutionary attempts to institute free public schooling, kept education a privilege of the well-to-do. Scholarships were not entirely unknown, but the government's policy of offering the lion's share to the children of officers, judges, and other state servants – men typically wealthier and more educated than their fellow citizens – only confirmed the prevailing social inequalities. Several schools, known collectively as the *Prytanée français*, did provide a free education to orphans, the

16 AG, X^b 431, General Schauenbourg, 'Revue d'inspection du 43ème régiment' (30 Vendémiaire XIII).
17 J.-B.-A.-M. Marbot, *Mémoires du général baron de Marbot*, 2 vols (Paris, 1983), vol. 1, p. 134.
18 Quoted in Dansette, *Napoléon*, p. 187.
19 J.-P. Bertaud, 'Napoleon's Officers', *Past and Present* 112 (1986), p. 94.
20 These examples are drawn from AG, X^c 253, 'Bataillon complémentaire, 32ème demi-brigade d'infanterie de ligne' (IX).

sons of soldiers, and other children of the 'inferior classes'. But in keeping with Napoleon's belief in the futility of social engineering, these charity schools sought merely to give their students 'an education suited to their existence'. In the regime's global conception of its educational institutions, the *lycées* were intended to furnish France with lawyers, doctors, and officers, while the *Prytanée* would train skilled (and appropriately grateful) craftsmen.[21] Napoleonic education was not supposed to facilitate social mobility, but rather offered a politically acceptable means of perpetuating the existing social hierarchy.[22]

The regime's desire to raise the social level of the officer corps was also intended to restore a sound foundation to hierarchical subordination. Although they had won their spurs during the Revolution commanding citizen-soldiers, Napoleon and his inspectors recalled with admiration the precise gradations of the royal army in which a sharp 'line of demarcation' distinguished the officers from the common soldiers.[23] The Revolution, in their view, had gone too far in the opposite direction. In their reviews, the inspectors found subordination too relaxed and relations between the ranks too comfortable. Baraguey d'Hilliers described the state of discipline in the 83rd demi-brigade as 'very lax, very un-hierarchic', and expressed dismay at the 'great familiarity' between officers and their men.[24] General Suchet encountered such a lack of subordination in the 75th demi-brigade that he felt it necessary to harangue the officers: 'the interest and existence of the army', he intoned, 'is linked to discipline'. 'Passive obedience ought to link the inferior to superior.'[25]

Napoleon was determined to reinforce the military hierarchy. To sharpen gradations of rank in an army still infused with an air of civil equality, an army politically and socially unable to return to the genealogically-based distinctions of the Old Regime, it was imperative to find a new marker of difference capable of replacing noble status as the basis of the officer's authority. For Napoleon, this could only come from possession of a superior education, in his view the 'sole legitimate basis of inequality'.[26] But some officers, perhaps lacking Napoleon's more acute sense of the ambient political environment, were less tactful. Marshal Marmont, Napoleon's former classmate at the exclusively-noble royal military school at Brienne, was one of these. 'To prepare the structure of obedience', he wrote, it was necessary to reinforce the

21 Cited in Dansette, *Napoléon*, p. 238.
22 On the use of education as a social filter, see P. Bourdieu and J.-C. Passeron, *Reproduction in Education, Society, and Culture*, trans. R. Nice (London, 1977); and Bourdieu, *La noblesse d'état: grandes écoles et esprit de corps*, (Paris, 1989).
23 AN, AF IV 1115, 'Réflexions sur l'avancement' (n.d.).
24 AG, X^b 298, Baraguey d'Hilliers, 'Revue d'inspection' (15 Prairial XI).
25 AG, X^b 260, Suchet, 'Revue d'inspection' (13 Thermidor XI), and AG, X^b 293, Suchet, 'Revue d'inspection' (5 Prairial X).
26 Quoted in Dansette, *Napoléon*, p. 288.

officer's authority with not only 'instruction', but also 'illustrious birth' and 'elevated social position'.[27]

Enhancing the social composition of the officer corps also served political and administrative ends. Destined (as in the Old Regime) to occupy prominent places in the Imperial Court, in the foreign service, and in local government, the officers required what Napoleon termed 'civil qualities'.[28] The 'military character' of the Consular (and later Imperial) Court was unmistakable. The upper reaches of the officer corps furnished many of its highest dignitaries, like General Duroc (*grand maréchal du palais*), Marshal Berthier (*grand veneur*), and General Caulaincourt (*grand écuyer*).[29] Other officers, like *chef de brigade* Colbert, a descendant of Louis XIV's minister, were employed by the regime in diplomacy.[30] Although only the most prominent and best-connected officers were named to these positions, military men of more modest social rank were frequently tapped to serve in the local civil administration. According to Louis Bergeron, Guy Chaussinand-Nogaret, and Robert Forster, they constituted a 'sort of reservoir on which state and society drew to exercise private as well as administrative activities'.[31] The prefectoral corps took more than thirty per cent of its personnel from the military. Nearly sixty officers served as mayors of major French cities.[32] And in every department military men were present in the broad Napoleonic elite, the *notabilité*. Over two thousand officers became *notables*.[33] To underline the pre-eminence of the military, the regulations on precedence placed officers ahead of civilian officials in official ceremonies.[34] As leading representatives of the new regime, the officers' 'private conduct' was closely scrutinized by the government to ensure that it reflected the public dignity with which they were entrusted. To this end, the government monitored military marriages by gathering information on the 'persons, fortune, and family' of prospective brides.[35] These sustained efforts to raise the social standing of the

27 Marshal Marmont, duc de Ragusse, *The Spirit of Military Institutions*, trans. F. Schaller (Westport, CT, 1974 [reprint from 1864 edition]), p. 228.

28 A.-C. Thibeaudau, *Bonaparte and the Consulate*, trans. G.K. Fortescue (New York, 1908), p. 140.

29 P. Mansel, *The Court of France, 1789–1830* (Cambridge, 1988), p. 57. Mansel may overstate the contrast between the military tone of the Imperial Court and the civilian ethos of Versailles before the Revolution.

30 *Correspondance de Napoléon Ier, publiée par ordre de l'empéreur Napoléon III*, 32 vols (Paris, 1858), vol. 8, pp. 298–9.

31 L. Bergeron, G. Chaussinand-Nogaret, and R. Forster, 'Les notables du 'Grand Empire' en 1810', *Annales : E.S.C.*, 26 (1971), 1066.

32 Bertaud, 'Napoleon's Officers', pp. 109–10. Bergeron, Chaussinand-Nogaret, and Forster note that the military officers represented the second largest professional category (after *agriculteurs* and *fermiers*) from which the mayors were recruited.

33 L. Bergeron and G. Chaussinand-Nogaret, *Les 'masses de granit': cent mille notables du Premier Empire*, (Paris, 1979), pp. 42–3.

34 J.-P. Bertaud, 'La "petite guerre" des honneurs sous Napoléon', *L'histoire*, 66 (1984), pp. 64–70.

35 AG, X^c 98, General Ney, 'Revue, 4ème cavalerie' (14 Ventôse X); and AG, X^b 260, General Suchet, 'Inspection, 39ème demi-brigade' (13 Thermidor XI). See also, AN, 138 AP 17, Daru, 'Observations sur les marriages des militaires' (n.d.).

officer corps and assign it a prominent role within the regime suggest that the Napoleonic seizure of power, far from ensuring the triumph of the bourgeoisie as some have argued, actually initiated the attempt to achieve a more complex social settlement based on the reconciliation of the potentially conflicting values of wealth, family, and service.[36]

To add new lustre to the social composition of the officer corps, it was not enough to purge the aged, infirm, crapulous, and plebeian. It was also necessary to encourage young men from good families to join the officer corps, something they had been reluctant to do during the years of republican rule. To make military careers more attractive to such people, Napoleon reinstituted the practice – which had been abolished by the Convention as perpetuating the germ of aristocracy – of granting them direct officer commissions. He believed that as long as an extreme republican conception of equality continued to determine officer recruitment policy – forcing everyone to begin their service as simple soldiers – the right kind of people would continue to reject the military profession. Only direct access to officer rank, distinction from the soldiery, and a head start up the ladder of advancement could persuade elite families to send their sons into the military profession.

Napoleon also conceived of direct officer recruitment as a means to achieve his overriding political ambition: the revival of monarchical authority and the creation of a dynasty that would continue to flourish after the death of its founder. Already in year VIII, the new constitution had empowered him to 'name and dismiss' officers (article 41), as well as bestow 'national awards' on military merit (article 87). These prerogatives provided the First Consul with a potent means of attaching entire families to his regime. Through his control over nominations to the officer corps, elites would grow accustomed to 'seeing only [Napoleon] as remunerator'.[37] A monarchical ethos of reciprocity – based on the exchange of social distinction for service – would once again join the upper echelons of French society to their sovereign.[38]

While committed to restoring a monarchical polity in France, Napoleon never broke openly with the meritocratic principles of 1789. In the regime's efforts at direct officer recruitment, no formal exclusions were pronounced and young men from all walks of life continued to win commissions. But in his quest to revive monarchical authority, Napoleon shunned meritocratic institutions antithetical to the concentration of power in his own hands. This is why he rejected proposals to recruit officers by competitive examination: it

---

36 For a discussion of this attempted fusion, see my article 'The *Ancien Régime* Origins of Napoleonic Social Policy', *French History* 14 (2001), pp. 408–23.

37 Miot de Mélito, *Mémoires* (Paris, 1858), vol. 1, p. 309.

38 J. M. Smith has discussed the evolution of absolutist traditions of monarchical-noble reciprocity during the Old Regime in his book, *The Culture of Merit: Nobility, Royal Service, and the Making of Absolute Monarchy in France, 1600–1789* (Ann Arbor, 1996).

would deprive him of the indispensable monarchical prerogative of nomination. In Napoleon's view, the advocates of examination were overlooking 'essential considerations' and 'entirely misunderstood the political objects at which we ought to aim'. The 'important point', he insisted, was that 'the government should have the means of recompensing the family of a deceased soldier or civil servant who has done good service, or of rewarding a deserving servant of the state during his lifetime'. 'Do you not think', he asked with barely concealed sarcasm, 'that this object altogether outweighs the advantage of rewarding boys who are able to satisfy the examiners that they know a little Latin and the four rules of arithmetic?'[39] During his fifteen-year reign, Napoleon would use his control over military appointments not to revive exclusive privileges, but rather to reconstruct a monarchical political order. The ideals of 1789 would be formally respected. Meritocracy would be preserved, but at the same time transformed into an engine of monarchical centralization.[40]

The war (and perhaps also Napoleon's political prudence) ensured that it would be several years, however, before centralized institutions of direct officer recruitment could be created. But soon after the Brumaire coup, unit commanders began, without formal authorization, to award commissions to young men from good families. In year VIII, for example, Mathieu Dumas, an Old Regime military noble charged with raising a reserve cavalry corps, bestowed officer rank on 'volunteers from the best families who clothed, mounted, and equipped themselves at their own cost'. This *belle jeunesse* included some of the most illustrious names of the former Second Estate: Ségur, Lameth, Choisy, and others.[41] At the same time, in the regular army, commanders also began to entice young men from well-connected families to join up by offering them accelerated promotion to officer rank. Jean-Baptiste-Antoine-Marcelin Marbot, a general's son, was commissioned in the 1st Hussars after just one year of service. Although he figured as a soldier in the regiment's muster rolls, Marbot enjoyed preferential treatment and minimal duties. Even though regulations assigned two soldiers to a bed, for example, he was allotted a bed of his own in the *sous-officiers'* quarters.[42] Others from similar backgrounds also received special treatment. Jean-Augustin-Michel Rampon, great-nephew of a serving general and future Imperial senator, was promoted rapidly to officer rank on the strength of his assurance that he

39 Thibeaudau, *Bonaparte and the Consulate*, p. 104.
40 Tocqueville made a similar observation in the notes he compiled for the projected sequel to *The Old Regime and the French Revolution*. In a revealing passage, he described how public offices, 'rendered revocable, hierarchized, and locked into the grand system of centralization', served to place 'all citizens under the hand of the central power and all those who possessed them in its strict and daily dependence'. *Oeuvres complètes*, ed. J. P. Mayer, 18 vols (Paris, 1951–98), vol. 2, *L'ancien régime et la Révolution: fragments et notes inédites sur la Révolution*, p. 316.
41 M. Dumas, *Souvenirs*, 3 vols (Paris, 1839), vol. 3, p. 178.
42 Marbot, *Mémoires*, vol. 1, pp. 54–88.

would 'follow in the footsteps of his great-uncle'.[43] When an aspirant could cite no hereditary traditions of military service, his family's wealth, social standing, and connections were often enough to secure a commission. Marc Vaucour, for example, received a commission because he possessed 'a certain *aisance* which would enable him to maintain himself honourably'.[44] In their social status, connections to the regime, and family traditions of military service, Marbot, Rampon, and Vaucour were typical of the kind of people that the regime would seek to bind to itself through the reinstitution of direct officer recruitment. In the commanding ranks of the army, the scion of the 'ancient military family', the 'nephew of the mayor', and the son of the 'rich landowner' would coalesce into a new elite of state service and dynastic loyalty.[45]

Although these unregulated practices would eventually furnish eighteen per cent of all direct officer nominees in the Napoleonic armies, they soon came under heavy criticism. Some observers felt that these methods risked seeing the officer corps 'perpetually recompose itself through the favouritism of generals or family members'.[46] Although Napoleon (true to the presuppositions of the Old Regime military culture in which he had been raised) certainly wanted to encourage hereditary military vocations and the growth of a family spirit within the regiments, he also disapproved of these anarchic expedients, mainly because they challenged his own power over nomination and threatened to create networks of military clientage in which he had no part. Moreover, he feared that these appointments, based primarily on favouritism, would be seen as 'an injustice by the rank and file'.[47] Soldiers would respect an officer who had proven himself on the field of battle or even in the classroom. But the revolutionary experience had amply demonstrated how soldiers might respond to officers who had no legitimate title to authority in their eyes.[48] Only a superior education and formal military instruction, Napoleon believed, could give untested young men authority over seasoned troops.[49]

Napoleon put this view into practice on 11 Floréal X (30 April 1802) with

43 AG, X^b 411, 'Lettre de Darricau au ministre de la guerre' (29 Ventôse XIII).
44 AG, X^c 134, 'Rapport fait au ministre de la guerre' (XIII).
45 AG, X° 9, 'Rapport présenté à l'Empereur' (7 Fructidor XIII).
46 *Correspondence de deux généraux sur divers sujets, publiée par le citoyen T**** (Paris, IX/1801), pp. 33–4.
47 Quoted in Dansette, *Napoléon*, p. 288. On the recruitment of 'sons of active citizens', young men from good families named directly to the officer corps to fill the vacancies left by émigré nobles, see ch. 3 of my forthcoming book, *The French Army, 1750–1820*.
48 The best treatment of the waves of insubordination that rocked the French army at the beginning of the Revolution can be found in S. F. Scott, *The Response of the Royal Army to the French Revolution: The Role and Development of the Line Army, 1787–1793* (Oxford, 1978), pp. 81–123.
49 P.-L. Roederer, *Mémoires sur la Révolution, le Consulat, et l'Empire*, ed. Octave Aubry (Paris, 1942), p. 142.

the opening of a new military school, the *École spéciale militaire*.[50] By 1814, it had furnished the army with over four thousand officers.[51] By enabling him to place such large numbers of young men in military careers, the school gave Napoleon his first and most potent means of building an elite of state service beholden to his regime, of 'attaching fathers to the government through their sons'.[52]

Analysis of their letters of application reveal that elites understood this to be the principal political function of the new school and that they had mastered the rhetoric attached to the monarchical ideal of reciprocity – faithful service for honorific recompense – that Napoleon sought to foster. Writing on behalf of his son, General Schauenbourg, who had begun his career as an officer during the Old Regime, promised that a favourable response would provide a 'new incentive for me to increase, if possible, my zeal for the service and my great devotion to the person of the Emperor'.[53] The prospect of a place at the military school could also encourage elite families which had never served the state to cast their lot with the new regime. Asking for a place for his son, a lawyer named Morlac assured Napoleon that, if granted, his whole family 'would never forget that it was from your hand' that this precious gift had come.[54] The importance of military education in reviving a monarchical ethos of reciprocity binding social elites to their new sovereign cannot be overstated. Indeed, it was precisely because of its intimate link with the monarchical ideal of the polity that the Convention had abolished formal military education in September 1793.[55]

In other ways, however, Napoleonic military education differed fundamentally from its Old Regime predecessor. Unlike the royal military school, which was reserved for *gentilshommes* until early 1790 and for the sons of officers thereafter, the *École spéciale militaire* respected the ideal of the career open to talents. Neither plebeian birth nor civilian profession constituted a formal barrier to admission. If a family could pay the annual tuition of 1,200 francs, its son was eligible for a military education. And indeed, sons of émigrés and revolutionary officers, *parlementaires* and lawyers, *seigneurs* and *propriétaires* all rubbed shoulders at the school, making it one of the most

50 Loi sur l'instruction publique … décidant en outre l'établissement d'une École spéciale militaire, (11 Floréal X). First housed in the château at Fontainebleau, the school was moved to Saint-Cyr in 1808.

51 G. Bodinier, 'Du soldat républicain à l'officier impérial: convergences et divergences entre l'armée et la société', in A. Corvisier (ed.), Histoire militaire de la France, vol. 2, De 1715 à 1871, ed. Jean Delmas, p. 295.

52 Roederer speaking before the Legislative Body on 11 Floréal X, Archives Parlementaires, series 2, vol. 3, p. 572.

53 AN, AF IV 1148ᵇ, 'Lettre et mémoire du général de division Schauenbourg au ministre de la guerre' (12 February 1808).

54 AN, F¹⁷ 6756, 'Lettre de Morlac, avocat' (2 August 1808).

55 For a more developed discussion of republican attitudes toward military education, see ch. 4 of my forthcoming book, The French Army, 1750–1820.

important Napoleonic theatres of political reconciliation and elite formation.[56] Fully one-third of the students were related through blood or clientage
to the *grands notables*, an indication that an even higher percentage were similarly linked to the lesser *notabilité*.[57]

Although no group was formally barred from admission, the school's
political function and the substantial tuition payments demanded ensured
that all but the prominent and wealthy would effectively be excluded.
Families of *propriétaires* accounted for eleven per cent of the students, business, manufacturing, and banking families another eleven per cent, and the
liberal professions six per cent. Peasants and artisans were almost totally
absent, the latter group represented solely by the most prestigious trades
(jewellery, clockmaking, bookselling, etc.). Within this elite student body,
service families were over-represented in comparison with the general
Napoleonic *notabilité*. Civil servants, thirty-four per cent of the *notables*,
accounted for nearly forty-seven per cent of the students. And while only
2.35 per cent of *notables* were military men, 23.4 per cent of the students were
the sons of officers, making the military the largest single socio-professional
group from which the school recruited. In all, seventy per cent of the students
came from families serving in the administrative, judicial, or military institutions of the regime. This pronounced preference for service suggests the ideal
toward which Napoleonic social policies were striving.[58]

As mentioned above, letters of application and recommendation – devot-
ing more attention to the service records of fathers and uncles than the qualifications of applicants – testify to the revival of an ethos of hereditary service
among Napoleonic elites. These recognized that family traditions of service
were the most effective key to unlocking the gates of the military school. For
example, the Courville boys, children of a naval officer, boasted that their
'family has consecrated itself to the service of the state from time immemorial'
and that they desired admission in order to 'follow in the footsteps of their

56 Figures on the social composition of Napoleonic military schooling given in this paragraph are
   based on the 1,184 students whose socio-professional backgrounds are indicated in AG, 4 Y^b
   31–32, 'Registre de contrôle: Ecole spéciale militaire'. Comparative figures on the *notables* are
   from Bergeron and Chaussinand-Nogaret, *Les 'masses de granit'*, p. 43.
57 Generally, the *grands notables* were those who figured on the lists of the thirty highest-taxed,
   sixty highest-taxed, and sixty 'most distinguished by their fortune and their public and private
   virtues'. For this calculation, I used the series of works on the *grands notables* edited by Bergeron
   and Chaussinand-Nogaret.
58 The government's bias in favour of public service, particularly of the military kind, was even
   more pronounced in its scholarship policy. Of those admitted to the *École spéciale militaire*, nearly
   fifty per cent of military families and twenty per cent of judicial and administrative families were
   granted *bourses*. Scholarships were also used to attach non-service families to the regime,
   although much less frequently. Only ten per cent of commercial and financial families and five
   per cent of landowning families received such aid. Despite the small proportion of scholarships
   devoted to non-service families, the fact that they received any assistance at all indicates that
   Napoleon viewed military education not merely as a means of recompensing state service, but
   also as a way of bringing new groups into his service elite. AG, 4 Y^b31–2.

ancestors'.[59] Another applicant, Ponsort, emphasized his family's 'constant devotion to the profession of arms'. His lineage, he explained with pride, had even produced a 'de Ponsort who, during the League, had maintained the cities of Chalons and Soissons in obedience to Henri IV'.[60] Seeking to obtain places for her four sons, 'all destined for the career of arms', the widow Lafitte noted that 'for many centuries, the authors of their days have distinguished themselves in this career' and promised that her 'children will make themselves worthy of them'.[61]

Although military service was clearly perceived by applicants as one of the most compelling arguments they could advance in their quest for places at the school, they did not hesitate to invoke family traditions of civil service whenever possible. As well as detailing the services of his maternal grandfather, a general in the former royal army, Cugnon d'Allincourt also described in great detail the 'important services' that his other grandfather had 'rendered in the civil order'.[62] Writing on behalf of her youngest son, Madame Chaurand emphasized 'the constant service' of her first-born, 'who, during the recent events of Saint-Domingue, had been employed in the civil administration ... and had the honour of dying at his post'.[63] Under Napoleon, an established pattern of family service – and, better still, death in the service – was clearly perceived by place seekers as constituting the strongest title to the bounty of the state.

Nonetheless, an hereditary tradition of service was not absolutely necessary to obtain a place at the military school. Candidates lacking such credentials were often able to ensure successful candidacies by invoking their families' stature, alliances, and wealth. The young Daubenton won admission because he was the 'nephew of the famous naturalist'. A candidate named Boilly secured a place because he was the son of the 'distinguished painter and a close relative of M. Arnault, member of the Institute'.[64] For an applicant named Martinez, it was enough to be 'honoured by the benevolence of Her Majesty the Empress' to gain admission to the school.[65] Even in the absence of service credentials, an illustrious name, or potent patronage, applicants could still effect successful candidacies simply by citing their family's fortune as a title to consideration. Bouire-Beauvallon, whose father claimed an income of four hundred thousand francs, was one student who owed the

---

59 AN, F¹⁷ 7140, 'Lettre de Millot de Fontaines, chef de bureau à la marine, tuteur des mineurs de Courville, à Fontanes' (14 July 1810).
60 AN, F¹⁷ 6756, 'Note sur la profession et le service des parents du jeune de Ponsort' (10 June 1810).
61 AN, F¹⁷ 6761, 'Lettre de Lafitte, née Coufitte, à Fontanes' (n.d.).
62 AN, F¹⁷ 6760, Presentation slip for Cugnon d'Allincourt.
63 AN, F¹⁷ 6756, 'Lettre de madame Chauraud à Fourcroy' (28 July 1808).
64 AN, F¹⁷ 6757, Presentation slips for Daubenton and Boilly.
65 AN, F¹⁷ 6757, Presentation slip for Martinez.

success of his demand to wealth alone.[66] Such examples show that Napoleon not only conceived of military education as a way of maintaining vocations of hereditary service in families where they were already well established, but also as a way of initiating these traditions in strata of the elite which had never served the state before.

Despite the government's desire to integrate civilian elites into the renascent culture of state service, they remained under represented at the military school throughout Napoleon's rule. This should not, however, be interpreted as evidence of disinterest, revulsion, or even political opposition on their part. Rather, it reflected the fact that the capacity of the school was permanently stretched to its limits. Even efforts to increase the output of the system of military schooling – such as radically truncating the programme of instruction and creating a second school (devoted exclusively to forming cavalry officers) at Saint-Germain-en-Laye – failed to meet the demands of war and the ambitions of the Napoleonic elite.

Applicants frustrated in their desire to attend the school were not, however, forgotten by the regime. They were encouraged to participate in other institutions of direct officer recruitment. Of these, the most efficient in producing new officers were the *vélites*, training corps for future officers attached to the Imperial Guard. Created in year XII, they gave families with less pronounced wealth, influence, and service records a way to gain direct commissions for their sons. Moreover, offering one's son to the *vélites* not only demonstrated loyalty to the regime, but also saved the young man from conscription.

To become a *vélite*, a young man had to be physically fit and rich enough to pay for his own upkeep – two hundred francs a year, according to the regulations. The relative modesty of this fee ensured that access to the *vélites* would be open to a wider social spectrum than could hope to enter the military school. Although the sons of a few generals, Old Regime nobles, administrators, and judges opted for the *vélites*, most were recruited from civilian, non-service backgrounds.[67] Less than twenty per cent came from families involved in the civil service: 12.3 per cent were from the judiciary, 5.3 per cent from the administration, and a mere 1.5 per cent from the military. The rest were from families which could claim no records of state service whatsoever.

The *vélites* were generally of more modest social condition than students at the military school. More than half of the student body came from

66 AN, F¹⁷ 6757, Presentation slip for Bouire-Beauvallon.
67 Socio-professional data are taken from a sample of 1,237 foot-grenadier *vélites*. AG, 20 Yᶜ 12, 'Grenadiers à pied: vélites'. It is likely that the mounted *vélite* units recruited from more distinguished families than the foot unit analyzed here. Unfortunately, however, socio-professional information was not recorded for these units.

property-holding backgrounds. Forty-six per cent appear in the muster rolls as *propriétaires* and *rentiers*, presumably families that lived off rent and investment income, neither working for a living nor exercising a public function. This large contingent of what in contemporaneous England might have been called the landed gentry was accompanied by a more compact group (ten per cent) of apparently less wealthy and more industrious landowners – *agriculteurs*, *laboureurs*, *fermiers*, and *vignerons*. The remaining twenty-five per cent of *vélites* came from the world of commerce (thirteen per cent), the liberal professions (five per cent), and the artisanate (seven per cent). In all, the 1,799 *vélites* who passed from the corps to *sous-lieutenances* in the regular army accounted for twenty-seven per cent of all directly-commissioned officers.

As is well-known, Napoleon attached great importance to rallying Old Regime nobles to his regime. One of the ways he sought to do this was by naming their sons directly to the officer corps. He awarded commissions to young men from illustrious French families – including a Castellane, a Talleyrand-Périgord, a Latour d'Auvergne, and two Montesquieu-Fezensacs – on the strength of their name alone. The same honours were also accorded to young foreign grandees – including a Hesse-Darmstadt, a Radziwill, and a brace of Hohenzollerns.[68] Napoleon also formed two new units, the quasi-proprietary La Tour-Maubourg and Issembourg regiments, to provide nobles 'who had served against their country in the emigration' with a chance to redeem themselves by serving his regime as officers. These regiments also took in as officers men 'whose service would bind influential families to the government' and young military nobles who 'did not have any service'.[69]

Napoleon's most successful attempt to recruit young men distinguished by their 'education, birth, and taste for the military' was the formation in 1806 of the *Gendarmes d'ordonnance*, a regiment inspired by the Old Regime *Gendarmerie*.[70] To give it particular lustre, Napoleon enlisted some of the most brilliant names of the Old Regime, including a Montmorency, a Monaco, and a Savoie-Carignan, to serve as officers.[71] To reinforce its exclusive social tone, aspirants had to equip themselves at an estimated cost of 1,800 francs and pay six hundred francs annual upkeep.[72] To encourage recruitment, the departmental prefects were directed to solicit, hat in hand, the cooperation of the most prominent families within their departments. But families possessing sufficiently blue-blooded ancestry, established service

68 For an excellent discussion of this practice, see A. de Montesquieu-Fezensac, *Souvenirs sur la Révolution, l'Empire, la Restauration, et le règne de Louis-Philippe* (Paris, 1961).
69 AG, X^h 8, 'Rapport à l'Empereur' (19 March 1806). Information on the personnel in these units is found in AG, X^h 8 and 11, and 2 Y^b 1115–17 and 1123–24.
70 AN, F⁹ 1033, 'Lettre du conseil d'administration du corps de MM les Gendarmes d'ordonnance à pied de Sa Majesté l'Empereur et Roi à M. le préfet du Lot et Garonne' (19 February 1807).
71 AN, F⁹ 1032, 'Formation du corps de la Gendarmerie d'ordonnance à cheval' (n.d.).
72 AN, F⁹ 1032, 'Lettre de Kellermann au ministre de l'intérieur' (10 November 1806); and 'Lettre de Kellermann au ministre de l'intérieur' (7 April 1807).

traditions, and enough money, however, were difficult to find in some departments. The prefect of the Creuse informed the Minister of the Interior that, while several families from the 'agricultural class' had expressed interest in the *Gendarmerie d'ordonnance*, they were unfortunately not 'worthy by their education and fortune of the honour of serving in such a favoured manner'.[73] Other prefects, like those of the Ain, Aveyron, and Correze, were unable to provide any recruits at all because the handful of eligible families had already sent their sons to the military school.[74] In the richer departments, however, '*rentiers, commerçants, propriétaires*, and *ci-devant privilegiés*' flocked to the corps to demonstrate 'their devotion to the service of His Majesty'.[75] Many Old Regime nobles joined up as simple *gendarmes*: Vergennes, Albignac, Saint-Pern, Forbin, and Salm-Salm among them.[76] Nearly half of the approximately four hundred *gendarmes* bore names with the particule. While not a firm indication of veritable noble ancestry, the ubiquity of the particule in the muster rolls of the new *Gendarmerie* was an unmistakable sign of its aristocratic pretensions.

Despite these attempts to raise the social tone of the military profession by recruiting sons of notables directly as officers, the regime could never break its dependence on the promotion of soldiers from the ranks to maintain the regimental cadres at full strength. Such advancement, sometimes awarded on the battlefield by Napoleon himself, is largely responsible for perpetuating the myth that the regime's meritocratic commitment extended equally to all echelons of the social hierarchy.[77] But Napoleon was only a reluctant practitioner of this revolutionary tradition. He would have much preferred that 'soldiers become officers only with great difficulty' and in no circumstances account for more than one-quarter of the cadre in any given regiment.[78] Napoleon's confidant, Daru, recommended limiting this proportion even more drastically, to one in six.[79] In practice, however, the constant bloodletting of war prevented the government from even approaching these proportions. Even at their peak performance in 1809, the military school, *vélites*, *Gendarmerie d'ordonnance*, and all other institutions of direct officer recruitment together accounted for only forty-three per cent of newly-commissioned officers.[80]

73 AN, F⁹ 1033, 'Lettre du préfet de la Creuse au ministre de l'intérieur' (28 November 1806).
74 AN, F⁹ 1033, 'Lettre du préfet de l'Ain au ministre de l'Intérieur' (28 November 1806); 'Lettre du préfet de l'Aveyron au ministre de l'Intérieur' (5 December 1806); and 'Lettre du préfet de la Correze au ministre de l'Intérieur' (27 November 1806).
75 AN, F⁹ 1033, 'Lettre du préfet de la Loire Inférieure au ministre de l'intérieur' (1 June 1807).
76 AG, 20 Yᶜ 134, 'Gendarmes d'ordonnance à pied et à cheval.'
77 For a good description, see Philippe-Paul, *comte* de Ségur, *Napoleon's Russian Campaign*, trans. J. D. Townsend (Alexandria,VA, 1965), p. 4.
78 Quoted in Dansette, *Napoléon*, p. 289.
79 AN, 138 AP 15, Daru, 'Officiers et sous-officiers d'infanterie et de troupes à cheval' (n.d.).
80 This figure is based on the personnel records of the following regiments at the AG: 3rd infantry (Xᵇ 347–8), 43rd infantry (Xᵇ 431–2), 44th infantry (Xᵇ 433–4), 4th cuirassiers (Xᶜ 100), and 2nd dragoons (Xᶜ 135).

Gilbert Bodinier has estimated that no less than seventy-seven per cent of all *sous-lieutenants* commisioned between 1802 and 1814 had begun their military careers as simple soldiers.[81] While taken by Bodinier as clear evidence of the failure of Napoleonic attempts to raise the social level of the officer corps, this raw figure cannot be accepted at face value. Although it suggests that soldiers promoted from the ranks dominated the officer corps, it actually says nothing about their subsequent advancement, nor, consequently, their relative weight in the superior ranks of the army, both at the head of regiments and in critical staff positions. In fact, *sous-lieutenants* risen from the ranks found themselves at a great disadvantage in the competition for advancement with those who had entered the officer corps directly. The former soldiers often received their commissions only after many years of service. They thus began their careers as officers later in life than the graduates of military schools, *vélites*, *gendarmes*, and others of their kind. This temporal lag was exacerbated by seniority requirements for promotion to the ranks of lieutenant and captain – the next, indispensable rungs on the ladder of the military hierarchy – that ensured that the former rankers would fall behind a further six years. Because of their initial handicap and these seniority requirements, officers who had begun their military careers as soldiers would necessarily arrive at superior rank – if they arrived at all – at a relatively advanced age.

In practice, the regime rarely promoted such officers higher than the grade of captain. As the existing Thermidorian and Directorial laws on advancement – those of 14 Germinal III and 18 Nivôse IV – already gave the executive control of promotions above the rank of captain, Napoleon did not need new authority to establish a glass ceiling between the lower and upper echelons of the officer corps. An examination of the professional destinies of captains who had been serving at that rank when Napoleon seized power reveals the existence of this invisible, unacknowledged barrier. The experience of the 138 captains serving in a sample of six infantry demi-brigades in year VIII shows that personnel who had begun their military careers with a commission enjoyed a substantially greater chance of promotion to superior rank than their peers who had entered the army as common soldiers.[82] Twenty-five per cent of those who had been elected directly to officer rank at the formation of their National Guard volunteer battalion would eventually be promoted to a superior grade. Thirty-three per cent of those who had embarked upon their military careers with a direct commission in the regular army could expect the same kind of advancement. In contrast, only three per

81 G. Bodinier, 'Du soldat républicain à l'officier impérial', p. 294.
82 This sample was based on the following sources at the AG: 3rd (2 Y^b 119–21 and 2 Y^b 401), 32nd (2 Y^b 221–5), 39th (2 Y^b 252–6), 43rd (2 Y^b 267–70), 44th (2 Y^b 271–5), and 75th (2 Y^b 375–8).

cent of captains who had first enlisted in the army as common soldiers received any further promotion. Former rankers may have dominated the subaltern ranks (*sous-lieutenant*, lieutenant, and captain), but they certainly did not dominate the officer corps. Without pronouncing any formal distinctions between different categories of officers, Napoleon had succeeded in dividing the military profession into two classes.

The superior officers thus formed both a professional and social elite. A significant minority were the sons of Old Regime nobles, vaulted to high rank by a regime eager to rally to its cause the illustrious names of the former monarchy. In the six regiments sampled above, for example, one finds among the superior officers a Custine, a Faudoas, a Coetlosquet, a Carignan, and an Adobrandini-Borghese. Others, fully one-quarter of the total, were *grands notables*, the cream of the Napoleonic elite.[83] Of course, some of these – like Pierre-François-Jean-Gaston Bisson, son of a lowly drum-major who had been raised in his father's regiment as an *enfant du corps* – had achieved professional and social prominence by dint of their own efforts.[84] However, most of the superior officers of the *grand notabilité* were not self-made men, but rather, had mobilized their family's social connections and wealth to advance their military careers. Typical of such officers was Emmanuel Attanoux. Son of the *bourgeois co-seigneur* of Roquebrune in Provence, Attanoux used his family's influence to win election as captain of a local National Guard volunteer battalion in 1791.[85] Napoleon sought to consolidate the superior officers' social position through the liberal distribution of titles in his new nobility. Of the 144 superior officers in my six demi-brigade sample, seventy-nine (fifty-five per cent) were ennobled: three as counts, forty-three as barons, and thirty-three as chevaliers.

Napoleon's *de facto* division of the officer corps into two classes – those, directly-commissioned, who would occupy the superior ranks and those, promoted from the common mass of soldiery, who could at best hope to wind down their long careers as captains – set the pattern for the nineteenth-century French officer corps. Had the Empire not succumbed in 1815, military school graduates, *vélites*, *gendarmes d'ordonnance*, and other directly-commissioned officers would have furnished the next generation of military leaders, once the last warhorses of the Revolution had faded into the sunset. Even with the demise of the regime and the subsequent attempts of the Bourbons to fill the army with its supporters, Napoleon's directly-commis-

83 For this estimate, the superior officers from the six-regiment sample detailed in footnote 82 have been cross-referenced with the series on the *grands notables* published by Bergeron and Chaussinand-Nogaret. Officers from departments not covered in the series were excluded from the calculation.

84 M. Vitte, 'Saône et Loire', Bergeron and Chaussinand-Nogaret (eds), *Grands notables*, vol. 16, p. 63.

85 F. d'Agay, 'Var', *Grands notables*, vol. 18, pp. 188–9.

sioned officers still made their presence felt at the highest ranks of the army. A survey of the professional destinies of the first five hundred graduates of the *École spéciale militaire* confirms their importance.[86] Of the 229 who survived the Napoleonic wars and remained in the military after 1815, 161 (seventy per cent) rose above the rank of captain. Of these, forty-three became generals and 118 superior officers. Far from tampering with the bifurcated career structure Napoleon had created, the Bourbons reinforced it through their institutional reforms and personnel practices. Although only one-third of officers recruited between 1815 and 1870 had graduated from the military school, they almost monopolized the upper ranks. On the eve of the Franco-Prussian War, they accounted for three-quarters of all superior officers in the army. Their predominance was even more palpable at the rank of general and in staff positions.[87] Napoleon had succeeded in creating a professional structure which, by preserving social gradations without pronouncing formal social exclusions, offered a way to resolve the tension between equality of opportunity and hierarchical selection inherent in the revolutionary idea of careers open to talent – and, indeed, in every meritocratic system of social distinction.

Changes in the social recruitment of the officer corps after Brumaire were less a reflection of a new, specifically Napoleonic understanding of the qualities that constituted military merit than a byproduct of the new regime's overriding, monarchical ambitions. Napoleon's initial attempts to streamline the officer corps illustrate the extent to which his policies remained faithful to earlier notions of merit held by the military reformers of the Thermidorian Convention and Directory. By removing the ageing, physically incapacitated, incompetent, and immoral in the purges of years VIII–X, Napoleon did little more than carry through to completion a programme of military rejuvenation already envisioned – and partially executed – before his seizure of power. And, as in Thermidorian and Directorial reconfigurations of the officer corps, political criteria played little role in decisions to retain or retire officers. If an officer possessed energy, intelligence, experience, expertise, bravery, and probity, Napoleon's inspectors were just as willing to overlook his political views as had been republican reformers like Carnot, Dubois-Crancé, and Aubry. In his initial steps toward greater military professionalism, Napoleon merely extended the later Republic's efforts to base officer selection on what Howard Brown has termed 'impersonal criteria' and 'bureaucratic screening'.[88]

86   AG, X° 9, 'Ecole spéciale militaire de Fontainebleau: Etat nominatif des élèves du no. 1 au no. 500 et leur position au 1er janvier 1847'.
87   P. Chalmin, *L'officier français de 1815 à 1870* (Paris, 1957), p. 370.
88   H. G. Brown, 'Politics, Professionalism, and the Fate of Army Generals after Thermidor', *French Historical Studies* 19 (1995), pp. 133–52. The preceding discussion of Thermidorian and Directorial conceptions of military merit is based on this article.

But as Napoleon moved to establish a dynasty, the qualities he sought in officers began to change. To an extent, this shift reflected the return of the older notions of hereditary vocation which had led Old Regime military reformers to encourage the father-to-son recruitment of the officer corps.[89] But beyond this, it was an unintended – although probably unavoidable – consequence of Napoleon's attempt to preserve the meritocratic ideals of 1789 within a monarchical political framework. Initially, meritocracy and monarchy were complementary goals, for both were predicated on inequality. The hierarchical nature of early revolutionary meritocracy, so energetically denounced by egalitarian republicans, was not inherently incompatible with the social gradations of a monarchical polity. Indeed, Napoleon believed that to build his monarchical power, it was necessary to revive a vigorous system of meritocratic distinctions. Only by bestowing places, riches, and honours on exemplary public functionaries, he reasoned, could he constitute a loyal elite capable of serving and perpetuating his dynasty. Over time, however, the monarchical ethic of reciprocity was bound to subvert the principle of careers open talent by forcing the monarch to recruit successive generations of state servants from the increasingly narrow circle of those families who had already served it. Whereas revolutionary meritocracy held out no special consideration for the children of meritorious public servants, thus allowing the state to seek out merit in the population as a whole, the monarchical model of polity tended to restrict the government's bountiful gaze to the existing pool of service families. Although this hardly influenced Napoleon's initial efforts to build a new elite – the revolutionary tabula rasa allowed him to recruit broadly from the socially diverse group of 'new men' who had served the Republic – the tendency toward auto-recruitment would grow ineluctably stronger with time. As the founding generation of the Napoleonic service elite aged, the regime would find itself obliged to look to its children to replace it, thus leaving fewer and fewer openings for families which had not yet served the state. In the long run, Napoleon's reimposition of a monarchical ethos of service and recompense could not help but undermine the revolutionary ideal of the career open to talent.

89 This rationale is discussed at length in D. D. Bien, 'The Army in the French Enlightenment: Reform, Reaction, and Revolution', *Past and Present* 85 (1979), p. 91.

7

A festival of the law: Napoleon's Jewish assemblies

Ronald B. Schechter

In late January 1806, on the way home from his victories at Ulm and Austerlitz, Napoleon passed through Strasbourg. There he heard complaints about Jewish moneylenders who, according to the Alsatian plaintiffs, were ruining the peasants through usury. After consulting with his Council of State periodically for the next four months, on May 30 he issued a decree designed to solve the perceived problem.[1] The decree stated that 'certain Jews, exercising no other profession besides that of usury have placed many cultivators ... in a state of great distress', and that it was necessary 'to come to the rescue of those of our subjects whom unjust greed has reduced to such miserable extremes'. The Emperor therefore ordered for Alsace and the recently annexed Rhineland a one-year suspension in the execution of all court judgements in favour of Jews whose non-commercial loans to farmers had been disputed. Yet he did not stop with this discriminatory act. He went on to convoke an 'assembly of individuals professing the Jewish religion and inhabiting French territory'. This group, which historians have come to identify simply as the Assembly of Notables, was to be selected by prefects and to include 'rabbis, proprietors and other Jews most distinguished by their probity and enlightenment'. The notables' task was to suggest ways of 'recalling their brethren to the exercise of useful arts and professions in order to replace, through honest industry, the shameful practices to which many of them have resorted from father to son over many centuries'. As a result of their counsel, Napoleon claimed that it would be possible 'to revive among those who profess the Jewish religion ... the sentiments of civil morality (*morale civile*) that unfortunately have become moribund among a large number of them by the state of abasement in which they have long languished'.[2]

---

1 R. Anchel, *Napoléon et les Juifs* (Paris, 1928), pp. 75–98; S. Schwarzfuchs, *Napoleon, the Jews, and the Sanhedrin* (London, 1979), pp. 45–51.
2 D. Tama, *Collection des actes de l'assemblée des Israélites de France et du royaume d'Italie, convoquée à Paris par décret de Sa Majesté impériale et royale, du 30 mai 1806* (Paris and Strasbourg, 1807), pp. 107–9.

When the notables convened in Paris on 23 July 1806, specially designated imperial commissioners presented them with a list of twelve questions about Jewish law and its relation both to the recently promulgated *Code civil* and the unwritten rules of civic virtue.[3] This questionnaire inquired into such matters as whether polygamy, divorce or intermarriage were permissible and under what circumstances, whether rabbis claimed any civil or police power, whether Jewish law prohibited any occupations or forms of military service, whether it maintained a double standard on lending practices toward Jews and non-Jews, and whether it encouraged fraternal feelings between the two groups. It was therefore meant to elicit a guarantee that there were no conflicts between the Jews' religion and their obligations as citizens, or, if there were, that citizenship and obedience to Napoleonic law would henceforth take precedence over religious obligations. Within three weeks the deputies produced a report stating that there was no conflict between Judaism and French citizenship obligations.

At some point, however, Napoleon appears to have doubted the authority that the assembly's report would carry with the Jews under his rule. Therefore, on 18 September he ordered the deputies to convoke 'an even more imposing, more religious assembly' charged with converting the answers to the twelve questions into points of doctrine that 'could be placed next to the Talmud and thus acquire, in the eyes of all Jews in all countries for every century, the greatest possible authority'. He named this new assembly the Grand Sanhedrin, after the rabbinical court of ancient Jerusalem, and stipulated, 'according to ancient usage', that seventy-one men be called to compose this august body, though he departed from the old form by requiring twenty-five of its members to be laymen.[4] After electing the Sanhedrin participants, the initial Assembly of Notables continued to meet during the next six months in order to establish a centralized system of Jewish consistories whose tasks included the enforcement of civic virtue as defined by the Sanhedrin. Yet public attention would shift toward the meetings of the Grand Sanhedrin in February 1807 as this extraordinary synod solemnly confirmed the Jews' duties as Jews vis-à-vis the Emperor, his laws and his non-Jewish subjects.

Although historians have written about the Assembly of Notables and the Sanhedrin, they have tended to use these meetings as an occasion for retrospectively praising or condemning Napoleon or the Jews, or both.[5] This judgemental approach tends to treat Napoleon's handling of the 'Jewish ques-

---

3 *Détail officiel de tout ce qui s'est passé à la première et deuxieme séances de l'Assemblé des Juifs* (Paris, 1806); and Tama, *Collection des actes*, pp. 132–3.

4 *Discours de MM. Les Commissaires*; and Tama, *Collection des actes*, pp. 237–40.

5 P. Sagnac, 'Les Juifs et Napoléon', *Revue d'histoire moderne et contemporaine* 2–3 (1901–02); two books by overtly anti-Semitic authors: J. Lémann, *Napoléon et les Juifs* (first published, 1891; reprint Paris, 1989); and A. Lemoine, *Napoléon Ier et les Juifs* (Paris, 1900); and a popular Bonapartist work, F. Pietri, *Napoléon et les Israélites* (Paris, 1965).

tion' for granted, whereas suspending judgement (if only temporarily) enables us to register a sense of surprise at precisely the course events took and, better still, to use their recovered strangeness as an opportunity to inquire into the little-understood political culture of the First Empire.

There is a general consensus that Napoleon's convocation of the Jewish assemblies were provoked by the complaints about usury that the non-Jews of Strasbourg had lodged earlier that year, and in this respect scholars have taken at face value the decree of 30 May 1806 in which Napoleon justifies his measures as responses to usury.[6] But one needs to ask whether the reputed effect followed necessarily from the supposed cause. Usury was a real problem in Alsace and the Jews, though not the only practitioners of the disreputable practice, were disproportionately engaged in it due to their exclusion from most other forms of livelihood.[7] More to the point, there is reason to believe that Napoleon was alarmed by the effects of usury on the Alsatian peasantry and held the province's Jews collectively responsible. Yet Napoleon had a number of options at his disposal. He could have left it to the courts to punish usurers, as indeed some members of his Council of State advised.[8] He could have ordered his legislature to enact a law on usury, which was still undefined in 1806. Indeed, this is precisely what he did in September of the following year.[9] Thus, if he created the Jewish assemblies to solve the problem of usury, he made that solution redundant within months by passing a law that dealt far more directly and efficiently with it.

Given the range of Napoleon's options, one wonders why the emperor chose, in addition to the measures enumerated above, to summon rabbis and Jewish laymen from the farthest reaches of his empire, to revive an institution that had died with the Roman destruction of Jerusalem and to have it convene publicly, in all pomp and solemnity, in the Hôtel de Ville. How would all this benefit Napoleon and his regime? Although Chateaubriand believed that Napoleon had financial motivations,[10] Napoleon knew better than to see in the Jews a significant source of wealth. Clearly he saw in them a wealth of *symbolic* opportunities. Famously aware of the power of symbols, he paid scrupulous attention to them in his own self-representation, a habit indicating a belief that the signs of power and legitimacy were inseparable from power and legitimacy themselves. He and his supporters accordingly used the ceremonial surrounding his Jewish policy to suggest his possession of these coveted attributes.

The act of liberating anyone, when performed publicly, constitutes an

6   Anchel, *Napoléon*, pp. 75–86; Schwarzfuchs, *Napoleon*, p. 45; and J. Katz, *Out of the Ghetto: The Social Background of Jewish Emancipation, 1770–1870* (Cambridge, Mass., 1973), p. 140.
7   Schwarzfuchs, *Napoleon*, pp. 29–30.
8   Anchel, *Napoléon*, p. 87; and Schwarzfuchs, *Napoleon*, p. 48.
9   Schwarzfuchs, *Napoleon*, p. 45.
10 F. de Chateaubriand, *Mémoires d'Outre-Tombe*, 2 vols (Paris, 1948), vol. 2, p. 381.

advertisement of the liberator's power. But emancipating the Jews in particular carried special advantages. It likened the liberator to the Messiah, the long-expected saviour of the Jews. Moreover, insofar as Napoleon highlighted the role of the Law in his Jewish policy, he likened himself to the famous Jewish lawgiver: Moses. One sees the Messianic-Mosaic Napoleon most vividly in an engraving by François-Louis Couché, *Napoléon le Grand rétablit le culte des Israélites, le 30 mai 1806*, designed to commemorate the calling of the Assembly of Notables. Centrally placed is Napoleon himself, crowned with laurels, clothed in his imperial robes and standing in front of his throne. With his right hand he holds a tablet bearing the inscription, '*Loi donnée à Moïse*'. Further to his right, the chief rabbi, in his ceremonial dress, gazes admiringly at him. In the left foreground two robed men with long hair and beards kneel before the emperor and extend their arms toward a seated female allegory of Judaism. Napoleon reaches out to the limp hand of the visibly weak woman, who can barely support the original Tablets of the Law with her other arm. She is leaning against a statue of a lion, evidently the Lion of Judah, which alludes to the ancient yet lost glory of the Jewish people, as do the adjacent oil lamp and large seven-stemmed candelabra. Visible in what appears to be a crypt is another female allegory of Judaism, the medieval Synagoga, her head bowed and arms folded across her shoulder, as she was typically depicted in the sculpture that adorned cathedrals. In the background on the far right is a mountain, no doubt an allusion to Mount Sinai.[11]

It was not necessary to take this message literally – indeed it had all the markings of allegory – to see its propagandistic meaning. Napoleon was enacting a *legal* liberation and therefore celebrating the object his regime fetishized: the law. Elsewhere, of course, Napoleon deliberately cultivated the persona of the legislator, repeatedly authoring constitutions, codifying laws and issuing decrees that carried the force of law. The Jewish assemblies gave him an additional opportunity to publicize to celebrate the cult of the law, which Napoleon had long used to legitimize a regime whose very origins in a coup d'état smacked of illegitimacy, even illegality. As Howard Brown has shown, a crucial feature of the Napoleonic regimes was the care with which they cultivated the appearance of legality.[12] Such an appearance, moreover, was all the more desirable in light of Napoleon's recent accession to a hereditary imperial throne of his own creation – to say nothing of the royal throne of 'Italy'. These innovations called renewed attention to the question of legitimacy, and the emperor therefore lost no opportunity to have himself cast in the cleansing light of the law. His Jewish assemblies provided just such opportunities.

11 F.-L. Couché, *Napoléon le Grand rétablit le culte des Israélites, le 30 mai 1806* (Paris, [1806]).
12 H. G. Brown, 'Domestic State Violence: Repression from the Croquants to the Commune', *The Historical Journal* 42 (1999), pp. 614–15.

Together the Assembly of Notables and the Sanhedrin constituted a veritable *Simchat Torah*, or Festival of the Law, but with this difference. The point of the traditional Jewish festival had been the celebration of God's Law or Torah. The Napoleonic *Simchat Torah* was to be a celebration of Napoleonic law. References to Napoleon's laws necessarily abounded in the two assemblies, the latter of which was open to the public and both of which were described in publications that included the principal speeches and written reports.[13] The very composition of the assemblies, which resembled law courts, if not legislatures, continually highlighted the law as the ultimate object of concern. Their task was to interpret, codify, canonize and decree. Although these mandates were overlapping and potentially contradictory, the important thing was that their object was always the law.

If Napoleon and his agents set the stage for an apotheosis of the lawgiver, however, they had little control over the script, and less still over the Jews' interpretation of the drama in which they had been invited to participate. The Assembly of Notables and the Sanhedrin were thus not merely an occasion for the emperor to receive the adulation of grateful subjects, they provided an opportunity for the Jews to interpret themselves and their culture. By calling on Jewish spokesmen to define their religion's relationship to the civil law and civic virtue, Napoleon gave them a voice. This observation may seem banal, but it is worth recalling that Jews had long been the object of description, and that, although they repeatedly answered the claims of non-Jews, only with Napoleon were they officially permitted, indeed, ordered, to present their side of the story. To be sure, their liberty to express themselves was limited. They were constrained by twelve leading questions, and it would have been most imprudent, for example, to suggest that some civil laws or obligations were not binding on the Jews, or that there was a double standard in lending rates for Jewish and non-Jewish borrowers. Yet given that Jewish leaders had insisted for generations that such suspicions were nothing but the fruit of prejudice and ignorance, it was highly improbable that anyone would have wished to depart from that position now that conformity to French standards was about to be (seemingly, at least) rewarded. The Assembly of Notables and the Sanhedrin provided an officially sanctioned forum for precisely the type of answer the deputies were inclined to give. Nevertheless, they did not limit themselves to mere assent or acclamation, and even if Napoleon had imagined the Jewish assemblies to mirror his plebiscites, the spokesmen were anything but laconic in their replies. Even simple 'yes' or 'no' questions provided the occasion for lengthy speeches, reports, prayers and sermons.

13 Tama's *Collection des actes* originally appeared in twelve issues available to subscribers under the title *Collection des écrits et des actes relatifs au dernier état des individus professant la religion hébraïque*. Tama refers to the wishes of his '*souscripteurs*' in *Collection des actes*, p. 153.

Just how did the Jewish notables represent themselves, their religion and their relationship to the French and imperial states and people?[14] How did they respond to and compete with non-Jewish descriptions of the situation? How did they co-author, as it were, their cultural text? The following pages should demonstrate that their performance on the Napoleonic stage did not merely involve the refutation of time-honoured prejudices, but that the Jewish deputies paradoxically turned long-standing negative stereotypes to their advantage.

Among the most damaging prejudices against the Jews was that their religion authorized usury and other immoral business practices. Consequently, the Sanhedrin refuted the persistent claim that Jews were prohibited from lending to fellow Jews at usurious rates but were authorized to engage in usury when lending to Gentiles, insisting that such a distinction was contrary to the Talmud.[15] David Sintzheim, the *Nasi* or Prince of the Sanhedrin, went further still. He argued that insofar as there were Jewish usurers, they practised their trade despite 'the terrible menaces of the God of Israel'.[16] Elsewhere, the deputies affirmed the Jewish work ethic through Biblical sources in praise of work, the rabbinical aphorism, 'Love work and flee from idleness', and the Talmudic precept that 'the family father who does not teach a profession to his son raises him to a life of banditry'.[17]

Moreover, the representatives attempted to disabuse their Gentile audience of the prejudice that Judaism inspired hatred for non-Jews. The Assembly of Notables invoked the Talmudic Noahide laws, the abbreviated code of moral conduct given to Noah and his family – who lived prior to the divine covenants with Abraham and Moses – and to all the 'nations' apart from Israel.[18] Because Christianity complied with these basic rules, the deputies argued, the Jews considered Christians to be their 'brothers'.[19] The Sanhedrin likewise cited the Noahides, along with other Talmudic dogma and more familiar Biblical passages, in its doctrinal statement on fraternity. In his speech to the modern Sanhedrin, Rabbi Abraham Cologna of Mantua, the *Haham* or 'Sage' of that body, cited the ruling of its ancient predecessor, in the

14 It is important to acknowledge that the Jewish representatives were not of one mind and that they disagreed vehemently over specific issues – intermarriage being the most controversial among them. Yet despite their differences of opinion, a relatively coherent style of self-representation can be identified.

15 Tama, *Collection des procès-verbaux*, p. 94.

16 *Ibid.*, p. 84. Sintzheim reiterated his point with the rhetorical question, 'Les talmudistes n'ont-ils pas signalé hautement les vices que nous censurons aujourd'hui?' *Collection des procès-verbaux*, p. 85.

17 Prov. 24, 27, 28–9; Avot 1, Kiduschin 1; Tama, *Collection des actes*, p. 181; and *Collection des procès-verbaux*, p. 81.

18 The Noahide requirements were: to adore God; to render and submit to justice; and to refrain from idolatry, murder, adultery and incest, theft, and the consumption of flesh from living animals. Sanhedrin 2.

19 Tama, *Collection des actes*, p. 171.

language of learned Christendom: *Pii cujuscumque nationis aeternae vitae participes sunt.*[20]

Yet the Jews did not restrict themselves to refuting longstanding prejudices. Indeed, an integral part of their strategy was to appropriate the very prejudices so long held against them and to give them a positive spin. Among the most persistent of these was the belief in their alleged legalism. Catholic theologians and anti-clerical *philosophes* alike had long criticized the Jews as overly scrupulous in venerating their laws.[21] By the time Napoleon came to power, however, the law had acquired a new prestige. Revolutionary leaders repeatedly invoked 'the law' to divert attention from the coercive nature (and questionable legality) of their policies, and the Directory in particular sought to distinguish itself from the reputed anarchy of its predecessors by insisting on its own respect for the law. Napoleon fetishized the law still further. Not only did the self-proclaimed Legislator attempt to secure obedience by issuing grand fundamental laws or constitutions based ostensibly on universal and 'natural' principles, he even deigned to concern himself with the particularities of civil law, including both the tangled mess of 'custom' and the relics of Justinian's digests, whence the celebrated *Code civil*. Indeed, recognizing that control over civil law tightened his grip on civil society, he treated the former as an instrument of his own power over the latter. The totemic status of the law provided an unprecedented opportunity for the people whose religion had long been derided for its legalism to proclaim proudly that they were indeed people of the law. Napoleon had given them a *Simchat Torah* and they were more than ready to celebrate the law in all its grandness and minutiae.

To be sure, the Jewish Festival of the Law involved much praise of Napoleonic law and of the emperor himself as, for example, 'the most beneficent of legislators'[22] and 'the Solomon of our century'.[23] Rabbi Cologna declaimed, 'Such is the character of the laws of Napoleon that the subject, in obeying them, exercises less an act of submission than satisfies his acts in his

---

20 The Grand Sanhedrin cited Lev 19:34, Mich 6:8, Avot 6:6 and Hirubin 7. Tama, *Collection des procès-verbaux*, p. 76. Cologna cited Sanhedrin 2. For Cologna's address see *Discorso* and Tama, *Collection des procès-verbaux*, pp. 8–9.

21 B. Pascal, *Pensées sur la Religion* (first published, 1661; reprint, Paris, 1952), §297, 317, pp. 190, 198; J.-B. Bossuet, *Méditations sur l'Evangile* (first published, 1704; reprint, Paris, 1966), p. 111; F. de Salignac de la Mothe-Fénélon, *Lettre à Louis XIV* (first published, 1694; reprint, Neuchatel, 1961), p. 69; *Sermons et entretiens*, in *Oeuvres*, (first published, 1706; reprint, Paris, 1823), vol. 17, p. 298; and C.-L. de Secondat, baron de Montesquieu, *De l'esprit des lois* (first published, 1755; reprint, Paris, 1958), book 26, ch. 7, p. 302.

22 Tama, *Collection des actes*, p. 182.

23 J. B. Segré, *Discorso pronunziato in italiano, a Parigi, li 15 d'agosto 1806, nel tempio ebraico; dal sign. Rabbino Segre ... all' occasione del giorno anniversaria della nascita di S.M. l'Imperatore dei Francesi e re d'Italia; tradotto in francese dalla sigra. Giulia-Theodora Cerf-Berr.* French title: *Discours prononcé en italien à Paris, le 15 août 1806, dans le Temple hébraïque ... à l'occasion du jour anniversaire de la naissance de S.M. l'Empereur des François et Roi d'Italie* (Paris, 1806); and Tama, *Collection des actes*, p. 206.

own advantage'.[24] This perfectly summarized the Napoleonic legal discourse and, perhaps inadvertently, identified the emperor as the ideal Rousseauian sovereign, whose laws one obeys without losing one's liberty.

Yet if the Jewish representatives were willing to laud Napoleon's activities involving the law, they were equally ready to praise themselves in their capacity as interpreters of the law. Sintzheim honoured his fellow rabbis by addressing them as *'docteurs'*.[25] Even the Sanhedrin's president, Abraham Furtado, the rich Bordelais with a reputation for secular learning, also called the rabbis *'docteurs'* or, more frequently, *'docteurs de la loi'*.[26] This was especially telling because the term *docteur*, when used by the *philosophes* to describe a theologian, Christian or Jewish, had connoted hair-splitting casuistry, jesuitical or pharasaic reasoning. That a partisan of the Enlightenment could use it as an honorific title was an eloquent sign that the study of the law, religious as well as civil, was now in favour.

The notables adopted other proud titles to indicate their legal expertise. Cologna called the Sanhedrin 'this assembly of sages' and referred to its members as 'respectable senators'.[27] Not to be outdone by his Italian colleague, Furtado displayed his classical erudition by designating the Sanhedrin 'this august areopagus'.[28] In his closing speech to that same body, Sintzheim referred to its delegates as 'legislators'.[29] One of the most strikingly bold claims of proficiency in the law, however, came from a member of the Assembly of Notables, who proclaimed, 'Our descendants ... will cover with benedictions these wise and venerable interpreters of the law.'[30]

24 Tama, *Collection des procès-verbaux*, p. 10.
25 [Sintzheim], *Discours*; and Tama, *Collection des procès-verbaux*, pp. 88, 89, 123, 124, 131. It is worth noting that Sintzheim addressed the Sanhedrin in Hebrew. Some if not all of his speeches were translated by Abraham Furtado. Since the original manuscripts are not known to exist, it is impossible to know precisely what term or terms Sintzheim used to express what Furtado translated as *'docteurs'*. Most relevant, however, is the fact that the translator, either Furtado or another member of the Sanhedrin, chose this term for the only version of the speech that would be comprehensible to non-Jews.
26 Furtado, *Rapport de M. Furtado au Grand Sanhédrin, en lui proposant les trois premières décisions doctrinales* (Paris, 1807); and Tama, *Collection des procès-verbaux*, pp. 29, 63, 77, 98, 111.
27 Abraham de Cologna, *Discorso pronunziato nella grande sinagoga di Parigi, all'occasione dell'apertura del Gran Sanedrin, dal Signor Abramo Cologna, rabino in Mantova, ex-legislatore e membro attuale del collegio elettorale dei dotti del regno d'Italia, deputato all'assemblea degl' Israeliti, e assessore del gran Sanedrin. Tradotto in francese dal signor Furtado, presidente dell'assemblea*. French title: *Discours prononcé à la grande Synagogue de Paris, à l'occasion de l'ouverture du Grand Sanhédrin ....* (Paris, 1807); and Tama, *Collection des procès-verbaux*, p. 6. Jacob-Samuel Avigdor similarly called the Sanhedrin a 'senate'. *Discours prononcé à l'Assemblée des Israélites de l'Empire Français et du Royaume d'Italie; par J.S. Avigdor (de Nice), secrétaire de l'Assemblée, Membre du Comité de Neuf et du Grand Sanhédrin* (Paris, 1807); and Tama, *Collection des actes*, p. 314.
28 Abraham Furtado, *Rapport*; and Tama, *Collection des procès-verbaux*, p. 27.
29 J. D. Sintzheim, *Discours prononcé par le chef du Grand Sanhédrin à la clôture des séances. Traduit par A. Furtado* (Paris, 1807); and Tama, *Collection des procès-verbaux*, p. 123. This speech only exists in Furtado's translation, so, as in the case of the term 'docteurs', the question of Sintzheim's original wording cannot be settled. Still, Furtado's decision to use the term *'législateurs'* is most relevant to the question of the Jews' self-representation.
30 Tama, *Collection des actes*, p. 156.

Their credentials as 'interpreters of the law' thus established, the Jewish representatives could confidently and authoritatively proceed with the business of interpreting the law. In particular, they emphasized the divine origin of Jewish law. Sintzheim called it 'the miraculous bush of our divine legislator', which is 'never consumed',[31] and a deputy at the Assembly of Notables similarly called God 'our divine Legislator' and 'our holy Legislator'.[32] Elsewhere the representatives referred to 'our holy law' or 'the divine law'.[33] Such laws were, by definition, perfect. Thus Sintzheim uttered the tautology, 'The law of the Lord is perfect',[34] and another reasoned similarly, 'The law of God ordains all that is just and good'.[35]

Moreover, the representatives made it clear that by 'law of God' or 'law of the Lord', they did not only mean the Pentateuch and the books of the prophets, but also the much maligned Talmud. This compilation of legislation and allegory, together with the rabbis who revered and interpreted it, had long been disdained by Christian theologians and *philosophes* alike. Yet the members of the Jewish assemblies took the Napoleonic Festival of the Law as an occasion to rehabilitate the Talmud and its rabbinic interpreters in the public eye. Indeed, the spokesmen were so aggressive in their defence of Jewish law that they were willing to denounce non-Jews who failed to recognize its qualities. Cologna complained that 'our faith' had been 'up to now misunderstood by some and calumniated by others'.[36] Furtado went further still, claiming that 'the majority' of non-Jews, 'enchained by popular prejudices ... imbued with the false idea that it was impossible to operate our regeneration, attributed to our dogmas effects that were only due to *their* laws, and reproached us for habits that they forced us to contract'.[37] Sintzheim went further still, arguing that those who accused Jewish law of authorizing usury epitomized 'the hatred, ignorance and intolerance of fanatical centuries'.[38] Elsewhere he denounced 'the ignoramus and the prevaricator who would dare advance that our law teaches us to cheat foreign nations! He profanes the name of Israel, he does not know the way of the Lord.'[39]

These were serious accusations: hatred, ignorance, fanaticism, prevarication, blasphemy. Among the accused, ironically, was the emperor himself, together with his commissioner Molé. Sintzheim and his colleagues could not

31 Sintzheim, *Discours*; and Tama, *Collection des procès-verbaux*, p. 125.
32 Marqfoy, aîné de Baïonne, *Discours prononcé sur la nature des réponses à faire aux 4e, 5e et 6e questions proposées à ladite Assemblée par les Commissaires de Sa Majesté Impériale et Royale* (Paris, 1806); and *Collection des actes*, pp. 197–8.
33 Tama, *Collection des procès-verbaux*, pp. 62, 91, 96.
34 *Ibid.*, 52.
35 Marqfoy, *Discours*; and *Collection des actes*, p. 199.
36 Cologna, *Discorso*; and Tama, *Collection des procès-verbaux*, pp. 7–8.
37 Furtado, *Rapport*; and Tama, *Collection des procès-verbaux*, pp. 29–30 (emphasis added).
38 Tama, *Collection des procès-verbaux*, p. 84.
39 *Ibid.*, p. 58.

have known that Napoleon had told Molé in the spring of 1806 that 'the evil' of usury 'comes above all from that undigested compilation called the Talmud, in which, next to [the Jews'] veritable Biblical traditions, one finds the most corrupt morality wherever relations with Christians are concerned'. Nor could he have known that Molé responded that among the authors of the Talmud were 'a large number ... inspired by the hatred of Christianity', and whose commentary included 'the most contemptible refinements on the art of extorting money'.[40] Still, they might well have suspected that Napoleon, like so many other non-Jews, harboured prejudices about the content of the Talmud. In any event, their drive to defend the 'Mosaic code' was so strong that they risked antagonizing their non-Jewish audience, including the emperor himself.

It did not suffice, however, for the Jewish leaders to defend their law. Napoleon had called them to the capital, according to his decree of 30 May, because many of their 'brethren' were lacking 'sentiments of civil morality'. If the law of Moses, being perfect, was not responsible for this deficit, the spokesmen were under pressure to account for it. In addition to taking on the role of legal scholars, then, the Jewish deputies at Napoleon's Festival of the Law made themselves into barristers on behalf of their co-religionists. Significantly, they made no attempt to refute the charges. They did not claim that the number of Jewish usurers had been exaggerated, or that Jews lending at legitimate rates were unfairly labelled as usurers, or that there were Christian as well as Jewish usurers. Instead they pleaded guilty with extenuating circumstances.

This defence strategy was not new. Montesquieu and Voltaire had emphasized the historical factors that induced Jews to deal in commerce more generally and money lending in particular, emphasizing the Church's condemnation of interest and the exclusion of Jews from other forms of livelihood.[41] In 1774 Pierre-Louis Lacretelle, quite literally a barrister, argued that persecution had provoked the Jews to cheat Christians both as a strategy for survival and out of an understandable desire for revenge, and that a 'decree of regeneration' providing them with equal right to the trades and professions would reverse their current state of moral depravity.[42] In the 1780s and into the Revolution, Jews and non-Jews reiterated the need for 'regeneration', and though they disagreed on the means to do so, they agreed that historical

40 Anchel, *Napoleon*, p. 93.
41 Montesquieu, *Esprit des lois*, book 21, ch. 6, p. 83; ch. 20, pp. 120–3; F.-M. Arouet de Voltaire, *Dictionnaire philosophique*, in *Oeuvres complètes de Voltaire*, ed. Louis Moland (Paris, 1877–1885), vol. 19, pp. 524–5; and *Essay sur l'histoire générale* (Geneva, 1756), pp. 9, 292–3.
42 [Pierre-Louis Lacretelle], 'LVIIIe cause. Question d'état sur les Juifs de Metz,' *Causes célèbres, curieuses et intéressantes, de toutes les cours souveraines du royaume, avec les jugemens qui les ont décidées*, vol. 23 (Paris, 1776), pp. 64–98. Published separately as *Plaidoyer pour Moyse May, Godechaux et Abraham Lévy, Juifs de Metz. Contre l'hôtel-de-ville de Thionville et le Corps des Marchands de cette ville* (Bruxelles, 1775).

circumstances had caused what they all regarded as a moral decline.[43] Finally, Napoleon himself had implicitly recognized the regenerationist position when he suggested in his decree of 30 May that usury was the product of 'the state of humiliation in which [the Jews] have long languished'.

Confident that their narrative would be recognized and that it would elicit a sympathetic response, the Jewish representatives told and retold the story of the Jews' fall from ancient greatness, miserable dispersion among hostile nations, then regeneration under Napoleon's auspices. Variations on this theme were slight, thus it would be laborious to cite the numerous examples from the proceedings of the Jewish assemblies. The speech of Berr Isaac Berr to the Assembly of Notables contains as good a specimen as any. It begins:

> More than seventeen centuries have passed since that ever memorable epoch when the Jewish people was subjugated by victorious and foreign legions ... rendered slaves, and dispersed by the hurricane of misfortune to all the corners of the inhabited world; always unhappy and persecuted, always remaining faithful to the belief of their ancestors, despite the executions and tortures, they present still today [an] imposing and incomprehensible spectacle to human reason, of an immobile column surviving the deluges of the centuries; and if the origin of this people recedes to the cradle of the human race, it seems that their remnants will continue until the days of its destruction.

Berr went on to describe the effect of persecution on the Jewish character:

> By turns the Jews were persecuted and disparaged in order to punish them for remaining faithful to the belief of their ancestors; the more they wanted to remain Jews, the more they ceased to be men. Mingling in the midst of civilized peoples, what useful citizens they would have become had a barbaric policy not made that impossible! Often humiliation and misery degraded us indeed.

Happily, however, this situation was about to change. Napoleon was the first ruler who deigned 'to convoke before his throne those who would be able to help him ease their misfortune and cure the plagues of Israel'.[44]

Berr's recounting of Jewish history contained all of the essential elements of the regenerationist template. Emplotted initially as tragedy, it employed a vocabulary designed to elicit sympathy. The Jews had been 'subjugated', 'persecuted', 'humiliated', 'degraded', all the while remaining stoically 'faithful' to their religion. Their moral decline received no elaboration, lest their specific misdeeds erode the sympathy of their audience. The mode of emplotment then shifted suddenly to comedy, as it always did in the regeneration

---

43 A complete bibliography of works treating the 'regeneration' of the Jews would be too long to reproduce here. Some of the most important books and pamphlets are reprinted in *La Révolution française et l'émancipation des Juifs*, 8 vols (Paris, 1968).
44 Tama, *Collection des actes*, pp. 160–1.

narratives after 1791.[45] Whereas the 'French nation' had been the *deus ex machina* during the Revolution, preparing the ground for the Jews' regeneration, now Napoleon himself assumed that role.

An integral part of the regeneration narrative, sometimes explicitly described and sometimes implicitly indicated, was an idealized origin, a Golden Age that preceded exile, persecution and moral corruption. It was this sense of a worthy beginning that informed Berr's suggestion that 'the origin of this people' dated from 'the cradle of the human race'.[46] Similarly, Furtado exalted the Jews as 'one the most ancient peoples in the world', and elsewhere referred to 'the antiquity of our origins'.[47] Indeed, the words 'antique' and 'antiquity' recurred continuously during the sessions of both assemblies. Sintzheim called the Jews 'the descendants of antique Jacob'[48] and Furtado referred to the Sanhedrin in particular as 'this antique body whose origins are lost in the night of time'.[49]

No doubt conscious of the value that Napoleon and so many of his European subjects placed upon antiquity, the Jewish representatives evoked their own ancient past as though its worth were unquestionable. Antiquity was synonymous with 'venerable antiquity', as Furtado assured the Sanhedrin and its non-Jewish audience: 'Contemplating this assembly of men who are commendable for their piety, knowledge and virtues, we believe ourselves transported to that venerable antiquity so well described in our sacred books.'[50] Elsewhere, a member of the Assembly of Notables referred to the Torah as 'the revered monument of our antique splendour', [51] and Cologna exhorted the Sanhedrin members to encourage 'useful professions' and military service as a means of 'reviv[ing] the glory of an antique people'.[52]

If antiquity was paired with 'glory' or 'splendour', however, it more frequently accompanied the more modest virtues of simplicity and equality. When asked whether 'the law of the Jews prohibits them from usury toward their brothers', the Assembly of Notables took the opportunity to construct an elaborate counter-image to the prevalent figure of the Jewish usurer. The Notables argued that interest on loans between Jews was forbidden because

---

45 Berr himself had written a similar narrative on the occasion of the first 'emancipation' of 1791, *Lettre d'un Citoyen, membre de la ci-devant communauté des Juifs de Lorraine, à ses confrères, à l'occasion du droit de Citoyen actif, rendu aux Juifs par le décret de 28 septembre 1791* (Nancy, 1791) [Reprinted in *La Révolution française et l'émancipation des Juifs* (Paris, 1968), vol. 8.]

46 Tama, *Collection des actes*, p. 136.

47 *Collection des procès-verbaux*, p. 27. Cf. Diderot: 'We know of no nation older than the Jewish nation.' *Encyclopédie*, s.v., 'Juifs, Philosophie des', 9:25.

48 [Sintzheim], *Discours*; and Tama, *Collection des procès-verbaux*, p. 128.

49 Furtado, *Rapport*; and Tama, *Collection des procès-verbaux*, p. 27.

50 Furtado, *Rapport*; and Tama, *Collection des procès-verbaux*, p. 27. Cf. Avigdor, who described the Sanhedrin as 'this Senate so celebrated in antiquity'. *Discours*; and Tama, *Collection des actes*, p. 314.

51 Tama, *Collection des actes*, p. 210.

52 Cologna, *Discorso*; and *Collection des procès-verbaux*, p. 12.

interest was foreign to their rustic society. They claimed that the intent of this prohibition, like that of the sabbatical and jubilee years in which debts were forgiven, was to 'tighten again among [the Jews] the bonds of fraternity, to prescribe reciprocal benevolence and to induce them to help each other disinterestedly'. Furthermore, the 'legislator' had wished to 'establish among them an equality of goods and a mediocrity of private fortunes'. The notables insisted that the sage laws had worked and that indeed 'primitive equality' reigned in ancient Israel.[53]

The Sanhedrin confirmed this view, and in a speech to that body Sintzheim offered a veritable *pastorale*:

All the monuments of history attest to the simplicity of our ancestors. The pastoral and agricultural life was their occupation, rustic games their sole pleasures. They had neither manufacture nor navigation; all the commerce with their neighbours had naturally to be limited to a few exchanges at a time when money was so rare and its various uses so limited. They lived in a happy ignorance of all those sumptuosities that are only known to the great and opulent nations. They enjoyed a happiness without pomp and knew how to practice virtues without renown.[54]

The trope of primitive or antique virtue enabled the Jews simultaneously to represent themselves as capable of regeneration and to critique European civilization as both corrupt and corrupting. The Sanhedrin as a body made this stance even clearer. In its doctrinal condemnation of usury, it asserted that the misunderstanding of the Mosaic legislation on moneylending came from an anachronistic attribution of 'the morals and habits of modern nations to the highest antiquity' and added, 'one falsely accords to the birth of societies what only belongs to their mature age, and too often to their decrepitude'.[55] By noting the 'decrepitude' of the morality of 'modern nations', the Jews attenuated their own guilt for having lost their ancient virtue. After all, they were not the only ones. Indeed, when one reads the Sanhedrin's judgment on modern morals together with the argument that non-Jews had forced the Jews into commerce and other corrupt activities, the implication is that the latter are less guilty than the former.

Closely associated with the idea of antiquity was that of perpetuity: Christian tradition had produced the image of the eternal Jew, but the Jewish deputies appropriated this cliché and turned it to their representational advantage. The negative side of perpetuity or the eternal character of an 'immobile column' was obstinacy. Yet the Jewish assemblies managed to spin this prejudice toward its positive aspect: fidelity. Indeed, Furtado explicitly substituted the positive for the negative connotation when he addressed the Sanhedrin. He observed that the 'religious laws' of the Jews 'remained in all

53 Tama, *Collection des actes*, pp. 189–91.
54 Tama, *Collection des procès-verbaux*, p. 87.
55 *Ibid.*, p. 67.

their vigour and were *faithfully* transmitted from generation to generation, across the torrent of centuries, of persecutions and revolutions of empires', and added, 'This rare *constancy*, which calumny has often slandered with the name of *obstinacy*, today receives the tribute of the eulogies that it deserves.'[56] Berr's observation that 'the Jews were persecuted and disparaged in order to punish them for remaining faithful to the belief of their ancestors' similarly served to revise the meaning of 'obstinacy'. Sintzheim made a comparable rhetorical parry when he declared that no people had 'suffered oppression with a more noble constancy or a more unshakeable steadfastness'. Like Berr, he insisted that this fidelity did not merely follow, but indeed caused, the wrath of non-Jews: 'everywhere we saw enemies rise up against us because we had remained faithful to our laws'.[57]

At the same time, and at the risk of contradiction, the Jewish spokesmen represented themselves as members of a larger French or imperial family. Family metaphors had long been used to conceptualize, justify and celebrate the grouping of human beings under various systems of law, government and administration. Historians of the French Revolution have shown the importance of familial imagery in the creation of its distinctive political culture.[58] The use of family language under Napoleon, here seen in relation to the Jews under his jurisdiction, might similarly reveal otherwise hidden aspects of imperial political culture. Specifically, one sees a proliferation of paternal allusions in the meetings of the Jewish assemblies. Molé had assured the Jews that they 'deserve ... such paternal treatment' as they were receiving.[59] By identifying the emperor as father, the Napoleonic state distinguished itself sharply from its revolutionary predecessor, in which the corresponding father figure had been executed, and instead adapted an image from the earlier familial configuration of absolutism. The Jewish spokesmen eagerly appropriated this paternal language. In their proceedings the adjective 'paternal' appeared frequently, modifying Napoleon's 'wishes', 'instructions', 'views', 'sentiments', 'solicitude' and 'goodness'.[60] They reinforced this association by repeatedly referring to Napoleon as a father. A deputy at the Assembly of Notables declared, 'The Government calls us to it as a father calls his

---

56 Furtado, *Rapport*; and Tama, *Collection des procès-verbaux*, p. 42 (emphasis added). Earlier Furtado had connected the immutability of the Jewish religion to its purity. He called the Sanhedrin 'striking homage to the purity of this religion that neither time, nor dispersion, nor the revolutions of empires have been able to destroy'. He went on to claim that the Jewish religion was 'eternal like nature, as durable as society', and that 'its principles have had to survive all human vicissitudes'. *Rapport*; and Tama, *Collection des procès-verbaux*, p. 28.

57 Tama, *Collection des actes*, p. 212.

58 See especially L. Hunt, *The Family Romance of the French Revolution* (Berkeley, 1992).

59 *Détail officiel*; and Tama, *Collection des actes*, p. 131.

60 Tama, *Collection des actes*, pp. 147, 277, 266; *Collection des procès-verbaux*, pp. 19, 11; *Collection des actes*, p. 135.

children.'[61] Cologna likewise asserted that the emperor 'act[s] with us less as a sovereign than as a father'.[62] Whether the Napoleonic father was scolding or protective was often an open question. Yet the image suggested that the Jews were equal to other imperial 'children'. One deputy made this clear by claiming, 'Catholics and Lutherans, Jews and Calvinists, His Majesty ... only sees in them children of the same father'.[63] This phrase suggested a relationship not only to the emperor, but to the Heavenly Father; indeed, it mirrored the conclusion to Grégoire's *Essai sur la régénération physique, morale et politique des Juifs*, no doubt familiar to much of the audience, in which the *abbé* addressed his readers as 'children of the same father', by which he meant God, and urged them to 'remove all pretexts to the aversion of your brothers, who one day will all be reunited in the same cradle'.[64] Elsewhere the line between the imperial father and God was blurred, as indeed Napoleon seems to have intended, and Sintzheim could call the emperor, rather improbably, 'the father of all the peoples'.[65] Yet if this comment deified Napoleon, it served to make the claim that the Jews were equal to the emperor-God's other children. Sintzheim elaborated on this change in status by thanking Napoleon for raising the Jews 'to the rank of your children'.[66]

A common paternity, whether in Napoleon or God, therefore implied the fraternity of all 'children'. The theme of fraternity was ineluctable at assemblies in which the participants were required to rule on whether Jews who were 'treated by the law as citizens' viewed 'the French' as their 'brothers'. Buttressed by numerous citations from the sacred texts, the assemblies unequivocally declared the fraternity between Jews and non-Jews in the French Empire. One deputy assured his co-religionists that if God sent them 'a second Moses', that legislator 'would say to us: love the Christians; cherish them as your brothers, unite yourselves with them, envisage yourselves as children of the same family'.[67]

Elsewhere, the spokesmen reinforced the impression that Jews were part of the French and imperial family. The Sanhedrin's ruling on 'civil and political relations' between Jews and non-Jews included the claim that 'everything obliges [the Jew] not to isolate his interest from the public interest, nor his

61 L. Cerfberr, *Discours pour l'ouverture de l'Assemblée générale des Juifs, prononcé le 26 juillet 1806* (Paris, 1806); and Tama, *Collection des actes*, pp. 157–9.
62 Cologna, *Discorso*; and Tama, *Collection des procès-verbaux*, p. 10.
63 Tama, *Collection des actes*, p. 154. Furtado similarly described Napoleon as the 'common father of all his subjects' and claimed, 'Whatever religion they profess, he only sees in them all the members of a single family.' Tama, *Collection des actes*, p. 136.
64 Abbé Henri Grégoire, *Essai sur la régénération physique, morale et politique des Juifs* (Paris, 1789) [Reprinted in *La Révolution française et l'émancipation des juifs* (Paris, 1968), vol. 3.], p. 194.
65 Sintzheim, *Discours*; and Tama, *Collection des procès-verbaux*, p. 130.
66 Sintzheim, *Discours*; and Tama, *Collection des procès-verbaux*, p. 130. Sintzheim's allusion was clearly to an adoption, an impression that was reinforced by a comment by Cologna, who had referred to the Jews as 'the orphans of debilitated Zion'. *Collection des procès-verbaux*, p. 3.
67 Tama, *Collection des actes*, pp. 143–4.

destiny, any more than that of his family, to the destiny of the grand family of the state'; furthermore, in the preamble to its decisions it reiterated the necessity of Jews to 'belong to the grand family of the state'.[68] Concerning the prevalent mistrust of Jewish statements as insincere, qualified or obscure, the deputies made ingenious use of the family metaphor to guarantee their honesty, and also to show their support for 'freedom of opinion', by declaring, 'we have explained ourselves ... before the very eyes of His Majesty, with the same frankness, the same freedom of opinion (*liberté d'opinion*) that we would have used in the bosom of our domestic hearths'.[69] As if to assure even further the sincerity of their words, they expressed family feelings in poetry and song. In an ode in honour of Napoleon's birthday, one deputy proclaimed his joy at becoming 'part of the grand and magnanimous family of Frenchmen'.[70] At the same ceremony, the assembly sang the familiar aria by Grétry, '*Où peut-on être mieux qu'au sein de sa famille?*'[71]

If the familial language of the Assembly of Notables and the Sanhedrin appears assimilationist, if not obsequious – and indeed historians have frequently interpreted the assemblies in this light – it is important to recognize that even in their most apparently subservient statements the Jews implicitly or explicitly placed their law above Napoleon's. 'The law of the Lord is perfect', Sintzheim assured his audience, and later, at the close of the Sanhedrin, he suggested the Jews' title to or possession of that object, claiming, 'the law *of Israel* is perfect'.[72] None of the representatives characterized Napoleon's laws as perfect. Elsewhere Sintzheim glorified the divine law, remembering the martyrs who had suffered 'because we remained faithful to our laws, to those laws that the Lord himself gave us by his revelation in the midst of lightning bolts and thunder'.[73] Napoleon was an admirable legislator, but his laws came without thunder and lightning. Nowhere was the difference between divine and Napoleonic law clearer than when Sintzheim congratulated the Sanhedrin for having 'succeeded in reconciling [God's] holy law, his pure law, with the institutions of this wise monarch who puts all his trust in the God whom we adore'. There was clearly no competition between the 'holy' and 'pure' laws of God and the 'institutions' of a 'wise monarch'.[74]

Similarly, the Jewish representatives assimilated (i.e. appropriated) the values of civic virtue, or, to use Napoleon's phrase, civil morality. Again, however, they made it apparent that these values were 'Hebrew' or 'Israelite' in origin, and implicitly congratulated their non-Jewish compatri-

---

68 Tama, *Collection des procès-verbaux*, pp. 78, 95.
69 Tama, *Collection des actes*, p. 245.
70 *Ibid.*, p. 234.
71 *Ibid.*, p. 183.
72 Sintzheim, *Discours*; and Tama, *Collection des procès-verbaux*, pp. 58, 127 (emphasis added).
73 Tama, *Collection des actes*, p. 212.
74 Sintzheim, *Discours*; and Tama, *Collection des procès-verbaux*, p. 127.

ots for having discovered belatedly what the Jews had long known. When Napoleon asked them about fraternity they suggested that they had invented it, or, more precisely, that their ancestors had practised this virtue before any laws protecting it had to be codified. Thus Furtado claimed that the fraternity Napoleon hoped to see encouraged between Jews and their non-Jewish neighbours only conformed to 'an eternal law of sociability contemporary to the origin of the species' and 'a universal law that preceded all apparatus of religious and political institutions'.[75] In other words, it was long familiar to the Jews, who, as the representatives repeatedly assured, were coeval with human origins and as 'eternal' as the natural laws that 'institutions' such as Napoleon's were now said to be following. Similarly, as has been shown, the deputies repeatedly implied that equality was not an invention of the French Enlightenment, Revolution and Napoleonic successor states, but of those who had practised the 'primitive equality' so elusive to modern people.

Paradoxically, then, the act of accommodating the legal codes and official morality of the Napoleonic regime to the Jewish religion implied the superiority, priority, and universality of the latter while suggesting the imperfection, youth and specificity of the former. In a sense, then, just as a bishop's or pope's consecration of a temporal ruler implied the approval, hence the superior moral position, of the Catholic Church, the rabbinical confirmation of the Napoleonic state amounted to a reversal of the hierarchical relations initially envisaged by the emperor. Now it was Judaism that was 'deigning' to confirm the rights of Napoleon. Finally, the practice of consecration took on a nearly literal form in numerous benedictions by the *docteurs de la loi d'Israël*. Repeatedly the Jewish representatives stated that God had 'chosen' or 'elected' Napoleon, and in the process likened him to the anointed kings of Israel. Referring to God's project of restoring Israel to its ancient dignity, Berr Isaac Berr asked, 'To whom could the accomplishment of such designs be confided? Is it not to him alone, to the mortal whom heaven has chosen as the elect of its heart, to whom it has confided the fate of nations, because he is the only one capable of governing with wisdom'.[76] Rabbi Sintzheim made the connection between Napoleon and the Biblical kings even clearer. In a sermon to the Assembly of Notables, he began by citing the following passage from the Book of Isaiah:

This is my servant whose defence I shall take; this is my elect in whom my heart has placed all of its affection. I shall spread out my spirit upon him, and he shall render justice unto the nations; he shall not be at all sad nor precipitous when he exercises his judgement on earth, and the islands shall await his law. I am the Lord who has

75   Tama, *Collection des procès-verbaux*, p. 101.
76   Tama, *Collection des actes*, p. 162.

preserved you, who has established you to be the reconciler of the people and the light of the nations.[77]

To remove any doubt as to the identity of this ruler, Sintzheim proclaimed of God, 'He has chosen Napoleon to place him on the throne of France and Italy; he has chosen him as I indicated in my text.' Elsewhere he recounted the recent imperial victory at Ulm, 'This fortress was occupied by an innumerable army of enemies, but as soon as the elect of the Lord appeared, one saw the accomplishment of what Isaiah said (ch. 41, v. 10): "All those who combat you shall be confounded; all those who oppose you shall be reduced to nothing and shall perish."'[78]

On the surface the use of such quotations might seem obsequious. Yet what the Jewish representatives proffered with one hand they took away with the other. By making him a 'servant' of the Lord, who in turn fought his battles, Sintzheim deprived the emperor of his autonomy and his famed 'genius'. By praising him as the only 'mortal' capable of 'governing with wisdom', Berr both emphasized the mortality of the man who no doubt preferred to be described as immortal and indicated that his 'wisdom' was defined in terms of its conformity with the law of God, in other words, *their* law.

In his concluding address before the Sanhedrin, Sintzheim put the following words into God's mouth:

Who is the one who shall come to the aid of my people? ... I have named him my elect one (*mon élu*); my will has chosen him to be the dominator of the nations and to distribute benefits to men. The hero ... shall be the liberator of Israel; the hero who shall overturn the throne of the mighty and raise up that of the humble is the hero whom I destine to raise from the dust the descendants of antique Jacob ... I have called him, I have sanctified him, and all the nations shall recognize by his deeds that I have not at all reproved my people and that I have not at all removed my affections from the midst of Israel.[79]

This imagined speech epitomizes the multivalency of the rhetoric employed by the Jewish representatives. There is a superficially slavish quality to the image of Jews languishing in the 'dust' prior to their liberation at the hands of Napoleon and a corresponding sense of Napoleon's unsurpassed, even messianic greatness. In this respect Sintzheim's words correspond to the Couché engraving of the emperor preparing to raise the figure of Judaism from the ground. Yet here Napoleon's grandeur is limited by God's 'will', which has chosen him as a mere instrument of the Jews' salvation, while their subservience is mitigated by the fact that God has retained his favor for

77 *Ibid.*, p. 211. This is a paraphrase of Isaiah 42: 1–6.
78 *Ibid.*, pp. 215–16.
79 Sintzheim, *Discours*; and Tama, *Collection des procès-verbaux*, pp. 128–9.

'Israel'. By implication, this fidelity, mirroring the quintessentially divine quality of immutability, is contrasted to the incontinence of 'the nations' who have persecuted the Jews. It is the positive face of obstinacy, and Sintzheim eagerly appropriates this quality, which is moreover implicit in the term 'antique', on behalf of his co-religionists. Thus assimilation (in the sense that Napoleon attempted to mandate) met resistance. Not only does God refer to the Jews as 'my people', suggesting a celebration of their persistent difference. That difference absorbs the alterity of the Empire as God *sanctifies* its ruler. This sanctification alludes to the perfection of the Jewish religion and, by implication, the virtue of its practitioners. If Napoleon 'raised' the Jews from the dust, then, they raised him to the status of consecrated Jewish king.

If the Jews were able to subvert the official version of their 'regeneration', it is because the discourse of regeneration was neither monolithic nor the exclusive property of the Napoleonic state. And this is the real historical significance of the Jewish leaders' cultural performance in 1806 and 1807. That performance reveals the paradoxical limits to Napoleon's control over the very discourse meant to justify his political authority. The moment he ceded that powerful weapon, which the French so elegantly and succinctly call *la parole*, he risked the discursive competition of subject-citizens who, in the best of all possible Napoleonic worlds, would have limited themselves to plebiscitary acclamation.

8

Arbitrary detention, human rights and the Napoleonic Senate

Michael D. Sibalis

They shot, beneath the windows of our prison cell, without any sort of trial, the four Breton sailors ...; they assassinated officially ... my friend Raoul de Saint-Vincent; they drove my friend Christoval to cut his own throat with his razor; and the newspapers knew nothing about it, and the Commission for Personal Liberty regularly drew its splendid salaries, that goes without saying; and the Conservative Senate carefully conserved the inviolability of arbitrary rule.

The target of this biting passage by Charles Nodier, published in 1829, was Napoleon's Senate and specifically the Senatorial Commission on Personal Liberty, accused of shirking its assigned constitutional duty of protecting French citizens against state tyranny.[1] Most historians who have studied the Senatorial Commission have condemned it no less unambiguously than Nodier, though in more measured language, as a dismal failure. Only Isser Woloch has recently portrayed the commissioners as generally 'liberally oriented men of 1789' and the Commission itself as 'an irritant to the police and justice ministries' that 'did yield results from time to time'.[2] Whatever their verdict on the Senatorial Commission, these historians drew on only a fraction of the relevant historical documentation: the minutes of the Commission's meetings, the ledgers registering petitions received and, more rarely, six cartons of its dossiers and official correspondence.[3] All of them,

1 C. Nodier, *Portraits de la Révolution et de l'Empire*, J.-L. Steinmetz and J. d'Hendecourt (eds), 2 vols (Paris, 1988), vol. 2, pp. 116–17.
2 F.-A. Aulard, 'La liberté individuelle sous Napoléon I', in his *Études et leçons sur la Révolution française 3* (Paris, 1902), pp. 290–313 [originally published in *Revue du palais 2* (June–Aug 1897), pp. 539–53]; J. Le Sciellour, *La liberté individuelle sous le Consulat et l'Empire* (Paris, 1911); J. Thiry, *Les attributions du Sénat du Premier Empire concernant la justice et les droits individuels* (Paris, 1922); M. Vovelle, *Théodore Desorgues ou la désorganisation* (Paris, 1984), pp. 194–9; I. Woloch, *Napoleon and his Collaborators: The Making of a Dictatorship* (New York and London, 2001), pp. 192–7, 204–5.
3 Archives Nationales (hereafter AN), CC 60, 'Registre des délibérations de la Commission, 13 Prairial an XII–27 mai 1814'; CC 61–62, 'Registres d'enregistrement des pétitions'; CC 63, 'Table des pétitionnaires'; O² 1430–1436, case dossiers. See J. Charon-Bordas, *Commission de la liberté individuelle (1802–1814): Inventaire* (Paris, 1989), which has minor errors, largely from transcribing poor handwriting in the original sources.

however, neglected the relevant police records, although a full understanding of the Commission's work requires matching up its cases with the copious files of the Ministry of General Police. These clarify many points often unclear in the Commission's own dossiers: the correct spelling of scribbled names, the exact identity of petitioners, the precise motives for police action against them, and even their ultimate fate.[4]

But an even better reason for examining more closely the cases that came before the Senatorial Commission on Personal Liberty is that they provide telling examples of how bureaucrats, policemen, prosecutors, and judges flouted the rights of French citizens during the Napoleonic era. The Napoleonic state was high-handed in dealing not only with political opponents – presumably the people most likely to claim that a dictatorial government had violated their liberty – but also with ordinary criminals (whether convicted or merely suspected) and with a broad spectrum of social misfits, including the insane and the indigent. The records of the Senatorial Commission and the police reveal a tension at the very heart of the Napoleonic political settlement between a human rights tradition inherited from the Enlightenment and the French Revolution and an imperative desire to re-establish and maintain law and order, whatever the cost in terms of arbitrary measures by the government machine.

Origins and composition of the Senatorial Commission

A declaration of universal and natural human rights – the 'rights of man' – was an integral part of the revolutionary project of limiting monarchical authority by establishing safeguards against abuses of governmental authority.[5] Of all the individual rights recognized in 1789, freedom from arbitrary arrest and imprisonment was probably the most valued; the *lettre de cachet* and the Bastille had come to represent the very essence of Old Regime despotism in the popular imagination.[6] Unlike the constitutions of 1791, 1793 and 1795,

---

4   For example, the Commission recorded one name (O² 1430, #26) as Lhambarel or Lhanarel, which Bordas, *Inventaire*, transcribed as Lhambarel or Lhouarel; he was Lhannard (AN, F⁷ 6285, doss. 5797–BP; F⁷ 8072, doss. 106–R). Aulard, 'La liberté individuelle', could not identify a petitioner named Coussaud or explain his arrest; the Commission's papers (which he ignored) include two dossiers on Jean-Jacques Coussaud (AN, O² 1434, #412; 1435, #158) and a police file recounts in detail his life, career, and offences (F⁷ 6333, doss. 7019–BP). Vovelle, *Théodore Desorgues*, assumed that Claudine Duflocq, *femme* Chaumette, was widow of the revolutionary P.-G. Chaumette; she was only an obscure 'anarchist' arrested in a police roundup (O² 1436, #72; F⁷ 6272, doss. 5588–BP).

5   K. M. Baker, 'The Idea of a Declaration of Rights', in D. Van Kley (ed.), *The French Idea of Freedom: The Old Regime and the Declaration of Rights of 1789* (Stanford, 1994), pp. 154–96; and L. Hunt, *The French Revolution and Human Rights: A Brief Documentary History* (Boston and New York, 1996).

6   H.-J. Lüsenbrink and R. Reichardt, *The Bastille: A History of a Symbol of Despotism and Freedom* (Durham, NC, and London, 1997).

however, the Constitution of 13 December 1799 (22 Frimaire VIII) did not include any declaration of rights. Cambacérès, Napoleon's Second Consul and then his Arch-Chancellor, wrote in his memoirs: 'If this [omission] was intentional on the part of the drafters, I would observe that a declaration of rights would have been a danger because of the difficulty of keeping maxims from encroaching on legislation'.[7] Nor did subsequent constitutional modifications adopted in 1802 and 1804 add any such declaration; only the more liberal Additional Act of 1815 timidly listed a few 'citizens' rights' in Title VI. At best, certain articles of the Constitution of 1799 enumerated specific liberties. Article 46 in particular guaranteed against the 'crime of arbitrary detention' by specifying that although the Minister of General Police could arrest conspirators against the State, he had either to release them or to remand them to the courts within ten days. It was ostensibly in order to defend this particular freedom that the Organic Senatus-Consultum of 18 May 1804 (28 Floréal XII) that created the Napoleonic Empire also established the Senatorial Commission on Personal Liberty (articles 61 to 63).[8]

Some historians have maintained that these three articles resulted from a deal struck between Napoleon and his Senate.[9] When Napoleon took the title of Emperor, the senators sought, as the price of their consent, an extension of senatorial powers, hereditary senatorships (which they failed to get), and reinforcement of the Senate's constitutional role as defender of the people's rights. An unpublished memorandum appended to the Senate's formal address urging Napoleon to assume the imperial dignity proposed that '[t]he Conservative Senate, guarantor of the civil rights of citizens, shall name two commissions, each composed of seven senators, one to receive petitions relative to personal liberty, and the other petitions relative to freedom of the press'.[10] Isser Woloch has written that 'Napoleon ... readily agreed to [these] proposals by the Senate that confirmed its symbolic role as guardian of liberal values', but in fact his initial reaction was to fly into a rage at a session of the Council of State: '[The Senate] feigns to see itself as guardian of the country's liberties; but what better guardian could these have than the prince? ... The Senate's claims recall the English constitution', which he described as totally unsuited to France.[11] Napoleon eventually did agree, however. Why? Most likely he recognized that he had little to lose from

7   J.-J.-R. de Cambacérès, *Mémoires inédits*, ed. L. Chatel de Brainçon, 2 vols (Paris, 2000), vol. 1, p. 456.

8   J. Godechot, *Les Constitutions de la France depuis 1789* (Paris, 1970).

9   For example, J. Thiry, *Le Sénat de Napoléon (1800–1814)* (Paris, 1932), pp. 144–6; Woloch, *Napoleon and his Collaborators*, p. 192.

10 AN, CC 3, 'Sénat Conservateur: Procès-verbal des séances', pp. 13v–14v, 'Mémoire joint au message adressé par le Sénat au premier consul, le 14 floréal an douze'.

11 Woloch, *Napoleon and his Collaborators*, p. 118; J. Pelet de la Lozère, *Opinions de Napoléon sur divers sujets et de politique d'administration, recueillies par un membre de son Conseil d'État* (Paris, 1833), pp. 61–6.

institutions that gave his regime a shining liberal veneer but could in reality do almost nothing to mitigate its authoritarianism.

There was, moreover, a recent precedent for the Senatorial Commission on Personal Liberty. Article 55 of the Organic Senatus-Consultum of 16 Thermidor X (4 August 1802) weakened the Constitution's guarantee against arbitrary detention by stipulating that 'the Senate ... determines the time for which individuals, arrested by virtue of article 46 of the Constitution, must be remanded to the courts, when this has not been done within ten days of their arrest'. The Senate subsequently named a special commission, which met several times in September 1802, to examine the case of every prisoner currently being held without trial as a security risk.[12] Napoleon furthermore asked that the commission widen its scope by looking into the cases of all men and women incarcerated without trial for any other reason, including brigands and thieves imprisoned on simple order of local authorities.[13] Napoleon clearly intended both to assuage public opinion and to legalize retroactively the government's past disregard of constitutional liberties:

> The First Consul attaches great importance to this work, in which the public will see a veritable guarantee given to civil liberty. ... Indeed, the Constitutional Act [of 1799] guaranteed to persons arrested for conspiracy freedom or trial within ten days, and the government, for reasons that are easy to understand, not being able to observe exactly this particular provision, will see its operations regularized by act of the Senate.[14]

Similar considerations probably inspired Napoleon's decision only two years later to accept a similar but more permanent senatorial commission.

Handling petitions

The Senatorial Commission on Personal Liberty comprised seven senators elected by their colleagues to a four-month term and eligible for re-election. Sixteen men served as commissioners between 1804 and 1814. Many had been moderates or even royalists during the French Revolution; several had known proscription and arrest under the Reign of Terror.[15] Such personal

---

12 AN, F⁷ 6998, for minutes of four meetings, the first undated, the others 28 Fructidor and 1er Jour Complémentaire X and 3 Vendémiaire XI (15, 18 and 25 Sept 1802).

13 AN, F⁷ 6998, 'Note pour le Grand Juge', Vendémiaire XI (Sept/Oct 1802).

14 AN, F⁷ 6324, doss. 6389–BP, 'Rapport au Grand-Juge', 1er Jour Complémentaire X (18 Sept 1802).

15 The members and their periods of service were: J.-J. Lenoir-Laroche, 2–06–04 to 28–02–11; F.-A. Boissy-d'Anglas, 2–06–04 to 13–02–13; J.-L.-C. Emmery, 2–06–04 to 13–01–09; A.-J. Abrial, 2–06–04 to 27–05–14; T. Vernier, 2–06–04 to 1–02–06; J.-.P. Sers, 2–06–04 to 5–03–05; N. Vimar, 2–06–04 to 22–10–04; L.-N. Lemercier, 22–10–04 to 27–05–14; F. Cacault. 5–03–05 to 1–02–06; M.-A. Cornet, 1–02–06 to 30–12–09; B. Journu-Aubert, 1–02–06 to 28–07–09; L.-J.-B. Gouvion, 13–01–06 to 27–05–14; J.-V. Colchen, 28–07–09 to 27–05–14; M. Lejeas, 30–12–09 to 27–05–14; C.-E.-J.-P. Pastoret, 28–02–11 to 27–05–14; and F.-G. Van Dedem Tot den Gelder, 13–02–13 to 27–05–14. Biographical information from J. Tulard (ed.), *Dictionnaire Napoléon* (Paris, 1987).

histories ought to have made for commissioners prepared to fight tooth and nail against arbitrary imprisonment; that, after all, was their job. Any individual French citizen detained without trial beyond ten days could petition the Commission for redress. If the senators found imprisonment 'not justified by the interests of the State' (an exception that in practice left the door wide open to abuse), they could 'invite' the minister concerned either to release the prisoner or to send him or her to trial. If the minister failed to comply after three such summations, the commissioners could ask the Senate to indict him for trial before the Imperial High Court, composed of senators, senior officials, and high dignitaries.

From its first session on 6 June 1804 to its last on 27 May 1814, the Senatorial Commission met every two or three weeks for a total of 221 times.[16] It handled a total of 551 distinct cases.[17] Although a minister could himself notify the Commission of his intention to detain an individual for more than ten days and explain why, thereby soliciting prior approval for his action, this happened only once, in July 1806 when the Minister of General Police informed the Commission that he planned to hold indefinitely three men plotting to assassinate the Emperor.[18] Otherwise, either aggrieved citizens themselves petitioned the Senatorial Commission or friends or relatives did so on their behalf. Most petitions were handwritten, usually in the petitioner's hand, although hired scribes occasionally wrote out and may even have drafted petitions. The tone was sometimes matter-of-fact and sometimes highly overwrought in asserting wronged innocence. Petitioners usually blamed their plight on bureaucratic error, mistaken judges, or the machinations of some personal enemy. Many tried to appeal to the senators' presumed sense of justice or to flatter them with phrases like this one: 'Oh! commission blessed by the People! friends of justice, defenders of atrociously oppressed innocence, come to my aid.'[19] Government officials themselves, unable or

16 AN, CC 60 contains the minutes. There were eighteen meetings in year XII; twenty-eight in year XIII; four in year XIV (three months); twenty-four in 1806; seventeen in 1807; twenty-five in 1808; twenty-five in 1809; twenty-one in 1810; seventeen in 1811; twenty in 1812; nineteen in 1813; and three in 1814.

17 The commonly given figure of 585 cases is erroneous. The Commission's ledgers end with case #585, but there are blanks opposite cases #426 though #442 (for which there are no dossiers either). Furthermore, six cases have two dossiers each (#570 and #422; #376 and #513; #152 and #333; #149 and #375; #186 and #397; #331 and #417; #488 and #525; #551 and #583), two dossiers cover the Aubin-Goujon case involving seven people (#363 and #446), and several single dossiers pertain to two or more distinct cases (#190, #193, #252, #296, #575, and #585).

18 Bibliothèque Nationale, Le49 28, *Rapport fait au Sénat dans sa séance du 30 vendémiaire an XII, par le Sénateur Lenoir-Laroche au nom de la Commission Sénatoriale de la liberté individuelle* (Paris, n.d.), pp. 4, 7; AN, O² 1435, doss. 'Affaires générales', Minister of General Police to Commission, 4 July 1806. These were Bonnard and Le Simple, allegedly paid two hundred guineas by the British to kill Napoleon, and Guillet de la Chevrière, denounced by the British cabinet minister whom he approached.

19 AN, O² 1430, #53, petition by Jean Sutières, 14 Messidor XII (3 July 1804).

unwilling to take on the police, might encourage the victims of arbitrary police methods to petition the Commission. For example, the journalist Henri Delloye appealed to numerous authorities after his arrest in April 1805 for defying an order by the prefect of the Ourthe to stop publishing a periodical that attacked local administration. This clearly violated Delloye's legal rights under existing press laws, but every official to whom he turned replied that he could not help someone held by police order and suggested that he instead try the Senatorial Commission.[20] Of course, prisoners who wanted to petition the Senatorial Commission had to persuade their jailers first to supply them with pen and paper and then to allow their letter to go forward. They also had to pay postage; in 1807 the Minister of Finance refused a senatorial request to exempt letters to the Commission from postal charges.[21] A state prisoner named Philippe Corneille complained in 1809:

Nothing equals the inquisitorial tyranny exercised [in prison] when it comes to letters. One cannot write to the Senatorial Commission on Personal Liberty, to the Ministers, even to His Imperial Majesty, without giving one's letters to the jailers, who send them all to the prefecture of police, where they vanish. Only those [letters] that the prisoners can conceal from their tyrants reach their destination.[22]

The Senatorial Commission did in fact receive Corneille's letter, but his complaint was not entirely unfounded. Jean Honnert, imprisoned in the fortress of Ham, was permitted to petition the Commission in February 1805, but the police intercepted and held back a second petition in January 1810 after the commandant protested that in it Honnert 'vomits forth the most atrocious insults against me; I am depicted entirely as a tyrant'.[23] In January 1810, Heinrich Heymann, held in the Château d'If since 1808, gave the commandant his petition to the Commission in an unsealed envelope. The commandant sent it to the Ministry of General Police, with a note appended: 'Please, if you find it appropriate, ... forward it to its address.' But he also drew attention to Heymann's intemperate language: 'this State Prisoner does not express himself tactfully enough. The [use of the] word *arbitrary* under a Government and a Police as enlightened and as just as ours, both displeased and offended me.' The Ministry filed away the petition and the senators never learned of Heymann's attempt to contact them.[24]

---

20 AN, O² 1431, #165; F⁷ 8134, doss. 7656–R; F⁷ 8424, doss. 7490–P. Deloye was released in July, perhaps because of the Commission's intervention, and exiled to Dijon.
21 AN, CC 60, 14 Jan. 1807.
22 Archives de la Préfecture de Police, D/b 144, 'Observations sur les Prisons adressées à Sa Majesté l'Empereur & Roi et aux grands fonctionnaires de l'Empire', 15 Nov. 1809, published as 'Les prisons sous le Premier Empire', *Revue pénitentiaire* 30 (1906), p. 253.
23 AN, F⁷ 8074, doss. 210–R, commandant Dillenius to councillor of state Réal, 26 Jan 1810. For the earlier petition, O² 1435, #154. Honnert's police file is F⁷ 8073, doss. 146–R.
24 AN, F⁷ 8526, doss. 8090–P3, Heymann to Commission, 22 Jan 1810; commandant to councillor of state Pelet, 23 Jan 1810.

Whenever the Senatorial Commission received a petition, its president assigned one member to the case and himself wrote to the appropriate minister (almost always the Minister of General Police) for his version of events. Although ministers generally answered promptly, the Commission sometimes had to send follow-up letters when responses were slow in coming; sometimes, too, the Commission wrote again months or years later to inquire about the final decision in a case already discussed.[25] This correspondence was unfailingly polite and even cordial, but ministers were no less determined to defend their authority against outside interference. The Commission's second case set the tone for dealings between the senators and the police. Having received a petition from one Claude-Etienne de Salignac-Fénélon, the Senatorial Commission wrote to ask the police why they were holding him without trial. The facts were simple enough. Napoleon had personally ordered the arrest in 1803 after Salignac-Fénélon proposed a toast to 'Louis XVIII' at a dinner in Dijon and predicted the First Consul's assassination. But as a worried ministerial official explained in an internal report, the Commission's inquiry potentially threatened the confidentiality of police files:

To respond to the Senatorial Commission's question, it was necessary to divulge details about this individual ... which ought to be known only to the police. What would happen then, if, not satisfied with a detailed report, the Commission also asked for communication of the documents? ... Not only could we not turn over the documents without serious risk, but to give the Commission knowledge of *all* the motives concerning our prisoners would also expose us to indiscretions that could compromise state security.

Such fears proved unfounded. The Commission accepted a general report on Salignac-Fénélon's misdeeds and the Minister's determination that 'given the circumstances in which we find ourselves, the interest of the State does not permit that he be granted his liberty'.[26]

Such blithe invocations of security would always be enough to satisfy the Senatorial Commission. The senators invariably accepted ministerial explanations without ever prying further into a case, asking for additional documentation or challenging the reasons for an incarceration. The police bureaucracy never had to worry about justifying one of its decisions to the senators. Only once did officials at the Ministry of General Police invoke – in confidential internal correspondence – the Senatorial Commission as pretext for liberating a prisoner, and this was in highly unusual circumstances. In June

25 For example, AN, F⁷ 6231, plaq. 2, pièces 137–38, president to Minister of General Police, 10 Vendémiaire XIII (2 Oct 1804), 'Tableau des [vingt] réclamations que la commission de la liberté individuelle a reçues pendant le dernier trimestre an XII sur lesquelles elle attend des renseignements et l'opinion définitive du Ministre de la Police générale'.

26 AN, O² 1430, #2, Minister of General Police to Commission, 26 Prairial XII (15 June 1804); F⁷ 6331, doss. 7001–BP, undated report to Minister of Justice.

1804, the Prefect of Police for Paris had ordered the arrest of Auguste Joseph Delagarde, an amnestied émigré, 'as a man devoted to the Bourbons ... and having more than once manifested his hatred of the Government and His Majesty the Emperor'. Soon afterwards, an official at the Ministry of General Police warned the Minister that 'given certain information which destroys the vague declarations that served as a pretext for the arrest, ... nothing can justify to the Senatorial Commission the decision taken by Your Excellency ... on the basis of the Prefect of Police's report'. It seems that Delagarde's real offence had been to seek repayment of twenty-eight thousand francs lent to one of the Prefect's friends. Police scruples had nothing to do with any commitment to human rights; here was a welcome chance for the Minister of General Police to discredit and rein in the Prefect, his bureaucratic rival. The Minister released Delagarde in October 1804, exiling him to his native Lille.[27]

The only time the senators ever came close to challenging the police occurred in 1807. Jean-Baptiste-Martin Lasalle was a Parisian merchant, arrested in September 1806 for publishing a pamphlet that denounced General Savary for cancelling three contracts that Lasalle had to supply the gendarmerie. (The police file shows that Savary had personally written to the police that they 'would give [him] much satisfaction by having [Lasalle] arrested'.) On this one occasion, the Commission went over the head of the Minister of General Police and wrote directly to the Emperor on 2 January 1807. Conceding in advance that Lasalle's detention was fully justified, they nonetheless urged Napoleon to have him released. The Emperor agreed, but Lasalle found himself back in prison within weeks, this time (in what may have been a put-up job) at the request of one of his creditors.[28] For once the senators showed firmness in seeking the release of a prisoner, but it was at best the exception that proved the rule.

The content of the petitions

It is by no means easy to classify the variety of cases examined by the Senatorial Commission on Personal Liberty, but the 551 cases divide into the following rough categories in descending order of magnitude: 159 involving criminal activity (including brigandage); 146 relating to some sort of political offence; 116 clearly outside the Commission's jurisdiction; fifty-seven vagabonds or beggars; sixteen men and women incarcerated at the request of their own families; and twelve interned madmen or madwomen. Another forty-five miscellaneous cases fall into no particular category. Each of these broad groups deserves examination, starting with those cases that lay beyond

27   AN, O² 1436, #98; F⁷ 6435, doss. 9072–BP (quotations from this dossier); F⁷ 8085, doss. 1509–R.
28   AN, O² 1432, #232; CC61, #232; F⁷ 6483, doss. 433–Série 2.

the Commission's reach and concluding with the sort of cases at the heart of the Commission's *raison d'être* – political offences.

About one in five cases involved grievances outside the Senatorial Commission's jurisdiction, usually because the petitioner was not actually in prison; these generally required no further investigation or deliberation.[29] Some of these cases, however, certainly deserved more than the peremptory treatment that the senators gave them, most especially those of deportees and exiles, who, while not technically prisoners, most certainly suffered from rather arbitrary police decisions. In 1804, the Commission received petitions concerning two of the 130 former revolutionary militants deported from France in January 1801, after the assassination attempt on Napoleon of 3 Nivôse IX (24 December 1800). Louis André wrote while still in prison awaiting deportation, but the senators refused to intervene. Étienne Michel's wife told the Commission that her husband had just been shipped overseas to an undisclosed destination; the senators recommended that she seek the Emperor's clemency.[30] The Senatorial Commission thus let slip the chance to remedy one of the regime's most arbitrary decisions – the deportation for political reasons of men guilty of no actual crime (the attempt on Napoleon's life was the work of royalists, not revolutionaries); of course, the government's action had been authorized at the time by a decree of the Senate.

Nineteen additional petitions came from men and women sent into 'internal exile', that is, expelled from their ordinary place of residence to live elsewhere in France under the surveillance of local authorities. This was a convenient and cheap way for the government to punish accused troublemakers, including minor political opponents, without any expenditure for incarceration (exiles had to support themselves).[31] A petition from Nicolas Joseph Perret, exiled from Paris in 1804 for stealing a watch (a crime he denied), noted the threat to liberty inherent in this practice: 'No one would be assured of sleeping at home the next day, and it would be necessary to shut down the law courts, because these [municipal] clerks

---

29 For instance: several men in the Paris debtors' prison asked for the right to receive visitors, a municipal secretary claimed that he had been wrongly accused of forging the mayor's signature and unjustly fired, a landowner near Avignon protested against the expropriation of his land to build a canal, a young man sentenced to five years' hard labour for fraud wanted this commuted to simple imprisonment, and a nobleman claimed that he was erroneously under surveillance as a returned émigré. AN, O² 1431, #198; O² 1432, #285; O² 1432, #264; O² 1436, #543; and F⁷ 6594, doss. 3788–Série 2; O² 1431, #520.

30 M.J. Sydenham, 'The Crime of 3 Nivôse', in J. F. Bosher (ed.), *French Government and Society 1500–1850* (London, 1973), pp. 295–320. For André: AN, O² 1436, #115; F⁷ 6272. doss. 5588; F⁷ 8337, doss. 2030–R3. For Michel: O² 1430, #47; F⁷ 6586. doss. 354–Série 2.

31 M. Sibalis, 'La Côte-d'Or, terre d'exil: Les résidents sous surveillance pendant le Consulat et l'Empire', *Annales de Bourgogne* 64 (1992), pp. 39–51; 'Internal exiles in Napoleonic France', *Proceedings of the Western Society for French History* 20 (1993), pp. 189–98.

would take over the recognition, prosecution, and judgement of all cases behind closed doors and without right of appeal.'[32]

The police insisted from the start that the senators had no right to concern themselves with internal exiles. Jean Baptiste Houdaille was among the very first to petition the Senatorial Commission from prison, after his arrest in April 1804 on suspicion of royalist conspiracy. The police released him in late July, but expelled him from Paris and Houdaille petitioned again: 'Such an order [of exile] annihilates me, because it prevents me from looking after my business.' The Commission wrote to the Minister of General Police that it 'has found this request important enough to be communicated to you' and asked him 'to give it information as to the conditions put on Jean Baptiste Houdaille's release, and to inform it of your definitive opinion on this matter'. Ministerial bureaucrats advised the Minister that the case was quite simply none of the senators' business: 'It does not appear, according to the articles of the Senatus Consultum ..., that this Commission has any jurisdiction over police measures [of this kind]. It mentions only imprisonment extended beyond ten days.'[33] The senators thereafter declined to deal with similar petitions and simply forwarded them to the Minister of General Police for his consideration.

More within its jurisdiction, but apparently not of great concern to the Senatorial Commission, were fifty-seven cases of vagrants and beggars. These were mostly men, aged anywhere from sixteen to seventy-seven, who had been interned against their will, generally in the poorhouse at St. Denis outside Paris (reserved for vagabonds) or the one at Villers-Cotterêts in the Oise (for deserving indigents from the Paris region). The Napoleonic government, like its immediate predecessors, wanted to bring about 'the extinction of mendicity' through a combination of poor relief and repression.[34] The police believed that poorhouses rescued beggars from poverty and idleness, while protecting society from mendicants who might otherwise turn to crime to survive. Sixty-year-old Guillaume Bienassis, 'an infirm veteran without resources', wandered for several years through eastern France before authorities in the Doubs took him into custody in 1809 and sent him to Paris, where the police placed him at Villers-Cotterêts. The Minister of General Police told the Senatorial Commission that 'in his own interest and that of society, [Bienassis] must remain there until he can prove that he has some means of existence'.[35] Likewise, the police arrested Michel Deglos in Paris in October

32 AN, O² 1436, #105.
33 AN, O² 1430, #42; F⁷ 6429, doss. 8742, Commission to Minister, 16 Thermidor XII (4 Aug. 1804), and 'Note à Son Excellence' (n.d.).
34 I. Woloch, *The New Regime: Transformations of the French Civic Order, 1789–1820s* (New York and London, 1994), pp. 266–76.
35 AN, O² 1434, #406, Minister of General Police to Commission, 29 Aug. 1810; F⁷ 8721, doss. 4942–G.

1809 after they caught him begging at shop doors, which they blamed on his 'laziness and bad inclinations'. The Minister of General Police 'thought that charity as much as public security required that this individual be kept in the prison of Villers-Cotterêts ... until good weather, bringing work in the countryside, might enable him to make himself useful and to live without begging'.[36]

The Commission dealt with police responses to other social ills as well. Sixteen petitioners owed their detention to relatives. The post-revolutionary settlement seemingly required the stabilization of family life, and many families in Napoleonic France turned to the police to buttress their authority over individual members in the same way that before 1789 they had asked the government for a *lettre de cachet*.[37] Families asked for police intervention when a relative threatened them with physical harm by acts of violence or economic damage by dissipation of the family fortune. In addition, criminal activity, habitual public drunkenness or sexual promiscuity (particularly a wife's or sister's) might bring dishonour on an entire family. In 1809, for example, Charles Marie Leclerc petitioned the Senatorial Commission against a series of arbitrary detentions at his family's behest. His story began in 1806, when his parents denounced their then thirty-six-year-old son as a man who 'has, since birth, by both his misconduct and his immorality, tormented his father and mother'. The prefect of the Oise and the local prosecutor reported 'that there is cause to isolate or exile this individual' and the Minister of General Police agreed.[38] Similarly, the Prefect of Police consigned Jeanne Adelaïde Bezuchet, *femme* Lagache, to a Parisian convent in 1813 on the grounds that 'her unbridled taste for libertinage has led her to exceed the bounds of propriety; she has become the scandal of her neighbourhood'.[39]

The cases of twelve petitioners who protested that they were unjustly held in a prison or asylum as clinically insane are less clearly arbitrary. One was the revolutionary poet Théodore Desorgues. A recent biography has revived the hoary legend that Napoleon's government regularly committed its opponents to mental hospitals, but in fact a law court placed Desorgues in Charenton asylum only after doctors certified him as genuinely mad.[40] There he may have crossed paths with the marquis de Sade, the most famous patient at Charenton, who petitioned the Senatorial Commission in June 1804,

36 AN, O² 1436, #410, Minister of General Police to Commission, 21 Nov. 1810 and 27 Feb. 1811.
37 S. Desan, 'Reconstructing the Social after the Terror: Family, Property and the Law in Popular Politics', *Past and Present* 164 (1999), pp. 81–121; A. Farge and M. Foucault, *Le Désordre des familles: Lettres de cachet des Archives de la Bastille* (Paris, 1982).
38 AN, O² 1434, #366; F⁷ 8136, doss. 7819–R.
39 AN, O² 1433, #546.
40 M. Vovelle, *Théodore Desorgues*; M. Sibalis, 'Un aspect de la légende noire de Napoléon: le mythe de l'enfermement des opposants comme fous', *Revue de l'Institut Napoléon* 156 (1991), pp. 9–26; 'L'enfermement de Théodore Desorgues: documents inédits', *Annales historiques de la Révolution française* 284 (1991), pp. 243–6.

claiming to have been unjustly interned for publishing an obscene book (*Juliette*) that he denied writing. The truth was that both the government and Sade's own family wanted to keep this troublesome man, whose behaviour was certainly bizarre and most probably insane, locked up in relative comfort.[41]

The police often handled ordinary criminals in the same arbitrary way, and 159 of the cases that came before the Senatorial Commission – the largest category at more than one-quarter of the total – involved felons. The most dangerous belonged to the armed bands of 'brigands', often composed of royalist insurrectionists or draft-dodgers who had taken to the hills, and who roamed the countryside attacking stagecoaches and isolated farmhouses.[42] A government pledged to internal order could hardly tolerate such lawlessness and the authorities treated accused brigands ruthlessly. Some prosecutors saw no point in even sending suspected brigands to trial, like the prosecutor of the Deux-Nethes, who in 1805 sought to justify to the Senatorial Commission the administrative detention of Joseph Vermoren and his co-defendants: 'nothing equals the ignorance and pusillanimity of our jurors ... who would certainly have acquitted them, and our brigands, emboldened by a scandalous impunity, would have continued along the course of their misdeeds'.[43] The Special Tribunals instituted in the early Consulate to conduct trials without benefit of jury were hardly known for their leniency,[44] but even when they acquitted accused brigands, the police still had their own way. The order for the arrest of Michel Chauvin (attached to his petition of October 1805) quoted instructions given by the Minister of General Police to the prefect of the Eure and dated September 1801:

The public interest demands ... that individuals against whom the courts have not found material evidence sufficient for conviction be kept under arrest when public opinion accuses them of brigandage. I consequently authorize you to execute this measure of public security with regard to those accused whom the Special Tribunal of the Eure has freed for lack of evidence.[45]

The authorities could be equally heavy-handed when it came to lesser criminals: not only murderers and arsonists, but even petty thieves. For instance, after a robbery in Nîmes in April 1808 the local police commissioner and mayor decided to arrest 'various suspect individuals', including Claude Gilly and Jacques Dufois. The police commissioner admitted that he had absolutely

41 AN, O² 1430, #32, F⁷ 6294, doss. 6029–BP.
42 J. Roberts, *The Counter-revolution in France, 1787–1830* (New York, 1990), pp. 59–76; J. Tulard, 'Quelques aspects du brigandage sous l'Empire', *Revue de l'Institut Napoléon* 98 (1966), pp. 31–6.
43 AN, O² 1431, #161.
44 H. G. Brown, 'From Organic Society to Security State: The War on Brigandage in France, 1797–1802', *Journal of Modern History* 69 (1997), pp. 661–95; 'Bonaparte's 'Booted Justice' in Bas-Languedoc', *Proceedings of the Western Society for French History* 25 (1998), pp. 120–30.
45 AN, O² 1435, #133, letter of 14 Fructidor IX (1 Sept. 1801); F⁷ 8075, d. 283–R.

no evidence against them, but argued that 'men branded by public opinion the way Gilly and Dufois are should be isolated from society'. Incarcerated in the citadel of Nîmes, Dufois eventually petitioned the Senatorial Commission two years later and the Minister of General Police deigned to order his release in June 1810.[46] In other instances, the police did not even have specific crimes in mind and merely deemed someone 'a person of bad character' (un mauvais sujet); that in itself could be sufficient grounds for detention. Joseph Rouelle (or Rouvel) was in his seventies when the police commissioner of Boulogne-sur-Mer arrested him in 1805 or 1806, describing him as a dangerous intriguer in a strategic coastal town ('adroit, shameless, speaking almost every language, he is mixed up in everything') and suggesting that 'a perpetual incarceration in Bicêtre prison or elsewhere seems to me the only guarantee that one can have against this execrable man'. The Minister of General Police agreed and transferred Rouelle to Bicêtre Prison in Paris, where he remained, despite his appeal to the Senatorial Commission, until April 1814.[47]

Prosecutors and judges themselves even connived at the process by which prefects and policemen substituted themselves for the law courts, as several cases reviewed by the Senatorial Commission illustrate. The courts twice acquitted Claude Tabalard, a weaver from Lachapelle (department of the Allier), once of murder in July 1810 and then of arson in July 1811, after the homes of two witnesses against him at his first trial mysteriously burned down. The prosecutor's 'deep-seated conviction' of his guilt and a request from the local prefect were enough for the Minister of General Police, who ordered his imprisonment in Lyon.[48] In September 1811, the Court of Assizes for the Eure acquitted Reine Denier, femme Cauchois, of arson, 'despite the strongest indications of guilt, but for lack of sufficient proof'. The court's chief justice, the local prefect, the commandant of the gendarmerie and forty witnesses at her trial got the Minister of General Police to keep her in prison nonetheless, because they feared her vengeance upon release.[49]

The police sometimes also held convicted criminals beyond the sentence imposed by the courts. As the Minister of General Police explained to the Senatorial Commission in the case of the thief Antoine-Marc Lambois, whom he retained in Bicêtre Prison in 1804 after the expiration of his sentence, 'one cannot be too careful in removing anything that might trouble good order and compromise public and personal security'.[50] Similarly, in April 1808 the police refused to release Léonard François Noiret after he finished his six-

---

46 AN, O² 1434, #405; F⁷ 8432, doss. 8751–P.
47 AN, O² 1432, #260; F⁷ 6579, doss. 3118–Série-2; F⁷ 6503, doss. 851–Série 2; F⁷ 8118, doss. 6287–R.
48 AN, O² 1433, #548; F⁷ 8241, doss. 7669–R2; F⁷ 8639, doss. 864–P3.
49 AN, O² 1433, #556; F⁷ 8120, doss. 6425–R.
50 AN, O² 1430, #58.

month sentence for theft. '[C]onsidering him to be a habitual and dangerous thief, especially during the winter', the Minister of General Police wrote to the Senatorial Commission, 'I have put him in Bicêtre prison, to be detained there until next spring.' In fact, Noiret did not get out until August 1812, more than four years after his legal sentence had expired.[51]

Although less numerous than strictly criminal cases, the petitions from 146 men and women detained for conspiracy or political opposition to the regime clearly lay at the heart of the Commission's concerns. The government consistently maintained that people of this sort could not be judged by the regular courts, but only by the Superior Police (*haute police*). For instance, in 1811 the prefect of the Seine-Inférieure stated the official line in reference to Pierre Ponce, detained in Rouen since January 1808 on suspicion of conspiring with the British. Attempts by a local prosecutor to assert the supremacy of the law courts only infuriated the prefect:

[T]his magistrate regards the detention of the aforementioned Ponce as arbitrary, illegal, and illegitimate, and ... reserves [to himself] the right to take a position on this detention, as if he had the power to annul actions taken by the Superior Police; as if he had the right to inquire into and judge the motives that determine police decisions; and as if it were not enough ... that this arrest has been made on a higher order from the Superior Police.

The prefect took particular offence at the prosecutor's suggestion 'that his office [as prosecutor] imposes on him the firm duty of repressing any attack on personal liberty'.[52]

Political prisoners, or so-called 'state prisoners', in Napoleonic France had committed offences of widely varying seriousness.[53] Some of the political cases that came before the Senatorial Commission involved little more than mistaken identity. For example, the police arrested the peddler Pierre Préjean (or Prigent) in the Maine-et-Loire in January 1804, after they misidentified him as a famous Chouan leader of the same name. Once his real identity had been established, they did liberate him in October 1804, but given 'the information ... designating Préjean as a man of very bad character, ... who escaped the severity of the laws only because of a lack of legal proof', the Minister of General Police exiled him to Dijon, where he lived in destitution until death set him free in 1807.[54] Others who petitioned the Senatorial Commission had done no more than make 'indiscreet' or 'subversive' remarks. Arbitrary detention of vocal malcontents avoided the unwanted but

51   AN, O² 1436, #372.
52   AN, F⁷ 6383, doss. 7807–BP, letter of 6 July 1811.
53   M. Sibalis, 'Prisoners by *Mesure de Haute Police* under Napoleon I: Reviving the *Lettres de cachet*', *Proceedings of the Annual Meeting of the Western Society for French History* 18 (1991), pp. 261–9.
54   AN, O² 1430, #63; F⁷ 3089, 'Feuilles de travail', 8 Thermidor XII (27 July 1804) and 13 Vendémiaire XIII (5 Oct. 1804); F⁷ 6200, plaq. 2, pièces 87–110; F⁷ 6378, doss. 7732–BP; Archives départementales, Côte-d'Armor, 1 M 35.

inevitable publicity of a public trial. In 1811, the prefect of the Lot had to decide what to do with Jean-Baptiste Reygasse Marmont (or Malmont), a local lawyer and 'fanatical Jacobin from the time of the Terror', who had openly criticized Napoleon as a usurper and praised the Spanish and English for attempting to drive him from the throne. The prefect decided against remanding Marmont to trial, because 'the hearing of such proceedings would be scandalous, in obliging the witnesses to repeat in public the blasphemies of this fanatic'. Marmont spent thirteen months in prison on simple administrative order.[55]

Even many so-called conspirators were small fry indeed, and no real threat to the regime, like seven illiterate Breton peasants, who could not even speak French, who petitioned the senators in 1805 from the Parisian prisons where they were languishing for their alleged participation in the royalist Debar conspiracy of 1803. They had done nothing more than harbour or guide Debar's men, whose identities and plans they apparently did not even know. Pierre François, for example, explained: 'A man whom I had never seen or met, having noticed me working in a field between eleven and noon, asked me to take him to a place one league away from where we were. ... I never believed that there was any harm in earning a thirty-sous piece.' The police themselves eventually decided that these peasants were so little dangerous that they soon sent them back to Brittany, in fact releasing one of them even before receiving an inquiry from the Senatorial Commission.[56] Other suspects, no less deserving of clemency, were less fortunate. Adam Louis de Wilhelm, a Knight of Malta and former captain in the Russian army, was arrested in Montreuil-sur-Mer in early March 1804 when he deviated from his authorized route to the Bas-Rhin. He said that he intended to visit his brother in Boulogne; the police feared he was an English spy and held him in various prisons until at least 1813.[57] They detained another individual in Paris and Bordeaux from 1806 until after Napoleon's fall in 1814 because he 'is hiding under the false name of François Dumont and obstinately refuses to provide any information that could identify him'. They suspected that he was 'perhaps a dangerous enemy of the Government, or guilty of some great crime'. He turned out to be an insignificant swindler and adventurer named Simon Fossey.[58]

Even acquittal by the courts (even courts martial) could not protect

---

55 AN, O² 1433, #559; F⁷ 8656, doss. 2526–P 3, prefect of Lot to councillor of state Pelet, 19 Sept. 1811.

56 AN, O² 1430, #628 (Pierre François); O² 1435, #130 (Yves Lecaz, Joseph-Jérôme Blanchard, Henri Lecan, Jean André); O² 1436, #113 (François Legras and Pierre Saumier or Le Sommier); F⁷ 3830–3831, scattered documents, 1803–05.

57 AN, O² 1430, #69; F⁷ 6415, doss. 8348–BP.

58 AN, O² 1433, #550; F⁷ 6571, doss. 2817–Série 2, police report, 30 Aug. 1810, and Prefect of Police to councillor of state Pelet, 20 Oct. 1810; BB³⁰* 188, register of state prisoners; Bibliothèque historique de la ville de Paris, NA 144, fol. 307–08, interrogation, 26 Nov. 1811.

someone perceived as a serious danger to Napoleon or the state from arbitrary police measures. In the spring of 1801, the police arrested François Jean Piogé or Pioger (nicknamed *Sans Pitié*), a Breton weaver and former Chouan. Piogé was hiding out in Paris under a false name, when the police noticed him observing the First Consul reviewing his troops in the Place du Carousel. A military commission acquitted him of conspiracy in January 1804, but, as Piogé wrote to the Senatorial Commission, 'it did not thereby return me to freedom and by a rather bizarre paradox, I found myself at one and the same time both innocent and guilty, innocent because it acquitted me and guilty because I was put back in prison'. He was still there in 1810, at which point he vanishes from the records.[59] Another military commission acquitted Charles Desol de Grisolles in 1804 on charges of spying, corresponding with the enemy and endangering national security, but 'considering that official reports indicate ... that the behaviour of Desol de Grisolles is suspect in their eyes, [the military commission] puts this individual entirely at the disposal of the Government', with the result that he remained in prison until 1814.[60] The senators saw numerous cases like these and yet, despite being fully informed in each instance of the flagrant illegalities at work, they remained surprisingly passive and did nothing significant to prevent arbitrary detention.

Conclusion

In 1811, Pierre Benjamin Bremg wrote to the Senatorial Commission complaining of 'the loss of [his] personal liberty' due to 'these men who often [hid] under the floorboards', poisoned his food and air and kept him awake at night with their noise.[61] Bremg was insane, of course, but his petition proves that many people in France, even madmen, looked to the Commission as their designated protector against oppression. Most of them would be sorely disappointed, none more than Jean-Jacques Coussaud, imprisoned without trial and then banished from Paris for 'the indiscretion of his talk about political affairs, [and] his violent character'. Coussaud sent in a flood of petitions – five in 1805, 108 in 1806, two in 1807, twenty-six in 1808 and twelve in 1810 – which document his transition from hopefulness through frustration to anger, which he vented freely on the senators: 'I want to believe that you have enough energy to fill courageously the honourable functions that are entrusted to you' (15 December 1805); 'I implore in vain your protection' (31 January 1806); 'you are the most barbarous or the most cowardly of men because you are deaf to all my claims' (3 October 1806); 'personal liberty has

59   AN, O² 1430, #44; F⁷ 6235, plaq. 7–8, pièces 620–712.
60   AN, O² 1436, #77; F⁷ 6398, plaq. 1 and 2, especially pièce 130, judgment of 6 Pluviôse XII (27 Jan. 1804).
61   AN, O² 1433, #479.

such very weak upholders in you that you are going to become objects of ridicule and public contempt' (25 October 1806).[62]

Was Coussaud's vitriol justified? The Senatorial Commission itself claimed a modest measure of success, despite what it described as 'inevitable delays' in dealing with a cumbersome police bureaucracy. By their own calculations, the senators obtained the release of forty-four of the first 116 petitioners whose cases they examined.[63] But this claim requires significant qualification. At no time did the Minister of General Police ever liberate a prisoner at the express request of the Senatorial Commission; indeed, the senators never explicitly asked for any such thing. What generally happened (as evidenced by the police records) was that an inquiry from the Senatorial Commission prompted the bureaucrats to look into the facts of a case in order to draft their response. In some instances, the Minister decided, either immediately or, more usually, somewhat later, that a prisoner could now be released. More often than not, however, he simply defended his decision to detain the petitioner without trial and the Senatorial Commission acquiesced without a murmur.

Whatever the senators might think of police procedures, they, like the rest of the ruling elite, looked to the police as an indispensable rampart against the perpetual threat of political and social chaos. They accepted the regime's authoritarianism because they sincerely believed that, in the aftermath of the French Revolution, meaningful liberty could flourish only under a state strong enough to enforce its authority and fully determined to do so. As Jean-Jacques Lenoir-Laroche, once Minister of General Police for ten days in 1797 and president of the Senatorial Commission on Personal Liberty in 1804, explained:

[I]f personal liberty is the first need of men in society, the security of the State is the first need of Governments. ... Civil liberty awaits the return of order to reappear, and order can be brought back only by the efforts of a skilled hand. [The Commission] will always consider itself to be a sentinel placed by the Constitution to see that the liberty of citizens is guaranteed against any truly arbitrary undertaking; but it will never lose sight of the fact that a State can maintain itself only by order, and by the firm, just and measured action of its government.[64]

If, as probably happened from time to time, the senatorial consciences were ever troubled by the flow of petitions that crossed their desks, in almost no single instance did the senators take meaningful action to defend a petitioner.

When all is said and done, Napoleonic France was a police state. The Ministry of General Police kept the nation under surveillance with a network

---

62 AN, O² 1434, #412 and O² 1435, #158; F⁷ 6333, doss. 7019–BP.
63 *Rapport fait au Sénat*, pp. 9–10.
64 *Ibid.*, pp. 6, 11.

of secret agents, sought to control all public expressions of opinion and detained alleged trouble-makers of every sort – from political opponents to ordinary criminals – by administrative order without formal charge or trial.[65] Howard Brown prefers to use the term 'security state' in order to emphasize 'the importance of surveillance and regulatory control in maintaining public order, rather than the use of coercive force to restore it'. This also underlines one of the principal justifications for the regime: the maintenance of political and social order after a decade of revolutionary upheaval. Brown describes the regime's dominant ideology as 'liberal authoritarianism', because even though 'hard-won civil and political rights would not stand in the way of preserving the social order in time of crisis', a liberal legal system did place some limits on the police apparatus.[66] And yet these limits were too easily breached, as our close look at the case load of the Senatorial Commission on Personal Liberty indicates.

A recent history of Napoleonic France has observed that 'in 1799 political stabilization seemed more urgent than respect for liberties that … had several times been flouted since 1789' (most notably, but not only, during the Reign of Terror and under the Directory). The regime intended 'to remain faithful to the work of 1789 by preserving certain of its great principles, but in taking care to demote liberty to the lowest of its priorities, after respect for property and social equality'.[67] France's social and administrative elite, horrified by the political and social violence of the 1790s and harbouring exaggerated fears of the foreign and domestic threats to the post-revolutionary settlement, accepted this situation. They put a high value – perhaps too high a value – on political stability and internal peace, and if this meant that the police had to ignore civil rights, so be it; that was the inevitable price of law and order. Even the otherwise liberally minded Antoine-Clair Thibaudeau, prefect of the Bouches-du-Rhône from 1803 to 1814, defended the police in his memoirs: 'The imperial police has been slandered. It was arbitrary, [but] that was in its nature; that's why in free countries people disapprove of a so-called [ministry of] general police.' But, he insisted, 'If one considers the obstacles and the perils that ceaselessly threatened the Emperor and the Empire, I can guarantee that in terms of arbitrary actions the imperial police remained far inferior to the police in states that were more solidly established.'[68]

The Napoleonic regime ultimately derived much of its support from its ability to guarantee law, order, and civil peace and to hold both royalism and

65 M. Sibalis, 'The Napoleonic Police State', in P. Dwyer (ed.), *Napoleon and Europe* (London, 2001), pp. 79–94.

66 Brown, 'From Organic Society to Security State'; 'Domestic State Violence: Repression from the Croquants to the Commune', *The Historical Journal* 42 (1999), pp. 597–622.

67 J.-O. Boudon, *Histoire du Consulat et de l'Empire* (Paris, 2000), p. 51.

68 A.-C. Thibaudeau, *Mémoires de A.-C. Thibaudeau, 1799–1815* (Paris, 1913), pp. 355–6.

Jacobinism in check. In such circumstances, upholding social and political order ranked well ahead of such ultimately abstract concepts as human rights and the rule of law. The Senatorial Commission, charged with protecting citizens against arbitrary and illegal imprisonment, never saw fit to challenge an arbitrary police and thereby consciously accepted police methods. The senators were not so much negligent of their duties (after all, they did consider every petition received and reviewed all cases within their jurisdiction) as they were ready to accept the policeman's view of how to enforce law and order. But then this was a view, it must again be stressed, widely shared at the time by the governmental elite, including the judiciary. Recalling with horror the 'excesses' of the French Revolution, minister, prosecutors, judges, and police were rarely willing to allow legal technicalities to stand in the way of detaining men or women who threatened – or merely *appeared* to threaten – the social, political, or even familial settlement achieved under Napoleon.

9

Napoleon and his artists: in the grip of reality

Annie Jourdan

On the eve of the French Revolution, under the influence of the sensualist and philosophical theories of the Enlightenment, the fine arts acquired an unprecedented moral and political role, and painters received an essential mission in the education of men and the formation of virtuous citizens. Long perceived as common artisans, artists struggled throughout two centuries to acquire the full status of creators. The foundation in 1648 of the Royal Academy of Painting and Sculpture facilitated this transition by assimilating artists roughly to the status of men of letters. However, the former more than the latter remained dependent on the King and the Church, even while henceforth finding themselves subject to the Academy's rules. Art criticism was born in the eighteenth century along with the advent of a public sphere and a tribunal of opinion. This criticism operated outside the Academy's official circle and soon contested its values. The *philosophes* added their voices to the debate in order to incite the fine arts to abandon the boudoirs of the wealthy and powerful and to put their talents in the service of loftier aims. Here Rousseau and Diderot came together to encourage artists to 'lift and stir the soul', to 'warm the heart with feelings of honour and glory'.[1] In the same period, society rediscovered the notion of genius – an innate impulse coupled with a divine and supernatural inspiration. This helped gradually to distance artists from the Academy because, if genius is innate, it certainly does not need rules. These various changes would accelerate during the Revolution when artists lost their traditional clienteles and therefore had to find work with the new government. In fact, the Revolution anticipated a sudden and irresistible regeneration of the arts and called upon artists to become the nation's teachers. Following the lead of their predecessors, many revolution-

---

1 D. Diderot, *Oeuvres esthétiques* (Paris, 1968), p. 524. Diderot praised Greuze for knowing how 'to touch, instruct, correct and elicit virtue'. On Rousseau and the arts, see my article 'Rousseau, critique des monuments et des arts', *Studies on Voltaire and the Eighteenth Century* 369 (1999), pp. 231–53. R. Chartier, *Les origines culturelles de la Révolution française* (Paris, 1990), pp. 32–52.

aries believed that speaking to eyes was better than to ears and that sight was the sense that yielded the most instruction. Therefore, art proved an important language for those who undertook to remake a people.[2]

Even more than the Enlightenment, which had raised the standing of writers and philosophers to unprecedented heights, the years 1789–99 rehabilitated the arts, with the strict proviso that they depict the splendid actions of the Revolution, its principles and its heroes – or martyrs. Those who had 'anticipated' the unbelievable event henceforth passed for visionary geniuses.[3] The architect Détournelle applied it to David, who, 'when a king was still subjugating France, first lit the torch of Liberty by drawing with an equally bold and learned hand the generous Brutus'. The impulse of liberty 'would lend a new flame to the fine arts', which in turn would stir up 'the spirit of Liberty'. They would regenerate morals, inspire love of the *patrie*, and carry men to virtue. The jury responsible for awarding the Grand Prizes of 1793 developed this idea in year II by imagining a republican art which would throw off the 'Academy's swaddling clothes'. It contrasted '*spirit, feeling, emotion, energy, truth and the virile character worthy of antiquity*' with the 'mechanism of art' as extolled by the Academy. After this, artists and legislators convinced each other that genius proliferated during great epochs and that the Revolution would lead to the birth of masterpieces.[4]

These expectations also became those of Vivant Denon, Director of the National Museum and soon Bonaparte's Minister of Arts. Denon established a link of cause and effect between Bonaparte's exploits and masterpieces of art. According to Napoleon himself, the development of the arts, sciences and letters 'could be favoured by special circumstances, by morals, and by an epoch'. Thus, circumstances had never been more favourable than under the Consulate and Empire. Public peace had been restored, the Hero of France continued his irresistible ascension, and the nation's glory had never been so great. Both emperor and minister expected an unparalleled artistic effervescence. In this sense, they were the worthy legatees of the previous generation. If they differed from them, it was because they no longer asked artists to regenerate the nation. What mattered now was that they portray the epic and celebrate the Hero of the modern age.[5]

2 On the status of artists over the centuries, see J. Lichtenstein, *La peinture*, (Paris, 1995), pp. 20–2, 721–3. See also H. Honour, *Le néo-classicisme* (Paris, 1998) (French translation) and E. Pommier, *L'art de la liberté. Doctrines et débats de la Révolution française* (Paris, 1991). Note that d'Angivillier, friend of the *philosophes* and admirer of Rousseau, had already steered the arts toward patriotism and virtue. See my book, *Les monuments de la Révolution. Une histoire de représentation* (Paris, 1997).

3 On the idea of genius in the eighteenth century, see A. Becq, *Genèse de l'esthétique française moderne, 1640–1814* (Paris, 1994), pp. 695–740, and T. Crow, *Painters and Public Life in Eighteenth-Century Paris* (New Haven, 1985), pp. 231–3.

4 A. Détournelle, *Journal de la Société républicaine des arts* (n.d.), p. 11 (emphasis added). *Collection Deloynes*, LVI, piece 1723 (séances du jury des arts).

5 N. Bonaparte, *Observations sur un projet d'établisssement d'une École spéciale de Littérature et*

The image that artists acquired in the eyes of enlightened opinion was the same image they gradually developed of themselves. David, and Girodet after him, were not afraid to re-use it for their own benefit. The chemist Chaptal, Bonaparte's Minister of the Interior, also testified to this certainty when he described artists as having 'a burning imagination and a highly excited nature' which enabled them to 'feel deeply'. And Chaptal recalled how they had suffered during the Revolution – an exaggerated claim, for, despite the disorder and other urgent priorities, the revolutionaries gave out awards, commissioned works, and opened vast competitions. True, these initiatives did not compensate for the loss of traditional clients, all the more so since the awards and remuneration were paid in thirds and usually in *assignats* which continued to depreciate over the years.[6] Therefore, artists only received sums much smaller than had been accorded them. Furthermore, ministers followed one another in rapid succession and promises made by one were not promises kept by another. Artists were reduced to soliciting the bureaucracy for what was due them. This was the case with the sculptor Lucas and the painter Peyron, who, in year VIII, tried in vain to recover the last third of a prize they had been awarded in year III.[7]

The recriminations of artists under the Directory or Consulate should not blind us to the fact that many of them had been wildly enthusiastic after the storming of the Bastille. David's eventful trajectory is well known – one of the first to advocate closing the Academies, the reproduction on canvas of the exploits and actors of the Revolution, and forming a revolutionary assembly of artists (which became the Commune des Arts). But he was far from the only one to sacrifice his repose and comfort for the revolutionary cause. Artists followed one another to the podium to pay their tribute to the *patrie* before 9 Thermidor. Chaudet, Martin, Houdon, Dupasquier, Chalgrin, Prud'hon, and Copia, as well as many others, offered statues, busts, paintings, drawings, and engravings. Artists' wives did not remain idle; led by Madame Moitte they came to donate their jewellery to the Assembly in the hope of contributing to the finest of revolutions. David, so often indicted for his 'greed', graciously gave his portraits of Marat and Lepelletier to the Convention, which then

---

d'Histoire au Collège de France in M. Vox, Correspondance de Napoléon, 1806–1810. Six cents lettres annotées (Paris, 1943), p. 196.

6 J.-C. Bonnet (ed.), La Carmagnole des Muses. L'homme de lettres et l'artiste dans la Révolution (Paris, 1988), especially A. Becq, 'Artistes et marché', pp. 81–95.

7 What Chaptal claims here is just what F. Boyer claimed in 1961 in order to denigrate the work of the Revolution: see 'Napoléon et les artistes', in M. Dunan (ed.), Napoléon et l'Europe (Paris and Brussels, 1961), pp. 41–8. Archives Nationales (hereafter AN), F[17] 1058 (various dossiers, including artists' requests for payment; among others, dossier 19). Lucas sought to recover the sums promised in 1793 for his statue of Equality, intended for the Panthéon and which he was still working on in year IV even though he had not received anything for two years. He restated his claim in year VI. Peyron had received two awards of encouragement, but still had to beg the bureaucracy to receive the last third of his first award.

adorned its walls, whereas the Salon of Liberty in the Tuileries Palace was decorated with works donated by French artists since 1789. The political commitment of artists was undeniable, at least as long as idealism and the utopia of regeneration prevailed.[8]

And yet, some painters and architects did emigrate. Fontaine, for example, left France for London in 1793. Fabre, a student at Rome when the Revolution began, preferred to remain in Italy rather than face the upheaval. Madame Vigée-Lebrun also went into exile. In contrast, however, Girodet, who was staying at the Academy of Rome at the start of the Revolution, rejoiced over the unprecedented events unfolding in France. 'Determined to die a republican', the young painter swore to reject any oath contrary to what he owed his country. Pajou *fils* said the same thing, and the future Baron Gérard followed the trend. The meetings of the Commune des Arts, just like those of the fine arts jury in year II, testified to artists' commitment to the Revolution and their hope of seeing the birth of a new art to fit new principles. We only need to read the words of Neveu, Topino-Lebrun, Gérard and Détournelle to appreciate their lofty ambitions.[9]

The high opinion artists conceived of their genius, their art and their mission no doubt influenced their attitudes and relationship to those who commissioned their work. How the nature and scope of these changes manifested themselves will be evident in what follows.

The revenge of artists on men of letters

The Directory, its spending limited by financial difficulties, was not very generous and yet became increasingly exigent. In the winter of 1799, the government, encouraged by its Minister of the Interior, François de Neufchâteau, imposed the subjects for the competition awards, instituted a jury to judge the morality and utility of the works exhibited at the Salon, and demanded that artists submit their projects to the government for encouragement awards. On the eve of the Consulate, artists complained of having too little work, of not receiving what was owed them, and of being under the thumb of men of letters – Neufchâteau was a writer and poet, and, since the

---

8 In year III, Moitte sent a petition invoking the sacrifices made in the Revolution's name and the many works he had lost since, before soliciting aid from the government. 'Last year', he wrote, 'I would not have dared to undertake the approach that I am risking today for fear of debasing myself'. G. Gramaccini, *Jean-Guillaume Moitte. Leben und Werk*, 2 vols (Berlin, 1993), vol. 2, p. 270.

9 Ph.-A. Coupin, *Les Oeuvres posthumes de Girodet-Trioson*, 2 vols (Paris, 1929), vol. 2, pp. 277–8; David, quoted in Détournelle, *Journal des arts* (1793), p. 17, or 'Rapport à la Convention nationale sur le Jury national des Arts' (Paris, 1793); on Pajou *fils*, who wanted to be 'somehow useful for the salvation of my fatherland', see H. Gérard, *Lettres adressées au Baron Gérard*, 2 vols (Paris, 1886), vol. 1, pp. 74, 202. On artists' patriotism, see the minutes of the fine arts jury in *Collection Deloynes*, LVI, piece 1723.

creation of the Institute, the fine arts shared the same class as Letters. They complained of being constantly attacked by critics, whether Ideologues or royalists. In fact, it was the period when Volney, an influential author and member of the Institute, wrote that the arts were 'a sterile use of work and a ruinous drain on wealth' and when Louis-Sébastien Mercier, the famous novelist and social commentator, railed against painting as 'the human spirit's childishness' which would breed idolatry and ruin states. But it was also the period when reactionaries, under the cover of art criticism, ceaselessly denigrated artists who remained faithful to the Revolution. David, in particular, was the target of the most venomous quills, but Hennequin, considered a fervent Jacobin, was not spared either.

The Consulate brought a new revolution that would have positive consequences for the fine arts and artists. Admittedly it was a gradual revolution, because Bonaparte's artistic policy did not take shape immediately. It first appeared in the colossal sums artists demanded, and then received. Once again, the first to lead the way was David, who demanded 24,000 francs from the king of Spain for *Bonaparte Crossing the Alps*. Girodet got 12,000 francs for his *Apotheosis of French Heroes* intended for the château at Malmaison. Gérard received 12,000 francs for his portrait of Joséphine. In 1802, the First Consul bought Guérin's *Phaedra and Hippolytus* and imprudently suggested that the painter set the price. The latter demanded 24,000 francs. This was the pattern for various commissions issued between 1800 and 1803. Bonaparte agreed to pay 120,000 francs for a colossal statue of himself by the Italian sculptor Canova and gave 16,000 francs to the famous student of David, the painter Gros, for his *Napoleon Visiting the Plague Victims at Jaffa*.[10] The enormity of these sums compared to those given during the *ancien régime* or Revolution testified to a lack of concern about prices, even a lack of understanding about the monetary value of art, and suggests an overvaluing of artistic production.[11] This trend was not to Denon's liking. Once he entered office in November 1802, he worked to put an end to the overbidding that risked putting the works of modern artists beyond the reach of individuals. Had Isabey not asked 20,000 francs for a simple drawing when there were very beautiful ones by Raphael which barely cost 3,000? Denon, who received only 12,000 francs a year as Director of the Museum, feared that this drift would harm the arts: 'It would be very bad for the arts if such prices took hold,

10 In year VII, awards for large history paintings had risen to 6,000 francs (Prize for First Class) and 4,000 francs (Prize for Second Class). The prizes for sculpture went from 4,000 francs to 2,000 francs. *La Révolution et l'Europe*, éd. des Musées nationaux, 3 vols (Paris, 1989), vol. 3, pp. 848–9.

11 These unusual expenses could be attributed to Joséphine, whose indifference toward prices is legendary, but she was not responsible for all the commissions and acquisitions. Thus, we are forced to conclude that Bonaparte himself was responsible for the excessive prices, due as much to ignorance as to ostentation, which meant that nothing was too expensive for the Hero.

because individuals and the government itself could no longer pay them, and, no longer able to obtain work, artists would die of hunger'.[12] And besides, if we pay such a high price for a drawing, what will we give 'to an artist who creates a twenty-five-foot painting'? Denon suggested giving Isabey 5,000 francs – a significant amount, after all, warranted by the large number of figures represented. Already early in the Consulate, when David was finishing his portrait of Bonaparte, Denon regretted that the King of Spain had paid so much for the painting, especially because David demanded 20,000 francs for each of three copies, and charged visitors a fee to come and admire it in his workshop. If Bruun-Neergaard is to be believed, the exhibition of the *Sabine Women* alone brought David more than 40,000 *livres*. The indignation of contemporaries is easily understood. The architect Détournelle went so far as to call it a 'mercenary exhibition of ... paintings' and Denon would work throughout his long tenure to rectify what he considered a venal system.[13]

In the light of these few examples, the idealism of revolutionary artists appears to have become blurred. Nevertheless, under the Consulate, many of them were fascinated by the strange figure of Bonaparte. David's enthusiasm after his first meeting is well known, as is that of Gros in Italy lamenting not being able to follow the new Alexander to Egypt. But Girodet was no less ecstatic. He also wrote letters to the general, prompting him to imitate the example of Athens and proposing a vast artistic policy. By 1800, he had conceived several works dedicated to the Hero – among others an allegory where Bonaparte appeared in the guise of Hercules – and executed the first drawings inspired by Ossian with the *Apotheosis of French Warriors* in mind. In a letter dated 6 Messidor X (25 June 1802), Girodet dedicated this work to the First Consul, to the 'hero who consoles France and who honours with his friendship and esteem, the warriors the nation laments'. He would later write that the painting had 'the originality and merit of aptness' because it was 'a triumphal monument in honour of the bravest men and, at the same time, it flattered the First Consul's taste for the poetry of Ossian'.[14]

An excess of zeal or enthusiasm toward the italianate Hero was not the exclusive privilege of painters. Sculptors and engravers rushed to propose works for the new patron. Thus, Bonaparte encouraged the publication of the *Historic Paintings of the Battles of Italy*, twenty-four prints drawn by Carle Vernet and engraved by Duplessi-Bertaux. The architect Poyet multiplied his initiatives in the vain hope of erecting a triumphal column on the Pont Neuf.

12   AN, O² 840, letter from Denon to Fleurieu , 18 Germinal XIII.
13   T. C. Bruun-Neergaard, *Sur la situation des beaux-arts en France* (Paris, 1801), p. 16; Détournelle, quoted in the *Journal des bâtiments des arts* (Paris, year X), no. 113, 73–75. In no. 110 this paper also criticized David's 'shameful speculation', having the public pay twice for his works.
14   Letter from Gros to his mother, 23 November 1798, published in P. Bordes, 'Antoine-Jean Gros en Italie (1793–1800): Lettres à sa mère', *Bulletin de la société historique des arts français*, année 1978 (1980), p. 243. Girodet, *Oeuvres posthumes*, vol. 2, pp. 284, 287–9, 338–44.

The sculptor Moitte multiplied proposals, including using the horses of Saint Mark. He would later create Desaix's tomb.[15]

The limits of allegiance

Whereas after 14 July 1789, artists had, one after another, offered the Assembly the products of their genius, their admiration for the First Consul did not lead them to donate their works to the government, but rather to solicit jobs, especially once rumours spread about the amounts awarded for the first commissions and about the generosity of the Bonaparte spouses. The lust for assignments and royal remuneration could only grow during the Empire when many works were commissioned.[16] It was as if artists wanted to forget the privations they had suffered and be compensated for the sacrifices they had made for the Revolution, as if they all wished to live well and were sure they deserved it. Some of their homes revealed a thirst for comfort, even luxury, visible in the decor around them. If we believe his visitors, David took over magnificent apartments, richly decorated in a neo-classical style.[17] Isabey had Percier and Fontaine carry out plans for a splendid studio. This did not prevent him from repeatedly complaining that he would be ruined if the government did not pay him what he was owed or did not buy some of his works. Hennequin, crowned by the Salons of years VII and VIII and assured of a brilliant career thanks to commissions from the government and Lucien Bonaparte, bought a house with garden and undertook to build a studio. However, having adventured into ill-considered expenses and been forced to take out onerous loans, he became so indebted that he had to leave France in search of work at Milan, Amsterdam and Brussels. The sculptor Moitte, whose household was carefully governed by a responsible wife, probably better illustrates the lifestyle and mentality of artists during the period. He too dreamed of acquiring a property, but prudently gave it up. The government's promises were viewed with scepticism. The artist asked for confirmations and advances before undertaking too large a project. The sums were paid in thirds, but fairly regularly. Madame Moitte easily managed to set aside some money without scrimping too much on daily expenses. As for David, he racked up jobs and sources of income. In 1811, his teaching alone earned him 10,008 francs a month and his title of First Painter paid 12,000 a year.[18]

15   G. Gramaccini, *Moitte*, vol. 2, pp. 280–6. On Poyet, see *Projets de places et d'édifices à ériger pour la gloire et l'utilité de la République* (Paris, year VIII); on the plans of year VIII and new ones in 1806, see AN, F^{13} 203.

16   See my book, *Napoléon. Héros, imperator, mécène* (Paris, 1998).

17   See the statements of Sir John Carr in A. Babeau, *Les Anglais en France* (Paris, 1898), p. 153.

18   The collection of prints by Percier and Fontaine (now in the Musée de Vizille) have been published, but it is not known whether Isabey was really able to carry out this sumptuous plan (I would like to thank Philippe Bordes for this information). See A. Schnapper, *David* (Paris, 1989), pp. 372–3. In 1822, David spent 180,000 francs on a residence on the boulevard des Italiens and later left a million francs to his children (*ibid.*, pp. 629 and 522). A. C. Moitte,

In contrast with the artists who lived well and accumulated riches, the painter Bergeret, assigned the drawings for the bas-reliefs on the Vendôme Column, insisted that he did not get rich under the Empire because he was paid in annuities which he had to discount at a forty per cent loss. This was certainly not the case with Isabey, given numerous tasks throughout the reign before becoming the Empress's drawing instructor. Nor was it the case with Gérard, the favourite portraitist of the imperial elite, who charged the outlandish sum of 6,000 francs for a single copy of the Emperor's portrait, 12,000 francs for a large portrait, and 14,400 francs for the one to be reproduced by the Gobelins tapestry makers. During the Empire, Girodet found himself commissioned to produce thirty-six official portraits of the Emperor, of which twenty-six had been finished by 1814 and for which he received 80,000 francs. As for Lejeune, he refused to sell whenever he considered the remuneration insufficient. Such was the case in 1810, when Denon offered him 6,000 francs for his *Battle of Somo Sierra* instead of 6,500. The affluence gained by most artists, the awards and commissions lavished by Napoleon, the formation of a fourth class at the Institute giving the fine arts autonomy, the concern displayed by the Emperor toward artists, his visits to Salons and his acquisitions, and the rewards and distinctions distributed under the Empire, (for it was not unusual for them to receive the Legion of Honour or medals at the close of Salons) – all this should have won over the arts and artists to the Master of France. It is worth investigating the extent to which this happened and whether it showed.[19]

In contrast with writers, whom Napoleon hoped in vain to stimulate and inspire but who could not accept the growing censorship and repression directed against reluctant or insolent authors, artists do not seem to have blatantly opposed the imperial dictatorship. In the past – recent or distant – if they happened to dispute one policy or another, they did it merely through allegory or ancient history in such a way that it was only visible to the eyes of true connoisseurs.[20] Besides, it was necessary to make a living before resisting.

Journal inédit de Madame Moitte (Paris, 1932), p. 92. In 1807, Mme Moitte had succeeded in setting aside 25,000 francs. On Hennequin, see Ph.-A. *Mémoires de Ph.A. Hennequin écrits par lui-même* (Paris, 1933), pp. 229–332.

19 P.-N. Bergeret, *Lettres d'un artiste sur l'état des arts en France* (Paris, 1848), p. 104; On Gérard and his success, see E. J. Delécluze, *Louis David. Son école et son temps* (Paris, 1860), p. 281; G. Bernier, *Girodet* (Paris and Brussels, 1975), p. 152; on Lejeune, see AN, 0^2 841; Schnapper, *David*, p. 369. Gérard had copies of his portraits made – by his students – for 1,500 francs and sold them to the government for 6,000 francs, whereas a less celebrated painter such as Bergeret received 300 francs for each of the drawings commissioned by the Sèvres manufactory. A. Dayot, *Napoléon raconté par l'image*, (Paris, 1902), p. 187. See also B. Foucart, 'L'artiste dans la société de l'Empire. Sa participation aux honneurs et dignités', *Revue d'histoire moderne et contemporaine* 17 (1970), pp. 709–19.

20 During the Revolution and Empire, as far as I know, Girodet was the first to produce pictorial criticism. Enraged by his model, Mademoiselle Lange, he transformed her into a modern Danaë for the Salon of year VII (1799). It could be suggested that the artist, once emancipated from the Academy and his status as an artisan, would become progressively less tolerant of criticism and take revenge on canvas. Here again, Girodet is emblematic. In 1812 he portrayed Napoleon in

Thus, what is striking during the Empire is that artists sought to live well and adopt a lifestyle in keeping with their genius, henceforth assured them, and the status of creative artists given them by the law of 1 Brumaire VII (22 October 1798). This conferred on artists the right to evaluate and fix the monetary worth of their own works, which also led to the escalating prices.[21] Furthermore, in contrast with writers who relied only on their quills, painters, sculptors and engravers had to pay for their materials and workers. Regular and significant income was thus essential. It is not surprising, therefore, to find a general indifference toward politics on the part of those who really loved their craft, especially on the part of those who had experienced the turmoil of the Revolution and who had suffered for being too overtly committed. In reading Madame Moitte's journal for the years 1805–07, for example, one notices that the couple were solely preoccupied by their own work – and their income. The sculptor, his friends, and his visitors were all more concerned with their art and their daily comfort than with Napoleon or the Empire. Admittedly, concern arose when alarming rumours circulated about a coming war. Yet the usual indifference is apparent in 1807, when, having been invited to be part of a delegation sent by the Institute to the Tuileries, Moitte resolved to participate, but grumbled about it. He returned satisfied. Napoleon had received them well and spoke to him 'in a very gracious manner'. He promised to come 'to his workshop to see the things he had heard greatly praised'.[22] And the very next day, in fact, the Emperor came to admire the tomb of Desaix. This testimony suggests that politics and official ceremonies no longer excited the sculptor and that, in order to coax him, Napoleon had to show interest and admiration for his works and encourage his labours through commissions or acquisitions. It was like this with many artists. Most of them were far more excited by finishing works, by their own success or failure, and by the cabals and quarrels between artists, than by the politics of the Empire. This applied just as much to Hennequin and Bergeret, who moaned about their troubles, the machinations of colleagues who nabbed their commissions, and cuts in the payments promised them. However, when recriminations did arise, they were directed at ministers or rival artists. The Emperor generally assumed the role of arbitrator – of 'true patron', as David

---

the theatre of Saint-Cloud: sleeping, waking up, looking around to make sure that nobody had noticed him asleep. See reproductions in A. Dayot, *Napoléon raconté par l'image*, pp. 206–7.

21   On this topic, see E. Pommier, 'De l'art libéral à l'art de la liberté. Le débat sur la patente des artistes sous la Révolution et ses antécédents dans l'ancienne théorie des arts', *Bulletin de la société de l'histoire de l'art français*, année 1992 (1993), pp. 147–67.

22   January 1807 in *Journal inédit de Madame Moitte*, p. 232. Note that there was a shift from 1790 when Madame Moitte had been at the head of a delegation of artists' wives who, following the example of Roman wives, brought their jewellery to the Assembly to serve the Fatherland in danger. Note that Moitte must have met Bonaparte at Milan when part of the Sciences and Arts Commission. See my book, *Napoléon. Héros, Imperator, Mécène* (Paris, 1998), ch. 2.

wrote to Wicar – provided one could approach him or get grievances to him, which was not an easy matter.[23]

David's case is particularly interesting in this regard, since he, more than anyone, played the role of a politically engaged artist. Certainly the Thermidorian experience cooled his revolutionary passion, but it is well known how much he admired the italianate general, especially since the general also admired him and from the start wanted to gain his allegiance. In contrast with writers like the Ideologue Volney and the dramatist Lemercier, who condemned Bonaparte's increasing personal power and the advent of the Empire, David apparently resigned himself to it. This is what one is led to assume by his famous quip, 'I've always thought that we were not virtuous enough to be republicans'. However, we should avoid jumping from this to the conclusion that his allegiance to Napoleon was genuine and constant.

Certain bits of evidence from the period invite searching his works for a muted form of opposition. For example, the German musician Reichardt insists on seeing a caricature in *Bonaparte Crossing the Alps*. He claims that this is a 'malicious invention of the painter'. As for the *Sacre*, anonymous critics and mockers are shocked by the 'disagreeable' heads of the spectators, 'by the dry and pale background, the inelegant poses, and the excessively heavy shadows'. They are sarcastic about the many figures 'looking into space' or 'looking at nothing'. *Arlequin au Musée* did not weary of interpreting the painting in highly political terms. The criticisms included objecting to the 'obviously false colouring' of the portrait of Napoleon in imperial garb and condemning the 'exaggeration' and 'theatrical affectation' of the *Distribution of the Eagles*.[24] These observations may corroborate Reichardt's thesis, but can they be taken seriously when we know that they were intended to condemn David as 'superintendent of the arts'? Finally, it is possible to detect, as Régis Michel has done more recently, a satire in the *Sacre*'s 'prodigious gallery of portraits, of an odd intensity, often grimacing, sometimes sinister looking'.[25] At the time, people criticized above all the fact that they were only sketched, not adequately finished. Furthermore, reactionary or academic criticism was mostly determined to denigrate the first painter of the Revolution. It is better not to draw a hasty conclusion, especially when considering the

23 Schnapper, *David*, p. 610. The comment is from 1808. David made clear that it was difficult to get an audience, but when one did, one often won out over the bureaucracy and ministers.

24 J.-F. Reichardt, *Un hiver à Paris sous le Consulat* (Paris, 1896), pp. 125, 302. On the *Arlequin au Musée*, see *Collection Deloynes*, XXXIII, piece 1132; on the 1808 portrait of Napoleon, see piece 1137, and on the *Distribution of the Eagles*, see *Journal de Paris* (1810), no. 316, 2233. This wholly negative commentary could be offset by the positive one from the *Journal des Arts* (1810), no. 45, 245.

25 R. Michel, *David, l'art et le politique* (Paris, 1988), pp. 105–9. The author indicates that, in contrast with the *Sacre*, where an ideological critique is not excluded, the *Distribution of the Eagles* is an apology for the regime. But, if one intended to criticize, so did the other. And, if that is the case, which is doubtful, could criticism not be found in the exaggerated poses that transform the oath into a parody of that in the *Oath of the Horatii*?

Distribution of the Eagles as an 'apology of the regime', as Michel has done. Otherwise, how can we explain that in one painting the painter enjoyed sati- rizing the court while in the other he celebrated the Empire and generals?

Claiming that David did not have explicit critical intentions is not to say that he was a faithful and constant admirer of the Emperor or that his alle- giance never failed or waned. However, rather than looking for the artist in opposition, we should consider the concept of disaffection. A first expression of this could be detected in the 1805 portrait of Napoleon in imperial costume, where the Hero appears as an arrogant and brutal parvenu, ready to do anything to retain the crown, and which the painter had entrusted to his student – malicious wags would say 'to his least skilful student'. It was a long time since David got excited about the idea of himself portraying the features of the great man.[26] In truth, David had a lot to do at the time, for Napoleon had entrusted him with four grand paintings, including the *Sacre*, shown in 1808, and the *Distribution of the Eagles*, presented in 1810. If there were disaf- fection, it is more evident in the mind-boggling sums the First Painter demanded from His Majesty and from his determination to secure them. Disaffection can also be read in his return to painting ancient history and in the fact that David never painted battle scenes based on contemporary history. He was the only one of the great painters of his day never to exhibit a modern military painting.[27]

If we believe Delécluze, David actually detached himself from Napoleon in the years 1812–13 when rumours of war provoked much concern. At the time, Napoleon's First Painter supposedly attacked the 'excessive warrior temperament' of the Hero and the new dynasty's growing absolutism. Delécluze claims to have heard him grouse, 'That's not quite what we wanted'.[28] As for Fontaine, Napoleon's architect, it was during this same period that an expression of disenchantment emerged. This disenchantment was due mainly to military problems and to the anxiety that invaded France every time the Emperor left for war.[29] As with numerous artists of the period,

26 He painted another version of the portrait in imperial garb in 1807 – a copy of which was sold to the King of Westphalia in 1808 and which Delécluze would also call 'theatrical'. Delécluze, *David*, pp. 346–7. On the last portrait of Napoleon, executed for the Englishman Douglas between 1811 and 1812, see Schnapper, *David*, pp. 433–6. Supposedly, the Emperor valued it greatly and wished to acquire it.

27 Other than David, among first-rate artists, we can name Prud'hon, who only made one painting dedicated to Napoleon in action, which was for the Senate. However, this latter specialized in portraits including those of Imperial personalities – from the Dutch minister Schimmelpenninck to Joséphine, to the King of Rome. He was also Marie-Louise's drawing instructor. See *Prud'hon ou le rêve du bonheur*, exhibition catalogue by the Réunion des Musées nationaux (Paris, 1997), p. 197.

28 Delécluze, *David*, pp. 340–1.

29 Fontaine, *Journal*, i, pp. 315, 376–9, 382. The economic crisis of 1810–12 reinforced strictly mili- tary concerns. To that was added the religious issue, which became exacerbated in 1811, setting the French Clergy in opposition to the Emperor. See J. Tulard, *Napoléon ou le mythe du Sauveur* (Paris, 1987), pp. 363–82.

like Moitte for example, Fontaine longed to work in complete calm. Everyone from dignitaries to marshals, from painters to sculptors, wished finally to enjoy the gains that had been made, a reasonable demand after so many troubled years. But such was hardly the case. One war rapidly succeeded another and the French feared seeing the Empire collapse – and with it, their conquests and privileges.[30]

Therefore, the uncertainty the Empire foisted on France appears to have been one of the main reasons for disaffection, certainly far more than imperial despotism. However, the fear of impending catastrophe was no doubt supplemented by injured pride, for Napoleon's tact was not infallible. He loved to parade his knowledge, opinions, and beliefs before imposing them. If he exasperated Fontaine by rejecting his carefully considered and repeatedly revised plans, he must have provoked the greatest irritation in the leading painter of his day when he interfered in judging fine art. Such was the case when he visited David's workshop in 1808. Napoleon admired the painting of the *Sacre* and enjoyed demonstrating that he recognized the figures. He then undertook a careful examination of them and passed on several observations to the painter. These should be called modifications rather than observations, because His Majesty demanded that 'the Pope be shown in a more active role' – that he appear to be giving his blessing – while the Cardinal legate should bear the Empress's ring. If we are to believe one critic – although, in this case, we ought not to – David, 'acknowledging appropriately the careful tact, refined taste, and profound thinking the Emperor displayed when he considered the sciences and arts, undertook to perfect his painting'.[31] If he did so, it was begrudgingly. This was not the only affront made to the genius of the century, who also had to modify his *Distribution of the Eagles*, eliminating Joséphine and, as a result, her ladies-in-waiting, which meant redesigning the painting.[32] These actions must have offended an artist as famous as David

30 On the subject of David, Delécluze rightly notes that every 'change of government was naturally the subject of deep concern for the man whom Napoleon's power had restored to high society'. Furthermore, his sons had jobs in the bureaucracy, his daughters had married generals, and he was First Painter – an honorific title, certainly, but one which crowned him as 'master of the school'. Delécluze, *David*, p. 341.

31 'Description du tableau du Couronnement' (drawn from the *Moniteur* of 16 January 1808), *Collection Deloynes*, XXXIII, piece 1116. Napoleon supposedly exclaimed, 'That's fine, really fine, David. You've read my mind. You've made me into a French knight.' Dayot, *Napoléon raconté par l'image*, p. 111.

32 In a letter to Thiénon on 16 September 1807, David fumed in couched language about changes requested by King Louis, 'Please, Sir, tell His Majesty to assist me and do not make me redo a person as crucial as that one, and then leave me in a predicament, because, as you know, in a painting everything is worked out and changing a person can lead to incalculable consequences and disorganize an entire side of a painting, and often the entire work.' Schnapper, *David*, p. 609. One of his students, Suau, indicated that an entire side of the composition (of the *Distribution of the Eagles*) was to be redone, 'which was neither pleasant nor enjoyable for the author'. P. Meslé, 'David et ses élèves toulousains', *Bulletin de la Société historique des arts français* 24 (1969), p. 95.

had been since 1789. No testimony appears to corroborate this hypothesis. However, the contrast between the adulation of the years 1789–94 and the imperial criticism was too strong for there not to be some truth in this supposition. The Master's criticisms were legion. Napoleon presumed to judge the *Sabine Women*, a painting he found cold, too cold – and too naked. He deprecated *Leonidas and his Soldiers at Thermopylae* because it depicted the vanquished. Finally, from 1810, when the *Distribution of the Eagles* was finished, to 1814, the Emperor commissioned no works from his First Painter.[33] *The Imperial Banquet* and *Family Gathering* were entrusted to Prud'hon and Gérard, later replaced by Regnault. Oddly, the marriage of 1810 was not the subject of any commission. And worse than that, when the decennial prizes were awarded, even if he wanted to see the *Sabine Women* crowned, the Emperor privileged *Napoleon Visiting the Plague Victims at Jaffa* over the large painting of the *Sacre*. Therefore, David could reproach Napoleon for not conferring on him the prerogatives that went with the post of First Painter.[34] But the esteem the Emperor displayed for the artist – at one point he considered creating a David Gallery where the painter's great works would be shown (following the example of the Rubens Gallery in the Luxembourg Palace) – the award of the Legion of Honour, the title of chevalier, which included being authorized to adopt a coat of arms, the financial privileges he enjoyed, all ought to have compensated for his wounded pride. No doubt this was one of the reasons for them.[35]

Fontaine's *Journal* is one of the most enlightening sources for learning even more about the Emperor's relationship with his artists. From 19 Brumaire to the abdication in 1815, the architect worked for Napoleon without questioning the validity of the Consular and Imperial dictatorship. What excited him was his craft. What tormented him was how to meet the complex demands of the Master without exceeding the budget. However, the *Journal* also reveals the limits of allegiance. In this Fontaine appears representative of a class of men whose talents set them apart from the crowd and brought them close to power, or rather dependent upon it. His observations about Napoleon over fifteen years reveal him to be admiring of the man who had accomplished so many feats and who combined virtue and genius. But the architect was harsh and critical about things related to the patron. Whether as First Consul or Emperor, Napoleon demanded speed, quality, and economy, which were difficult to reconcile. Fontaine accused him in a highly

33 A commission was planned for David to do decorative painting in the Louvre's interior (23 August 1813), but it seems this was not carried out. Schnapper, *David*, p. 619.
34 In a letter of 2 September 1812, David asked as First Painter to be put in charge of 'all the paintings that would grace the imperial palaces'. He received the reply that the job of the First Painter had been created in favour of M. David 'as an honorific distinction, but without functions'. It fell to Denon to propose the paintings. Schnapper, *David*, pp. 618–19.
35 Delécluze, *David*, pp. 347–8; letter from David to Douglas in 1812, in Schnapper, *David*, p. 476.

disrespectful tone of not being able to decide and of changing his mind too often. The great man is sketched as someone who shilly-shallied, kept demanding plans without ever implementing them, and who ordered grandiose ones for purely political reasons without any intention of completing them. Fontaine's attitude wavered between insolence or annoyance on the one hand, and admiration or satisfaction on the other. This illustrates rather nicely what other artists must generally have felt. Thus Fontaine, annoyed at Napoleon's fickleness and hesitations, the public exhibitions, the competitions and the excessive number of responsibilities entrusted to him, knew to resist silently. We see him determined to carry out the Emperor's orders 'without following them to the letter'. At least he interpreted orders according to his own feelings in the hope that Napoleon would see only zeal. This was the case with the restoration of the Louvre, when Fontaine decided to remain faithful to the laws of architecture at the risk of giving offence. Nonetheless, he continued to prefer dealing with the Emperor than with the 'know-it-alls and quibblers' of his entourage. And, in keeping with David, he considered Napoleon a difficult but reasonable interlocutor.[36]

Napoleon was not always conciliatory or kind. For example, in 1811 he fulminated against French architects, hatched the idea of appointing an engineer to govern them, and threatened them with Italian competition. However, shortly thereafter he decorated Fontaine with the Legion of Honour, accepted his election to the Institute and showered him with signs of benevolence and trust, then sent the Italian architect back to Rome without ever having accorded him the honour of a private audience. Undoubtedly, this was one of his famous tactics and we can conclude, like Fontaine, that it was one of the ways 'in which he gave himself an advantage in order to command obedience from all who surrounded him'.[37] Nevertheless, these ploys wounded those subject to them and risked detaching them from the Emperor of the French.

Named First Architect in 1813, Fontaine turned up his nose. The title mattered little if his responsibilities increased dangerously. Was it not going to turn ministers and colleagues, and no doubt the Emperor, against him? Discontent grew when it became clear that peace would not be signed. Like many of his contemporaries, the architect wondered when the interminable adventure would end. As a result, criticisms came to outweigh kudos. The Hero of 1800, admired so much as a general, became in 1814 a 'reckless leader' (*chef aventurier*). 'Drunk with ... success, he no longer had limits, moderation, or reflection. A blind ambition was his sole guide'.[38] The disappointment was even worse in 1815 when the Emperor returned to Paris after

36 Fontaine, *Journal*, vol. 1, pp. 88, 119–20, 167.
37 *Ibid.*, pp. 279–83, 298, 318–9.
38 *Ibid.*, pp. 347, 362, 379, 382, 384, 408.

Waterloo. 'Even his walk, his bearing, his expression, and his speech were characterized by an insensitivity that could be considered mental instability (*une absence de raison*). Prestige was destroyed; the extraordinary man was no longer recognizable and regret at seeing such a famous person embarrassingly survive his fall was the only feeling he inspired'.[39]

It took the first defeats for Fontaine fully to admit his disappointment. But at the same time as he glimpsed the ouster of Napoleon and condemned him for not dying in combat – 'on the field of honour' – in 1815,[40] he persisted in describing him as an extraordinary man. And he was not alone. Once he confronted the Restoration, which turned out to be just as disappointing, if not more so, the architect retracted his criticism. He undertook a rehabilitation of the Great Man starting in 1825. This led to a laudatory article published in 1833 under the title 'Napoleon, architect'. As time passed, Fontaine, who in 1816 had indicted Napoleon's caprice, hesitations, and distrust regarding buildings, transformed the Emperor into a man 'always concerned about the public good'; 'the numerous monuments, public edifices, and useful structures built during the short duration of his reign will long attest the greatness of his genius and the scope of his ideas'.[41] Time had softened his bitterness, since Percier and Fontaine, still continuing as First Architects, were in a position to compare and judge.

A final category of artists was that of the 'weathervanes' (*girouettes*): those who joined the mob or showered praise depending on the moment. The architect Poyet was one of these, adapting his plans according to circumstances and modifying his presentations for whatever arose. Thus a monument could be dedicated to the defenders of the *patrie*, to Victory, or to Napoleon before celebrating 'His Majesty Louis XVIII and the reunion of all good Frenchmen around the legitimate throne'. The painter Landon, author of the *Annales du Musée* and someone who had no reason to complain about the Revolution or the Imperial government, poured forth insults about the government that had just fallen as well as its predecessor. Without fearing ridicule, he accused 'those who through greed or to get ahead, and maybe pushed by harsh necessity, made a constant study of flattery and a habitual duty of sacrificing for circumstances'. Times changed. Henceforth, 'the man of genius ... convinced of the dignity of his art, can offer it as a worthy homage to his legitimate prince and, without being accused of adulation,

39 Nonetheless, during the Hundred Days, Fontaine admired Napoleon's moderation and sympathized with his fall. *Ibid.*, pp. 460–1.

40 Fontaine compared the government of 1825 dominated by priests and aristocrats with that of the Jacobins. He found intolerance and fanaticism in both. The comparison is surprising, but it says a lot about the impression left by the Empire, which was not as negative as is often thought. Among others, see *ibid.*, pp. 471–2. Fontaine also well describes the anxieties of 1816, including those of a number of artists. These reached the point where a significant group – including Le Breton, Debret, and the two Taunays, among others – left for Brazil. *Ibid.*, p. 510.

41 Percier and Fontaine, 'Napoléon architecte', *Revue de Paris* 52 (1833), pp. 33–45.

celebrate the virtues of a King whom Providence miraculously returned to the bosom of his people'. This strategy would pay off. After having been named a chevalier in the Legion of Honour in 1814, Landon suddenly replaced Dufourny as curator at the Louvre.[42]

From this perspective, we would undoubtedly condemn David – who became the whipping boy of many historians over the years because he had the audacity to love the Revolution, Robespierre and Bonaparte at the same time, and to aspire to glory and wealth. Even though he was enthusiastic about the italianate Hero on the eve of 18 Brumaire, he never fulminated against the Revolution. Even though he censured Napoleon's absolutism, he remained faithful to him in hard times and signed the Additional Act to the Constitutions of the Empire in 1815. In exile in Belgium during the Restoration, he would refuse to undertake humiliating entreaties in order to return to France, despite Gros' insistence and the good will of Charles X. As for Fontaine, who had less to fear from the Bourbons' return, he went to say farewell to Napoleon on the eve of his departure for Saint Helena and sympathized with his hardship. He later became a Bonapartist in the 1830s.[43]

These few examples demonstrate that not all artists were necessarily 'inclined to flatter those from whom they expected a salary and favours', as Delécluze claimed. There were a few, of course, such as Poyet and Landon, but there were also those who agreed to make compromises without abandoning their ideals or preferences. Such was the case as much with David and Girodet as with Fontaine and Moitte, or even Bergeret, who, besides the sketches for the Vendôme Column, continued to paint the troubadour scenes he loved. Under the Empire, writers were undoubtedly more reticent in the face of Napoleon's demands than were artists. It is rare to find many artists like Gros, willing to sacrifice their taste for ideal beauty to contemporary history painting. And yet, on the other hand, many pursued their careers without worrying too much about the expectations of the sovereign. This is how they became troubadour or landscape painters. And once again it was Denon who saw to it that they too received commissions or that their works were the object of acquisitions. Finally, there were some – and these are the most famous – who conformed to imperial demands as much as necessary, but devoted themselves to the things that truly inspired them as soon as their

42   Ch.-L.-P. Landon, *Annales du Musée* (1814), pp. 29–33; Fontaine, *Journal*, i, p. 528. Poyet had more cause than Landon to denigrate the Emperor, who had never minced words in criticizing the portico of the Palais-Bourbon; besides his university proposal had been rejected by the Minister of the Interior. Not that we would condemn every criticism made by contemporaries, much to the contrary; but Landon was all praise during the reign, like Poyet, who wanted to glorify the Emperor and his victories through a triumphal column on the Pont Neuf.

43   It is disconcerting to read the invectives crafted against David by Alfred Fierro in his *Histoire et dictionnaire du Consulat et de l'Empire*, edited by J. Tulard (Paris, 1995), pp. 703–4.

resources allowed. This was the case with David, Guérin, Girodet, and Regnault, who quit the Salon after 1812.[44]

From artistic genius to the difficulty of assessing the price of artistic production

In light of the preceding material, it is easier to understand that throughout his long career, Denon had to face artists' demands, or what contemporaries called 'financial speculation'. He complained about it early on, stating that the amount Bonaparte paid for *Phaedra and Hippolytus* threw 'these men's exalted heads into such disarray that it was no longer possible to raise objections to their exaggerated claims and bring them back to the modest simplicity of true artists'. Artists had tasted luxury and would never accept giving it up. For this reason, they became 'painting entrepreneurs' and 'thought that they only had to produce two or three works to obtain their fortune and to assure their reputation'. It got worse, for they decried the paintings (of marshals) produced by their colleagues. Now 'the real motive for this defamation is that only two thousand francs were paid for each of these portraits'. At this time – 19 February 1806 – just before the major commissions of 1806, Denon tried to persuade Napoleon to set prices once and for all. Twelve thousand francs would be paid for large canvasses and 6,000 francs for easel paintings. This good advice was in vain. Denon returned to press the point in April the same year, bemoaning the 6,000 francs still being paid for copies of Gérard's official portrait. In order not to appear 'to be the ruination of artists', he had been forced to agree to 4,000 francs for portraits of the princesses.[45] In fact, artists accepted a particular figure at the time of the commission, then changed their minds. They 'settled it among themselves that a monument executed for the government must make their fortune'. And instead of working they 'spent their time dreaming of other prizes and haunting the hallways of the bureaucracy'.[46] In effect, the problem was to decide on the value of artistic production. This is what Daru, the intendant-general, noted in response to the exorbitant prices demanded by David. He was clearly of the opinion that 'the sovereign must pay nobly for artistic works but ... even talent has a price which can not be arbitrary'. The price would be commensurate with the working time. This would not prevent giving extraordinary compensation to master works once completed.[47] The intendant-general was

44 Note that Girodet, even while reproducing an idealized image of the Emperor in the outfit of the *Sacre*, enjoyed sketching the great man in less respectable poses and restored his true corpulence. Compare the Saint Cloud drawings from 1812 and the ageing Napoleon, casually sitting on a chair, also from 1812. See note 20.
45 AN, O² 840, letter from Denon to Daru, 28 April 1806.
46 AN, AF IV 1050, letter from Denon, 7 May 1806. We have seen that in this matter they did their apprenticeship under the Directory.
47 AN, O² 836, letter from Daru to the Grand Marshal, 9 October 1807. Daru would have liked to end this 'undecided' affair.

convinced that 'time and effort can be appraised (*s'évaluent*)' and, like Denon, expected that prices could be set in advance.[48]

The artists' 'excessive' demands disconcerted the politicians in as much as these latter were rarely truly enlightened amateurs. It was left to Denon to make the claim that paintings by a living painter must not exceed 40,000 francs. By dint of persistence, David managed despite everything to get 65,000 francs for the *Sacre*, 40,000 for the other three large paintings (expected but not delivered) and 12,000 francs in salary, while being promised a bonus if the Emperor were satisfied. An identical problem arose regarding Isabey, who angled for 20,000 francs on the pretext that he had spent a year on his drawing showing Napoleon's visit to the factories at Rouen and that that was how much he had been paid for the one of the parade. Faced with Denon's refusal on the grounds that a drawing had never fetched such a price, Isabey did not get flustered and simply invoked the promise made to him by the Director of the Museum. Daru then took over by reminding the miniaturist of the many privileges he enjoyed: two posts 'which were worth two hundred *écus* to him and take none of his time', and a large number of portraits supplied to him every day. 'This exclusive privilege is not without utility' and the annual benefit was not insignificant. The message was heard. Isabey agreed to what he had been offered: 6,000 francs. But, in 1811, he returned to press his point and won.[49]

Thus, the problem of prices recurred throughout the Empire, and the government was frequently forced to ratify them. Because the Emperor demanded haste and diligence, ministers were forced to call upon seasoned artists. Denon had certainly considered turning to young artists who would be happy with 1,000 to 1,500 francs, but 'the execution would have been delayed'. However, Napoleon did not tolerate his orders not being executed immediately. In other words, the sovereign was generous when it was a matter of remunerating artistic prowess – master works or works quickly executed.[50] Also, in other words, artists very often won their cases, whether Denon liked it or not, because Napoleon was always 'pressed for time'.

These few examples illustrate better than anything else the extent to

48   Cretet confronted a similar, though slightly different, problem in the matter of appraising *Aldobrandines' Wedding*: 'Its value is totally in opinion and this opinion is constituted by factors which not everyone is capable of determining: these are age, rareness, and the enlightenment that can be drawn from it regarding the Ancients' state of art ... Not only was the proper knowledge necessary to appreciate it fully, but one must also be free of this superstitious veneration which is so understandably held for everything pertaining to Antiquity ... Some experts appraised the painting at 20,000 francs, others at 150,000.' F Boyer, *Le monde des arts en Italie et la France de la Révolution et de l'Empire* (Turin, 1969), pp. 207–8.

49   Isabey received 17,000 francs for a drawing of Napoleon at the Jouy factory and two other miniatures showing Their Imperial Majesties. Denon believed that the miniatures were valued too highly, but, despite everything, recommended satisfying the painter's demands – using the pretext of shipping expenses between Paris and Compiègne. AN, O² 840 and 836.

which the Empire was a time for reality – even if this reality was somewhat surreal. This was undoubtedly true for the Master; but it was also true for artists, especially those who enjoyed great renown. Henceforth, portraits could cost up to 25,000 francs. This is the price Alexander Douglas paid for David's *Napoleon* painted in 1812. As we have seen, modern statues earned up to 120,000 francs – whereas a piece from antiquity like the *Grand Pompée* was only evaluated at 60,000 francs. True, these exceptional payments were not enjoyed by everyone. Established painters of middling rank got only 1,500 or 3,000 francs for a canvas. Others, even though much admired, contented themselves with more modest payments. Such was the case with Robert Lefèvre, who received 3,000 or 3,500 francs for portraits of Napoleon, or the famous sculptor, Houdon, who offered his marble busts of the Emperor and Empress at the price of 3,000 francs. The enormity of the sums demanded by the leading painters and sculptors of the century, especially by those accepted as geniuses – like David, Gérard, Girodet, and Canova – is obvious upon seeing the budget of an artist's wife like Madame Moitte. Her daily expenses fluctuated between nine and twenty-eight francs according to the festivities planned, which brought the annual budget to around 5,400 francs, whereas in years of high spending it came close to 10,000.[51]

In tandem with financial remuneration given at the time of acquisition or commission, the Empire also gave out gold and silver medals in the form of awards. As has been noted, the great painters received the Legion of Honour, a transmissible title giving the right to a coat of arms and livery. Vien, the doyen and rejuvenator of the French School, was named a senator of the Empire and then a count. Just like the former Conventionnel, Thibaudeau, who could not resist adorning himself with the handsome title of chevalier, David the ex-Jacobin saw no problem daily sporting his medal and assuming a coat of arms: a gold palette embellished with two arms holding weapons.[52] After David, Gros, Girodet, Vernet, Prud'hon and Cartellier would each become chevaliers of the Legion of Honour. Thus, the period was a boon to the arts and artists. These latter acquired an eminent place in society thanks to the new image associated with them. They were no longer uneducated

50 AN, O² 840, letter from Denon, 23 March 1808. On Isabey, see AN, O² 836, letter of 9 January 1812.
51 This can be compared with a young officer's pay under the Empire, which reached 5,520 francs a year (1809). The couple's spending rarely exceeded 75 francs a month. *Mémoires de Madame de Rémusat*, ed. C. Kunstler (Paris, 1957), p. 359. Note that what David's students earned him monthly equalled close to the Moittes' annual spending – in the years of high spending.
52 Schnapper, *David*, p. 612. This was only granted to Thibaudeau in 1809. See Foucart, 'L'artiste dans la société', pp. 709–19. Foucart includes the following artists: a commander (Vien), an officer (David), and twenty-six chevaliers, including eighteen members of the Institute. Napoleon was even more generous with scientists, six of whom were named barons. Seventy-eight members of the Institute of the Academies were ennobled. N. Petiteau, *Élites et mobilités: la noblesse d'Empire au XIXe siècle (1808–1914)* (Paris, 1997), p. 458.

artisans, but geniuses, cultivated, sensitive and profound, capable of conveying the spirit of the century, even shaping it or foreseeing it.[53]

The bidding up of prices went hand in hand with this (over-)enhanced esteem. David, Canova and many others did not hesitate to have their talents paid for, confident that it would be done after careful consideration. These pretensions show that the issue was not really allegiance to the Emperor, but rather the artist becoming increasingly convinced of his own genius and of the leading role he played in society – and in the representation of power. It was as if he discerned the interdependence between himself and his employer. Seeing the consideration Napoleon had for the great painters and sculptors of his century, it seems he consciously or unconsciously shared this belief. The Restoration completed the rehabilitation of artists by adorning some of them with the title of baron and by continuing the artistic policy, in the hope of eclipsing it, adopted by the 'Corsican usurper'.[54]

53 David only wanted students who had learned Latin. The century had conferred an unprecedented role on knowledge. During the Revolution, artists claimed their liberty and the autonomy of genius, but they did not shrink from assuming the role of philosophers. David, *Rapport à la Convention nationale sur le jury national des arts* (Paris, 1793). T. Crow, *Emulation: Making Artists for Revolutionary France* (New Haven and London, 1995), pp. 26–30, shows nicely the value placed on knowledge in artistic settings beginning in the 1780s. See also Delécluze, who assessed artists according to their education, not only their talent.

54 On the artistic and cultural policies of Napoleon, see the chapter devoted to it in my book *Napoléon*, cited earlier. The present article offers the artists' point of view.

Index